Open Hatch
The Theater Criticism of Robert Hatch, 1950–1970

Open Hatch

*The Theater Criticism of
Robert Hatch, 1950–1970*

EDITED BY JAMES R. RUSSO

LIVERPOOL UNIVERSITY PRESS

Introduction and organization of this volume copyright © James R. Russo 2023.

The right of James R. Russo to be identified as Author and Organizer of this work has been asserted in accordance with the Copyright, Designs and Patents Act 1988.

2 4 6 8 10 9 7 5 3 1

First published 2023 by
Liverpool University Press
4 Cambridge Street
Liverpool
L69 7ZU

All rights reserved. No part of this book may be reproduced, stored in a retrieval system, or transmitted, in any form or by any means, electronic, mechanical, photocopying, recording, or otherwise, without the prior written permission of the publisher.

British Library Cataloguing-in-Publication data
A British Library CIP record is available

Paperback ISBN 978-1-78976-208-2

Typeset & designed by Sussex Academic Press, Brighton & Eastbourne

Contents

Acknowledgments	vii
Introduction	1

ESSAYS

"Circle in the Square" (1960)	18
"The New York Shakespeare Festival" (1960)	27
"Persistent Ibsenism" (1962)	34
"The Living Theatre" (1962)	38
"John Arden" (1962)	45
"Upstaging Scenery" (1962)	51
"The Actors' Studio" (1962)	55
"Repertory Defended" (1963)	61
"Orson Welles" (1963)	68
"Tyrone Guthrie" (1963)	77

REVIEWS

A Phoenix Too Frequent, by Christopher Fry, & *Freight*, by Kenneth White (1950)	90
Julius Caesar, by William Shakespeare (1950)	91
Billy Budd, by Herman Melville (1951)	92
Stalag 17, by Donald Bevan & Edmund Trzcinski; *Dream Girl*, by Elmer Rice (1951)	93
Mademoiselle Colombe, by Jean Anouilh (1954)	94
The Desperate Hours, by Joseph Hayes (1955)	95
The Dark Is Light Enough, by Christopher Fry, & *Silk Stockings*, by George S. Kaufman & Abe Burrows (1955)	96

CONTENTS

Bus Stop, by William Inge, & *The Master Builder*,   99
by Henrik Ibsen (1955)

The Three Sisters, by Anton Chekhov (1955)   101

Cat on a Hot Tin Roof, by Tennessee Williams (1955)   102

Inherit the Wind, by Jerome Lawrence & Robert E. Lee;   103
Trouble in Tahiti, by Leonard Bernstein; *27 Wagons Full
of Cotton*, by Tennessee Williams (1955)

The Honeys, by Roald Dahl (1955)   105

Damn Yankees, by George Abbott (1955)   106

The Maids, by Jean Genet (1955)   107

The Trial, by Franz Kafka (1955)   109

The Cherry Orchard, by Anton Chekhov (1955)   125

The Bourgeois Gentleman, by Molière, & *The Chalk Garden*,   125
by Enid Bagnold (1955)

A Hatful of Rain, by Michael Gazzo (1955)   127

The Lark, by Jean Anouilh (1955)   128

Pipe Dream, by Richard Rodgers & Oscar Hammerstein;   130
The Most Happy Fella, by Frank Loesser (1955-56)

The Iceman Cometh, by Eugene O'Neill (1956)   132

Measure for Measure & *King John*,   133
by William Shakespeare (1956)

Johnny Johnson, by Paul Green (1956)   136

Girls of Summer, by N. Richard Nash, & *The Happiest*   137
Millionaire, by Kyle Crichton (1956)

The Good Woman of Setzuan, by Bertolt Brecht (1957)   139

Troilus and Cressida, by William Shakespeare (1957)   140

Purple Dust, by Sean O'Casey (1957)   141

The Waltz of the Toreadors, by Jean Anouilh (1957)   142

A Hole in the Head, by Arnold Schulman (1957)   143

Exiles, by James Joyce (1957)   145

Orpheus Descending, by Tennessee Williams (1957)   145

A Moon for the Misbegotten, by Eugene O'Neill, & *New Girl*   147
in Town, by George Abbott (1957)

CONTENTS

Summer of the 17th Doll, by Ray Lawler, & *The Music Man*, by Meredith Wilson (1958) — 149

Endgame, by Samuel Beckett (1958) — 152

The Visit, by Friedrich Dürrenmatt, & *The Firstborn*, by Christopher Fry (1958) — 153

A Touch of the Poet, by Eugene O'Neill (1958) — 157

Epitaph for George Dillon, by John Osborne (1958) — 160

Gypsy, by Arthur Laurents (1959) — 161

The Tempest & *Henry V*, by William Shakespeare (1960) — 163

Krapp's Last Tape, by Samuel Beckett (1960) — 166

The Hostage, by Brendan Behan (1961) — 174

Period of Adjustment, by Tennessee Williams, & *A Taste of Honey*, by Shelagh Delaney (1961) — 178

Roots, by Arnold Wesker (1961) — 182

The Death of Bessie Smith & *The American Dream*, by Edward Albee (1961) — 183

Purlie Victorious, by Ossie Davis (1961) — 188

The Blacks, by Jean Genet (1961) — 189

A Man for All Seasons, by Robert Bolt, & *The Caretaker*, by Harold Pinter (1962) — 196

The Merchant of Venice, by William Shakespeare (1962) — 201

A Man's a Man, by Bertolt Brecht; *Oh Dad, Poor Dad, Mamma's Hung You in the Closet and I'm Feelin' So Sad*, by Arthur Kopit; & *Who's Afraid of Virginia Woolf?*, by Edward Albee (1963) — 203

The Dumb Waiter, by Harold Pinter; *Desire Under the Elms*, by Eugene O'Neill; & *The Milk Train Doesn't Stop Here Anymore*, by Tennessee Williams (1963) — 208

But for Whom Charlie, by S. N. Behrman (1964) — 214

Dutchman & *The Baptism*, by LeRoi Jones (1964) — 216

Hamlet, by William Shakespeare (1964) — 218

Baal, by Bertolt Brecht (1965) — 220

Troubled Waters, by Ugo Betti, & *Live Like Pigs*, by John Arden (1965) — 223

CONTENTS

Leonce and Lena & *Danton's Death*, by Georg Büchner (1966)   227

San Francisco Mime Troupe (1967)   230

Soldiers, by Rolf Hochhuth (1968)   231

The Memorandum, by Václav Havel (1968)   232

A Midsummer Night's Dream, by William Shakespeare; *Tartuffe*, by Molière; & *The Seagull*, by Anton Chekhov (1968)   234

We Bombed in New Haven, by Joseph Heller (1968)   237

Little Murders, by Jules Pfeiffer (1969)   240

Promenade, by María Irene Fornés (1969)   241

The Trial of A. Lincoln, by James Damico (1970)   243

Bibliography of Robert Hatch's Writings on Theater and Drama   246

Index   256

viii

Acknowledgments

Thanks to the following publishers and individuals for permission to reprint: *The New Republic, The Nation*, and *Horizon*; Peter Hatch, Gillian Hatch Gretton, and the estate of Ruth Bower Hatch (1914–2007).

x

Introduction

"Man on the Aisle:
Robert Hatch as Theater Critic"

Along with John Simon, Robert Brustein, Richard Gilman, and Stanley Kauffmann, Robert Littlefield Hatch, Jr. (1910–94) was one of the most potent, influential authors in the New York school of twentieth-century American arts criticism. Although (sadly) not well-known for his film criticism, Hatch was also a frontline drama critic for a time, for *The New Republic*, *The Nation*, and *Horizon*; and some remarks on this role of his—among his other roles as an editor and book reviewer—are in obviously in order in a volume titled *Open Hatch: The Theater Criticism of Robert Hatch, 1950–70*.

But, before discussing Hatch's work as a drama critic, I want to point out the difference between criticism and reviewing where the theater is concerned. Such a distinction is snobbish, if you will, indecorous, perhaps quixotic. But it seems to me that we are never going to get out of the miasma of deceit, self-pity, and wishful thinking that emanates from the theater in the United States as it does from no other medium, unless we begin to accept the distinctions that operate in actuality between actors and stars, dramas and hits, art and artisanship—and critics and reviewers.

Perhaps the greatest irony in a situation bursting with ironies has been the reiterated idea that the *critics* are killing the theater. Now we all know that when theater people or members of the public refer to the "critics," they almost always mean the New York reviewers. It is certainly true that the critics—those persons whom the dictionary describes as "skilled in judging the qualities or merits of some class of things, especially of literary or artistic work"—have long harbored murderous thoughts about the condition of American drama, but their ineffectuality as public executioners is legendary. The reviewers, by contrast, come close to being the most loyal and effective allies the commercial theater could possibly desire. (They are killing the *non*-commercial theater.) But not close enough, it would seem, for this "marriage" constitutes the case of an absolute desire encountering

1

INTRODUCTION

arelative compliance."As a corollary of its demand for constructive criticism the theater insists on absolute loyalty, and clearly receives a very high degree of it from reviewers, who are all "theater lovers" to one or another extent.

And that brings us to our second irony. For "loyalty in a critic," George Bernard Shaw wrote in 1932 in *Our Theatres in the Nineties,* "is corruption" (Vol. 3, 177). This richly disturbing remark comes near the heart of so much that is wrong in the relationship between the stage and those who write about it from seats of power or places of romantic yearning. From the true critics the theater generally gets what can only be interpreted as gross infidelity, the reason being—as Shaw and every other major observer of drama make abundantly clear, and as our own sense of what is civilized should tell us—that critics cannot give their loyalty to people and institutions, since they owe it to something a great deal more permanent.

They owe it, of course, to truth and dramatic art. Once they sacrifice truth to human beings or art to institutions, they are corrupt, unless, as is so frequently the case, they never had any capacity for determining truth or any knowledge of dramatic art in the first place; for such persons, corruption is clearly too grandiose a condition. But some reviewers, at least, are people of ordinarily developed taste and a little intellectual maturity, and it is among them that corruption—in the sense not of venality or outright malfeasance but of the abandonment of a higher to a lower good—operates continually and in the name of that very loyalty which is worn like a badge of honor.

The point about reviewers is that they exist, consciously or not, to keep Broadway functioning within staked-out grounds. They preserve it as the arena for theatrical enterprises that may neither rise above an upper limit determined by a line stretching between the imaginations of Lillian Hellman, William Inge, and Richard Rodgers, nor sink beneath a lower one marked out by the inventiveness and sense of life of Norman Krasna, Harry Kurnitz, and Garson Kanin. (These are names from Broadway's supposed Golden Age; they have changed, but nothing else has.) Whatever creeps into the spaces north or south of this Central Park of the imagination is adventitious, arbitrary, and hermetic; if it is good, if it is art, if it is *Waiting for Godot* (1953), its presence on the Street may confidently be ascribed to someone's idea of a joke that just might pay off. (Beckett's masterpiece was billed in advertisements as "the laugh riot of two continents.")

Outside the theater's hothouse, not part of its clubbiness, its opening-night ceremonies, or its cabalisms, unconsulted about the

INTRODUCTION

honors it awards itself every year, and owing no more devotion to it than the literary critic owes to publishers or the art critic to galleries, the serious critic of drama like Robert Hatch is left free—to do what? *To judge*. "There is one and only one justification for the trade of drama criticism," George Jean Nathan wrote, "and that is to criticize drama and not merely apologize for it" (Nathan, 64). Shaw went further:

> A critic is most certainly not in the position of a co-respondent in a divorce case: he is in no way bound to perjure himself to shield the reputation of the profession he criticizes. Far from being the instigator of its crimes and the partner of its guilty joys, he is the policeman of dramatic art; and it is his express business to denounce its delinquencies. (*The Drama Observed*, 969)

It is this idea of the critic as policeman that infuriates theater people to the limit of their anarchistic temperaments.

Go through the three volumes of Shaw's criticism, or police blotter, covering as many London seasons, and you will find that not once in any sequence of fifteen to twenty reviews was he anything but indignant at what he was called upon to see. Without pity in *Our Theatres in the Nineties*, he excoriated that theater, which sounds so much like our own, with its "dull routine of boom, bankruptcy, and boredom" (Vol. 2, 68), its performers' "eternal clamor for really artistic work and their ignominious collapse when they are taken at their word by Ibsen or anyone else" (Vol. 2, 76), its lugubrious spectacle of the drama as it "loses its hold on life" (Vol. 3, 181). Only when, once or twice a year, something came along that actually had a hold on life did Shaw's critiques turn enthusiastic and positive. But not "constructive"; you do not patronize or act generously toward artistic achievement—you identify it.

For if critics are not the makers of dramatic art, they are the persons most able to say what it is, and at the same time to establish the conditions under which it may flourish or at least gain a foothold. By being negative or *destructive*, if you will, toward everything else, they can help dramatic art to outlast the ephemera described as "smash" and "riot" and "socko," as "haunting," "riveting," and "stunning." And they will do their championing nearly always in the teeth of the coiners of these inimitable if vacuous terms. To the handful of great journalist-critics the English-speaking stage has had—Shaw, Max Beerbohm, Nathan, and Stark Young; Eric Bentley, Richard Gilman, Robert Brustein, Stanley Kauffmann, and finally Robert Hatch—we

3

INTRODUCTION

owe most of our knowledge of the permanent drama of our time, and in most cases we owe even the opportunity to read or see it.

When, for instance, the London reviewers were doing their best to drive Ibsen back to the depraved Continent (*Ghosts*, in 1882, was "unutterably offensive," "revoltingly suggestive and blasphemous," "a dirty act done publicly" [Archer, 209]), it was Shaw, along with William Archer, who fought brilliantly and implacably to keep open the door to a resurrected drama. Later, Nathan helped Eugene O'Neill past the roadblock of those newspapermen who characteristically admired his "power" while being terrified of his thematic and technical innovations. And, in the 1950s, the truly heroic work of Eric Bentley—both in introducing us to the most vital contemporary as well nineteenth-century European plays and in promulgating standards for a potentially mature American theater—is a monument to the critical spirit at its untiring best. When, for example, Jack Gelber's *The Connection* was savaged by the daily newspapers in 1959, it was salvaged through the combined support of Bentley and other magazine critics, just as, three years earlier, these intellectual critics had rehabilitated the American reputation of *Waiting for Godot* after its disastrous reception at the hands of such reviewers as Walter Kerr. (The process used to work the other way, too: in 1958, Archibald MacLeish's *J.B.* was more accurately evaluated by the weekly critics after the *New York Times* had called it "one of the most memorable works of the century" [Atkinson, A2].)

If the history of the modern theater, then, is one of mutual suspicion between playwrights and their audiences—or between playwrights and the audience's stand-in, the reviewer—the history of the postmodern theater in the United States is one of quick rewards and instant media replay. In this arena, serious writers fight not poverty and neglect but the fickleness of a culture that picks them up and discards them before they have had sufficient time to develop properly. Like any jaded culture, America's hungers not for experience but for novelty, while an army of media commentators labors ceaselessly to identify something new. In such an atmosphere, where unorthodoxy becomes a new orthodoxy and fashion the arbiter of taste, the function of the vanguard artist, sacrificing popularity for the sake of penetrating uncharted ground, is radically changed. The emblematic avant-garde figure is no longer the expatriate playwright, exiled from nation, home, and church, but rather Julie Taymor—catapulted from the lofts of the Open Theater and the Chelsea Theater Center (where she began) to the Broadway stage, where, through *The Lion King* (1997), she peddled visual emptiness and dramatic pabulum, in the

INTRODUCTION

guise of experimental technique, to fat cats and wide-eyed tourists at $100 at throw.

One of the causes of this condition can be found in the peculiar relationship between the American playgoer and the American theater critic, for never before has a handful of reviewers possessed so much power and lacked so much authority. The mediocrity of newspaper, radio, and television reviewing throughout the country is nothing new—it is the inevitable result, first, of the need for haste, and, second, of choosing reviewers from the ranks of journalism (from the sports page, say, or from what used to be known as the "women's department") rather than from literary or professional training grounds. What is new, and most depressing, is the scarcity of decent critics *anywhere*. It is almost as if the theater had been abandoned by men and women of intelligence and taste, only to be delivered over wholesale to the publicists and the proselytizers.

Among them was Clive Barnes of the *New York Times*. It was always difficult to take seriously the judgments of a man, like Barnes, who could speak in nothing but superlatives—who, in the course of a single year, said that five or six different actors were giving the most brilliant performances of their careers, called eight or nine resident companies one of the finest in the country, announced four or five plays to be the best of this or any other season, compared a young writer who had just completed his first play with the mature Chekhov, and identified Stacy Keach as the finest American Hamlet since John Barrymore, though Barnes was too young to have seen Barrymore's performance in the early 1920s. Barnes's use of hyperbole, with its promiscuous display of the word *best*, exposed not the splendors of the theater season but rather its bankruptcy, for it suggested that his need to identify works of merit or interest had far outrun the theater's capacity to create them.

Obviously, no theater can benefit in the long run from fake approval, partly because the critic becomes discredited, partly because the spectator grows disenchanted, partly because the theater practitioner begins to lose faith in his craft. The very rare work with serious aspirations thus gets lost in the general atmosphere of praise— either because it is ignored or unappreciated, or more likely because it is acclaimed in the same way as everything else. When the inspired and the routine are treated exactly alike, the act of criticism comes to seem arbitrary and capricious; when the corrective impulse is abandoned, the whole construct of standards breaks down. A serious *literary* artist can always hope for an understanding review or two in the midst of the general incomprehension, and anyway, regardless of reviews, his

INTRODUCTION

book continues to exist for future generations to discover. But the theater artist writes on air, and preserves his work only in the memories of those who see it. In the present critical atmosphere, even those memories are tainted. The marriage that must exist in any art form between the mind that creates and the mind that judges has for the most part dissolved in the theater, with the result that the art form itself is in danger of losing its purpose and direction.

I'm speaking only about the United States, of course. In London, Rome, Paris, and Berlin, critics like Robert Hatch are likely to be found writing for leading newspapers, rather than being relegated to the back pages of weekly, monthly, or even quarterly intellectual magazines. This is one of the reasons Hatch's theater criticism should be of interest to international readers, especially European ones: he is a public intellectual who writes for the educated reader from any country, not an arcane academic who preaches to a highly specialized and limited audience of fellow scholars; he writes like a citizen of the world rather than as a parochial American. Not only do Hatch's urbane style and wide knowledge of all the arts, past and present, tell us of his global outlook; so too do his choices of plays or productions about which to write.

Of his own volition, Robert Hatch stopped writing dramatic criticism for *The Nation* in 1970. Four years earlier, in 1966, Stanley Kauffmann, theater critic of the *New York Times*, was dismissed from his own post after only eight months and relegated to the back pages of intellectual magazines because, in his own words (equally applicable to Hatch's situation),

> the theater has always resisted serious criticism and tolerates it only when it is relatively powerless. A chief component of this condition is the attitude of much of its audience, who would probably be happier with a one-to-four-star rating service plus a brief synopsis. The theater's view of the matter is supported by most newspaper publishers and editors, whose standard in criticism is not quality but readability. The writer who can supply bright, readable copy, and supply it quickly, is an acceptable critic. (Kauffmann, 36)

The reasons for this journalistic development can be found in the history of American theater criticism, which has outlines that, not surprisingly, correspond to large socio-cultural movements.

To wit: as American society became less dependent on the theater for diversion (with the advent of film, radio, and the automobile), as

INTRODUCTION

the middle class turned into the pseudo-aristocracy, as new wealth gave more people a leisure that had once been restricted to a few, including the leisure to be elegantly bored, there arose a tribe of critics whose principal qualifications were urbanity, wit, and fundamental non-commitment to the theater. In the United States a chief haven for that kind of critic has been the *New Yorker*, which, from its outset as well as from its very insignia, has always had a strong streak of Anglophilia—promulgated over the years by such (unidentical) critics as Alexander Woollcott, Wolcott Gibbs, Brendan Gill, and Robert Benchley.

A quite different kind of reviewing also arose in America, out of the same root social causes. Newspaper and mass-magazine reviewing in the first half of the twentieth century was, understandably, in the hands of representatives of this new middle class, men and women who represented both the appetite for boredom and an equivalent appetite for cultural acquisition at a level that imposed no strain. Mr. Average Person filled the job to the average person's satisfaction, his virtue being that he or she knew just as little as the common spectator, and sometimes even less. But where American cultural and intellectual life had been relatively homogeneous in the nineteenth century, it was now dividing into major and minor elements—again, for a complex of social reasons.

One of the minority elements found its critical voice around the turn of the century, approximately, with the "arrival" of James Gibbon Huneker and the now-forgotten Percival Pollard. The theme of this "adversary" criticism was that American culture was provincial, puritanical, and benighted, and that mass-media criticism was banal when not together dumb. Huneker, who criticized several arts, developed these ideas about the theater specifically, and his themes, even when unspoken, persisted through the first five decades of the twentieth century—usually in magazines of oppositional stance with theater critics like Joseph Wood Krutch as well as the aforementioned Young, Nathan, and Bentley.

This schizoid situation, between popular reviewing and intellectual criticism, altered after the Second World War, again in response to social change. Higher education became democratized, culture "exploded," and the middle class became aesthetically radicalized— very strictly within the limits of middle-class values (themselves now somewhat circumscribed by television) but still with a lot of innocuous daring. The result is that today we live in a critical situation in which the vocabulary and stance (if not the literary style) of the mass-medium reviewer are very different from his predecessor's and much more like

INTRODUCTION

those the adversary critic. The dividing line is no longer a line; only the ends of the spectrum are clearly defined. But what is forgotten in the new joy about the "improvement" of mass-circulation reviewing is, fundamentally, that the critical spectrum still exists.

Furthermore, almost no one collects one man's mass-circulation theater reviews in a book, as Robert Hatch's selected dramatic criticism is collected here for the educated reader. For, unlike collections of film criticism, which, among other uses, serve as guides to movies that are "revived" in theaters, on television, and in VHS or DVD format, collections of theater criticism have no precisely parallel use. When one of the plays discussed is revived, the new production must in some way alter it. For this very reason, collections of theater criticism like Robert Hatch's have, I think, a special importance that more than compensates for their lack of "utility." In a sense, one part of the past—"unknown" or lesser known plays, for example, by long-forgotten dramatists—would not exist without them. Collections of performance criticism, then, are books of *witness*. Surely, like other critics, performance critics can help to illuminate works, can test, revise, and extend criteria, can capture qualities and pose questions (if not posit answers). But the unique reward of performance criticism is in its immediacy and the distillation of that immediacy, in the salvaging for posterity of pertinences.

Those pertinences, for Robert Hatch, always included acting (as well as directing and design), but the pertinences also included the play as a piece of literature. Thus Hatch's value as a drama critic resides in his values as a critic generally. For him, the drama should be something other than a repetitive theatrical game designed to comfort the bourgeoisie; it must be an art that renews itself as serious playwrights in every age reinvent their chosen form. Hatch admired all such writers, who know that art is not a complement to life but an increment; that drama is not psychology, sociology, philosophy, or political theory; and that the only new content is new form. He was thus always attentive, in his articles and reviews, to the manner in which plays are made, but he was never concerned with form as embroidery or decoration. Instead, dramatic forms for him were forms of new knowledge, a mutual freeing of the self—the audience's as well as the author's—from artistic and cultural conventions that limit our sense of possibility.

Robert Hatch's chief interest was always in discovering how new ways of presenting drama and unfolding consciousness aid in revealing character, transmitting ideas, and in general increasing the potential for capturing a sense of "felt life" on stage. Like Eric Bentley, he wisely

INTRODUCTION

saw the playwright as thinker—a shaper of modern consciousness— *and* as showman. The best playwrights, Hatch regularly suggests in *Open Hatch: The Theater Criticism of Robert Hatch, 1950–70*, are the ones who can turns ideas and problems, moral conundrums and philosophical complexities, into engaging theater. Yet even these fine dramatists, with the exception of Shakespeare, have never held the kind of central position in educated minds that the authors of fiction and poetry have. This must have something to do with the relative difficulty of seeing good performances of great plays, with the trouble most readers have in imagining how a dramatic text would sound and look on the stage (if not in their mind's eye), with (for English-speaking readers) a mistrust of translations that have often well deserved the mistrust they engender. And, I suppose, there is a larger suspicion that drama is an impure medium: commercially exploitable, subject to the vanity or stupidity of actors, unlikely to come off in the theater at all. One goes to a play expecting disappointment, and one usually finds just that.

Despite Robert Hatch's recurrent disappointment with the productions he saw over the years, his collected theater reviews have a genuine charm that comes, paradoxically, from their suggestion that the author did not entirely believe his own doomsday judgment on American theater and drama. That he stopped writing regular theater criticism in 1970, while he continued as a film critic for *The Nation* for thirty years, from 1954 to 1984 (having begun writing film-and-drama criticism for the *New Republic*, from 1948–52), deserves some comment, however. For theater criticism once attracted a number of writers of the caliber of Hatch: not only the aforementioned Bentley, Kauffmann, Brustein, and Gilman, but also Susan Sontag, Mary McCarthy, Kenneth Tynan, and John Simon—writers, in short, who could be expected to analyze a play or production intelligently, and to correct the misjudgments of the daily press. Today, this kind of corrective has practically disappeared, as the dissenting critics have departed, retired, or shifted to other fields like music. Most intellectual journals, on their side, have long since stopped carrying theater chronicles.

Moreover, John Simon's own virtually single-handed crusade, in *New York* magazine, to preserve high standards became vitiated by his uncontrolled savagery, his excessively punning style, his peculiar prejudices, his personal attacks on the physical appearance of actors, his obsessive campaign against real or imagined homosexuality on the stage, and, lastly, his turning of his critical fury into its own mode of performance for the amusement of television talk-show audiences eager to see the bad guy in person. Simon's "progress" (which finally

9

INTRODUCTION

ended in 2005, though he, too, continued to write film criticism—for the *National Review*) may suggest why so many other serious authors, like Robert Hatch, have abandoned the writing of all but occasional theater criticism, for it shows what may happen to a person of intelligence and discrimination when he or she observes too long the execrable products of the American theatrical scene (unmitigated, as in the case of film, by international imports in sufficient number and quality).

After all, it was Max Beerbohm, a similarly high-minded critic, who wrote the following words back in 1904—partly in indictment of himself: "A critic who wants the drama to be infinitely better than it is can hardly avoid the pitfall of supposing it to be rather worse than it is. Finding that it rises nowhere near to his standards, he imagines that it must be in a state of motionless prostration in the nethermost depths" (Beerbohm, 110). To counteract this tendency in himself, Beerbohm (like Shaw), when faced with an evening of despicable entertainment, went home and devised a substitute entertainment of his own, loosely disguised as a review. See in Beerbohm's *Around Theatres* (1924), for example, the little theatrical event this critic stages as his lead into a review of Victor Hugo's *Ruy Blas* (1838) in dismal English translation. Robert Hatch himself, it is true, lacks such playfulness—some would say triviality—but that may be because the American theater itself is almost wholly one of play, of child's play, even when it is ostensibly trying to be serious. And such a theater at one time required, I think, the stern but stimulating contempt, the acerbic yet arousing intolerance, of a Hatch.

Initially backing up Robert Hatch in his ire were the seminal essays of Francis Fergusson as well as Eric Bentley, comprising the academic artillery being fired (chiefly from Columbia) at the philistines in Sardi's and Shubert Alley, at the entrenched establishment of Lincoln Center and the Actors' Studio, and at the new breed of barbarians storming south of 14th Street past the Living Theater and toward other assorted dead ends. It is not too far-fetched to suggest that not only Bentley but also Fergusson, and later Robert Brustein and Stanley Kauffmann (themselves having moved, like Bentley, to the academy—in their case Yale—in the 1960s), represented an authentic revolution in the modern theater away from the championing of realism of the poetic as well as prosaic variety, toward an appreciation of a still (at the time) undetermined fusion of the ironic and the absurd. With tragedy in tatters and comedy in confusion, these modern critics turned to irony as the only link between the form or formality of theater and the flux of history. Chekhov, Pirandello, Brecht, and Beckett are neither

INTRODUCTION

tragedians nor comedians but ironists, and a genuinely ironic sensibility is something unheard of on Broadway. Hence, even on the infrequent occasions of revivals of Chekhov, Pirandello, Brecht, and Beckett, the ironies of their plays are swallowed up by the slobbering sentimentality of a realistic stage tradition; and it took an "ironic" critic like Hatch to point this out.

In this constantly contentious period of cultural history, Fergusson functioned as a remote Hegelian influence on the revolutionaries, Bentley played Marx as he translated Brecht, and Brustein was Lenin arriving at the Finland Station on the New Haven Railroad (which would eventually take him from Yale to Harvard). On the other side, Walter Kerr turned into the Kerensky of the revolution by betraying his academic origins to consort with the hated bourgeoisie, while the drama critics of the *Village Voice* (among them Gordon Rogoff and later Richard Gilman) became the left-wing revisionists of Off-Off Broadway. Stanley Kauffmann and Robert Hatch wound up, by turns, playing Trotsky with a tortured ambivalence that robbed them of nothing except professional stamina.

Open Hatch: The Theater Criticism of Robert Hatch, 1950–70 attempts to document, if not Hatch's longevity as a drama critic, then his range and perspicacity as one. With style and erudition Hatch discusses plays and productions from the following countries: England, the United States, France, Russia, Ireland, Germany, Switzerland, Italy, Czechoslovakia, Norway, Greece, and Australia. Contained in this volume are reviews of productions of such notable plays as *The Master Builder*, by Henrik Ibsen; *The Cherry Orchard* and *The Three Sisters*, by Anton Chekhov; *Cat on a Hot Tin Roof* and *Orpheus Descending*, by Tennessee Williams; *The Bourgeois Gentleman*, by Molière; *The Iceman Cometh*, *A Moon for the Misbegotten*, and *A Touch of the Poet*, by Eugene O'Neill; *Julius Caesar, Measure for Measure, Hamlet*, and *Troilus and Cressida*, by William Shakespeare; *The Good Woman of Setzuan* and *Baal*, by Bertolt Brecht; *Endgame* and *Krapp's Last Tape*, by Samuel Beckett; *The Caretaker* and *The Dumb Waiter*, by Harold Pinter; and *Who's Afraid of Virginia Woolf?* as well as *The American Dream*, by Edward Albee.

Open Hatch: The Theater Criticism of Robert Hatch, 1950–70 also features treatments of dramatists such as Jean Anouilh, William Inge, Jean Genet, Elmer Rice, Sean O'Casey, Friedrich Dürrenmatt, John Osborne, Brendan Behan, Arnold Wesker, Ugo Betti, John Arden, and Georg Büchner; discussions of a dramatization of Franz Kafka's *The Trial* and of Herman Melville's *Billy Budd*, as well as the only play by

11

INTRODUCTION

James Joyce, *Exiles*; and a selection of pieces on such subjects as the Living Theatre, Ibsenism, the Actors' Studio, Broadway and Off-Broadway, repertory theater, Shakespeare festivals, melodrama, scene design, Tyrone Guthrie, and Orson Welles.

I would like, in addition, to make note of some lesser-known dramatists whose work is treated in *Open Hatch: The Theater Criticism of Robert Hatch, 1950–70*: Michael Gazzo, Christopher Fry, Paul Green, Ray Lawler, Ossie Davis, N. Richard Nash, Robert Bolt, Arthur Kopit, S. N. Behrman, Shelagh Delaney, LeRoi Jones, Rolf Hochhuth, Joseph Hayes, Jerome Lawrence, and Václav Havel. That is, I should like to explain why Hatch's writings on these lesser-known and, in some cases, lesser dramatists have been included in this volume. My explanation is simple: *most* of what is done in the theater is lesser—mediocre or worse. Even so, the mediocre or worse is as much a part of the theater critic's subject as the good or better. Shaw himself wrote one of his best reviews about a long-since forgotten item called, of all things, *The Chili Widow*. Every critic grapples continually with *Chili Widows*. Such plays need to be identified and at least generically understood, both as a matter of clear vision and because every critic either has a touch of John the Baptist in him or her or that critic ought to quit. Critics ought to live in hope that true art is continually *en route*—and does in fact occasionally appear. Part of this proselytizing function is to make sure that false messiahs, peddlers, and charlatans are shown as such. But hope—non-delusionary, non-inflationary, non-self-aggrandizing *hope*—is the core of the critic's being: hope that good work will recurrently arrive; hope that (partly by identifying trash) he or she may help it to arrive; hope that the critic may have the excitement and privilege of helping to connect such good work with a good audience.

Look, then, through the index of the collected writings of any theater critic you admire, and note how many *Chili Widows* are listed, how few of the plays he or she discusses are ones that you have seen or would want to see or read. But the critic hoped and persisted; through hoping and persisting, even when the theater was bad, created a *literature*. The theater critic, like other critics, creates a literature about an art, a literature that has both art and the critic's life as its subject matter. If a purpose of art is to explore and distill one's existence, which art is greater: Edmund Wilson's criticism or Edmund Wilson's novels, plays, and poems? Or, to separate the functions in different people, who would hesitate to choose Robert Brustein's theater criticism over Robert Anderson's plays? When we read fine criticism in any field, that of Lionel Trilling and Northrop Frye, say,

12

INTRODUCTION

of Edgar Wind and Herbert Read, we often lose all sense of reading *criticism* and simply have a sense of *reading*. We are simply enjoying a kind of literature.

So the theater, finally, is a subject. That is why the critic writes and why the reader, even the one who rarely goes to the theater, reads. The theater is a complex, significant, reflective, implicative *subject*. The consumer-guide motive for, or function of, reviewing is quite secondary—though, like any human being, the critic naturally likes to see his enthusiasms prosper. Much more important, more central to the critic's being than any box-office influence he or she may have, is the realization that this person works in a concurrent plane to the theater, not a congruent plane. That is, the critic exists in a kind of para-reality to the theater's reality. His criticism is a body of work obviously related to, yet still distinct from, what the theater does; possibly influential, possibly not, criticism in the end is no more closely connected to the theater than is political science to the current elections. The critic knows that, on the one hand, there is the theater, with good and bad productions, and, on the other hand, there is criticism, which ought to be good about both good and bad productions. Life is the playwright's subject, and the playwright ought to be good about its good and bad people; the theater is the critic's subject, and the critic ought to be good about its good and bad plays.

One thing Hatch does not do in *Open Hatch: The Theater Criticism of Robert Hatch, 1950–70* is comment on the continuing revolution, or crisis, in dramatic criticism—a situation created these days, in part, by the advent of the Internet, where anyone can publish dramatic criticism, at any time, in a blog or other form of web page, on a media platform, etc. Is the quality of dramatic criticism therefore now declining, since anybody can upload his theater reviews, without editorial control (of the kind with which print critics such as Robert Hatch always had to contend) or careful vetting, to the Internet? Are the blogosphere and social networking sites just the virtual equivalent of "talk" or chatter where the theater is concerned—a pullulating buzz of artists promoting shows, audience members offering their opinions, badly written reviews by amateurs, and friends promoting friends? Or will dramatic criticism ultimately be enriched by such democratic, "immediate," often highly personal practice online, and will the print critic at the same time slowly disappear, even as print journalism itself is dying?

Indeed, have digital reviewing and even the uploading of entire productions to YouTube begun to impact the very way in which we see theater? Moreover, how do younger students of theater feel about

13

INTRODUCTION

these matters? How, especially, do those youthful theatergoers feel who do not know the work of print critics like Robert Hatch, yet might learn, from an acquaintance with his theater reviews, about something currently in short supply—critical standards and aesthetic values, historical perspective and social discernment, careful writing and close reading? These are legitimate questions that, naturally, only began to be asked some years after Hatch's death in 1994; such questions were inconceivable during his tenure as a drama critic in the mid-twentieth century, when print journalism was still king and the media landscape had not yet burgeoned to its present, inordinate—and sometimes overwhelming—size.

In sum, Robert Hatch was, and is, the critic many of us aspire to be—in print or online—as well as the champion of criticism in an art form, theater, more hostile to it than any other with the possible exception of film. The precision, wit, and wisdom of Hatch's writing thus chime in *Open Hatch: The Theater Criticism of Robert Hatch, 1950–70*, as he reveals—and revels in—his sense of cultural mission. Particularly impressive is the extent to which his writing in *Open Hatch* exhibits not only an application to drama of the highest standards, but also a love of good art in any form—theatrical, cinematic, painterly, musical, or literary. Speaking to this love, I would like to close with these words, written by Lionel Trilling about a great artist, F. Scott Fitzgerald, but equally applicable to Hatch, the *critic* as artist: "We feel of him, as we cannot feel of all moralists, that he did not attach himself to the good because this attachment would sanction his fierceness toward the bad—his first impulse was to love the good" (Trilling, 245).

Works Cited

Archer, William. "*Ghosts* and Gibberings" (1891). In Egan, Michael, ed. *Henrik Ibsen: The Critical Heritage*. 1972. London: Routledge, 1999. 209–214.

Atkinson, Brooks. "MacLeish's *J.B.*: Verse Drama Given Premiere at ANTA." *New York Times* (Dec. 12, 1958): A2.

Beerbohm, Max. *Last Theatres, 1904–1910*. Ed. Rupert Hart-Davis. London: MacGibbon, 1970.

Kauffmann, Stanley. "Drama on the *Times*." *New American Review*, no. 1 (Sept. 1967): 30–49.

Nathan, George Jean. *The Morning After the First Night*. New York: Alfred A. Knopf, 1938.

Shaw, Bernard. *Our Theatres in the Nineties*. Vol. 2. 1932. London: Constable, 1954.

Shaw, Bernard. *Our Theatres in the Nineties*. Vol. 3. 1932. London: Constable, 1954.

Shaw, Bernard. *The Drama Observed*. Vol. III: 1897–1911. Ed. Bernard Dukore. University Park: Penn State University Press, 1993.

Trilling, Lionel. "F. Scott Fitzgerald." In Trilling's *The Liberal Imagination: Essays on Literature and Society*. 1951. New York: New York Review of Books, 2008. 243–254.

16

ESSAYS

ESSAYS

"Circle in the Square" (1960)

A defunct nightclub at 5 Sheridan Square in Greenwich Village provided the makeshift premises for a group of players performing virtual theater-in-the-round: hence their name, Circle in the Square. Today their Circle is no longer in the Square, having been forced by threatened demolition to move to newer quarters in a ramshackle auditorium known as the Amato Opera on Bleecker Street farther south. Yet the name and identity of this hardy Off-Broadway company persist. For ten years the Circle has been operating under the same auspices, headed by the director José Quintero and the producer Theodore Mann. And in the New York theater, ten years constitute permanence.

Moreover, in an era when most theaters are controlled by real-estate companies, a house whose fortunes rest in the hands of the people who actually use its stage is a rare and invigorating phenomenon. Circle in the Square does not dominate the theater world of its town as the Haymarket, the Drury Lane, or the Princess dominated the theater of nineteenth-century London. But something like that could very well be the dream in its proprietors' eyes, and meanwhile they have made it one of New York's most edifying fixtures.

Like all enterprises that sail into the teeth of wise advice to the contrary, Circle in the Square has amassed a history lively with alarms and anecdotes. It has produced eighteen plays, four of which can be considered hits (though a hit Off-Broadway is by no means the bonanza that is understood by the term uptown). It was once closed for a year by the Fire Department and reopened (it is too bad, by the way, that another Off-Broadway theater is already called the Phoenix) only because Messrs. Quintero and Mann found it unbearable being without their own theater. Then there was the Chinese youth who overheard a group of Circle actors talking of their theater's imminent collapse at the bar in Louie's next door, and who came by the next morning to donate a thousand-dollar bill, which he pulled from his watch pocket. He has not, it is thought, been around since, and his motive for the gift was enigmatic to the point of parodying the mysterious East.

When Circle in the Square opened in 1950 with its first production, Howard Richardson and William Berney's *Dark of the Moon* (a musical fantasy that was cheered by the critics and won four awards), it had no theater license and therefore could not charge admission. A hat was passed between acts, and the company, camping in dormitories uptown, lived for weeks on communal spaghetti and other

18

"CIRCLE IN THE SQUARE" (1960)

high-bulk, low-overhead dishes. In an early program, the management solicited playgoers for clothes, hats, shoes, and accessories to form the basis of a costume department.

The backgrounds of the theater's founders are themselves interesting. Mr. Quintero, a native of Panama (he is presently the Panamanian consul in Jersey City, a relatively undemanding post that confers small diplomatic conveniences), came to the United States to study medicine at the University of California and became interested in the theater when he took a speech course to improve his English. Mr. Mann, having passed his New York bar examination, decided to spend a summer managing a stock company in Woodstock, New York, and has not yet found time to accept a client.

Roughly speaking, running a theater is a job half-creative and half-administrative, and from the beginning that is the way these two men have divided the work. Mr. Quintero is the director, and Mr. Mann is the producer; they work harmoniously by respecting each other's area of competence. The third member, present Circle management partner Leigh Connell, joined the team in 1955 as a script-reader and today serves as a talent scout and general artistic associate of Mr. Quintero. The plays that Circle in the Square offers reflect a Quintero–Mann–Connell judgment of how a contemporary theater should occupy and conduct itself.

If there is any pattern in Circle in the Square's fortunes so far, it is one of predictable disaster evaded by unpredictable luck. The fact that its guiding spirits fell into the theater by accidental circumstances, which today even they can scarcely explain, may be pleasantly ironic but is really a commonplace of such enterprises. And there is nothing in the record to explain why the Circle survived when most theater projects of a similar sort fail: it was no more carefully planned, professionally launched, or prudently managed. It survived essentially because its operators had a greater-than-average talent for the job.

What is important, and what does begin to define the nature and significance of Circle in the Square, is the fact that it should be thought of as having a history at all. Uptown in New York, theaters do not have histories, any more than hotel bedrooms have histories. They are efficient, highly specialized spaces for hire. Circle in the Square is nether efficient nor specialized. In its Sheridan Square period the theater had the form of a large, rectangular room with low ceilings and a floor space cluttered by many supporting columns. (Some readers may remember the old premises when occupied by the Greenwich Village Inn, one of the city's brassier centers of commercial

ESSAYS

Bohemia.) The new Circle occupies a one-time movie house, long also the home of peripatetic operatic offerings.

In ten years Circle in the Square has enjoyed four big successes, as previously noted: Tennessee Williams's *Summer and Smoke*, Alfred Hayes's *The Girl on the Via Flaminia*, Eugene O'Neill's *The Iceman Cometh*, and most recently Thornton Wilder's *Our Town*. Of the Circle's other productions, approximately half were acknowledged to be artistic successes. But all the plays were selected and produced by men for whom the theater is a profession and not, as is frequently the case on Broadway, a stimulating change from baccarat. The Circle is a "house" in the sense that a book publisher, an architectural office, or a law firm is a house—and in this sense no Broadway theater has been a house in living memory.

They have had flops—Victor Wolfson's *American Gothic*, Gregorio Martinez Sierra's, *The Cradle Song*, Francis Fergusson's experimental lyric play titled *The King and the Duke*—but flops are not necessarily disasters from a spectator viewpoint. In fact, failure in the theater can sometimes be as engrossing as success; what is disastrous is the play that aims at success not worth having (except in dollars). The latter kind is not staged at Circle in the Square—or for that matter elsewhere Off-Broadway. There is no sense in selling your soul for subsistence wages, and subsistence is all anyone can make downtown and over on the East Side.

The emergence of Circle in the Square (and with it the Phoenix, the Cherry Lane, the Theatre De Lys, and the Renata, among others) as a house with a reputation to build and guard has begun to effect the rehabilitation of New York's almost moribund theater audience. The theaters in the West Forties do not, for the most part, attract an audience; they attract a consuming public. These playgoers buy the prestige of having seen a hit, and they care no more about what makes a play live than about what makes a Cadillac purr. They spend a lot of money (largely expense-account money) and they support a number of good plays along with the expensively packaged vacuities, but they do not qualify as a participating audience; and their nervous competition to buy success is one of the factors that have changed the Broadway theater from a profession to a fabulous slot machine.

No one goes to the theater Off-Broadway for reasons of swank. The surroundings are insufficiently sumptuous, big names are scarce, the plays are typically either classics or revivals of works that failed to hit the uptown jackpot. The only reason, in short, for sallying off to one of these outlandish addresses is the hunger to see a play. And as the idea has spread that down in the Village and east of the Village are

"CIRCLE IN THE SQUARE" (1960)

several clusters of small theaters engaged in putting on plays that their proprietors admire, the almost forgotten pastime of theater-shopping has risen again in New York.

Because of the physical limitations of its former house, Circle in the Square has also been a leader in liberating the contemporary stage from conventional and often competitively ostentatious notions of what constitutes a professional theatrical production. A well-equipped, modern theater is a machine of almost limitless versatility, but complete freedom of means is not synonymous with the highest vitality. It is not just that the theater can produce an excellent illusion of reality (though a preoccupation with literal accuracy in sets and stage deportment often diminishes our drama); it is also that the theater can master almost any illusion. When audiences applaud a set as the curtain rises, they betray themselves . How can they possibly know that it is a good set until they have seen the play for which it was built? Have they come to some modern equivalent of the destruction of Pompeii, or . . . ? Illusion is essentially the prerogative of the playwright and his company, and the theater becomes mere playfulness when the designers take over the magic.

Off-Broadway is financially poor and physically makeshift; illusion is not easily achieved, but when it comes, it is from the right source. No one applauds when the curtain rises at Circle in the Square. For one thing, there is no curtain; for another, there is nothing on view to excite the most volatile hand-slapper. Placed about on stage there may be a few chairs and tables, perhaps a rug to designate a living area, a hanging lamp to light a dining table, leaf-twined trellis sections tacked up to mark a garden, a stepladder if action is to proceed on a second floor. All this is mere lumber, lifeless until the actors bring in the illusion. Then, however, the possibilities are limited only by the play's power to initiate illusion and the spectators' power to respond.

The necessity for both actors and audience to share commitment in the terms of the play is what so often gives the Off-Broadway theater an almost hypnotic vitality. Attendance at Circle in the Square is not a spectator sport; what your ticket buys is the right to take part in an exercise of the imagination. But this does not mean the Circle's facilities are a triumph of architecture. As in many of the Off-Broadway houses, the stages of both the old and new Circle in the Square are adaptations to available circumstances of theater-in-the-round. In the first Circle theater, the audience sat around three sides of the dance floor of the one-time nightclub, in slightly elevated tiers. The performers and spectators, virtually unseparated, were quite close to one another. The fourth side of the floor was blank, actually a series

21

ESSAYS

of shuttered loft doors that gave on the street. This provided the players with a wall that, figuratively and sometimes literally, they could back up to (often it was dressed with skeletal scenery). The Circle's directors have become so happy with the arrangement that they have almost exactly duplicated it in their new home.

Such a design is greatly superior to true theater-in-the-round, which, whatever its advantages of salable seat space, deprives a production of any tangible orientation and usually involves the actors in a melancholy vortical movement that resembles the slow emptying of a sink. The Circle's wall itself is a boon: the actor has thus a podium and a refuge; he can gaze "out there" without staring some cash customer out of countenance. Still, for the audience, this design does away with "upstage" or "downstage," with "stage left" or "stage right"—and it all depends on where you are sitting.

Relative position is a powerful tool in the theater, and a director deprived of it must develop a new style of his own. One reason for Circle in the Square's long survival is the style that Mr. Quintero devised to suit his hand-me-down theater arrangement. And, to flip the coin, the Circle's former primitive stage in a nightclub became the springboard from which Mr. Quintero has leapt in a very few years into the small circle of "name" directors. These are the men—Harold Clurman, Robert Lewis, and Elia Kazan prominent among them— whose services are bid for by Broadway producers and who, by selecting the plays they choose to undertake, affect the quality and direction of the commercial theater. Gaining critical acclaim for his work at the Circle, Mr. Quintero has been sought out as director for such varied, prestige productions as *I Pagliacci* and *Cavalleria Rusticana* at the Metropolitan Opera, Jane Bowles's play *In the Summer House* for Broadway, and Robinson Jeffers' *Medea* on television.

The influences that Mr. Quintero acknowledges as having the most impact upon him are the Catholic Church and Martha Graham. In this context, he refers to the pageantry of the Church, and once you know the source, the logic of the adaptation can be startling. Despite the surface incongruity of the notion, the spatial arrangements at the old Circle in the Square, re-created at the new, are not unlike those of a cathedral. Mr. Quintero does not assemble his performance on a box platform to confront a massed audience. He has one axis of action to work with and it passes through the center of his spectators. One does not think in terms of entrances left or right; players emerge from the darkness onto the stage from various entrances, including those the audience enters by.

"CIRCLE IN THE SQUARE" (1960)

The analogies with Church procedure here are obvious enough. Situated thus in the midst of his audience, Mr. Quintero can use processions, opposed choirs, leader and chorus, or wedges aimed to threaten or defend a focal point. These assemblages convey universally understood implications, and they say the same thing from whatever the point of observation. The effect sounds stiff when the forms are thus isolated, but Mr. Quintero rarely employs his geometry bare; like the sculptor's armature, it is the framework about which he constructs his play, articulating its parts into a communicative and subtly moving whole.

He also has a way of flinging his performers into the playing area like pebbles flung from a hand, a brilliantly effective way of swinging a scene instantly into full momentum or, alternately, of pitching the action to a blink of frozen suspense before climax. This device owes more, perhaps, to Greek than Gothic sources, or it may be a link with Martha Graham. The most obvious contribution of this great dancer is the high plasticity, or consciousness of himself as sculpture, that Mr. Quintero requires of an actor. Actors who are given no front or back for their impersonations are forced to be peculiarly aware of themselves in three dimensions. The twist of a back, the jut of an elbow, or the slope of a shoulder must all be simultaneously considered, for each of them is going to convey the dominant impression to some segment of the audience. In a sense, then, a Circle-in-the-Square performance is theater-as-sculpture rather than theater-as-mural.

The modified theater-in-the-round productions at the Circle result in performances that seem uncommonly fluid. Either in spite of or because of an almost embarrassing intimacy between audience and actors, the latter radiate a heightened aliveness that lends them stature. This is a lyric, impressionistic theater, very sensitive to emotional pressure, very responsive to shifting winds. It is necessarily—and by Mr. Quintero's choice—a poetic, allusive theater: it cannot be realistic, though it often deals in realism.

The limitations that had done much to form this admirable style were nonetheless limitations: no loft from which to fly scenery; no bridge behind a proscenium from which to direct lights; in short, almost no apparatus for illusion save talent. Over the years, Mr. Quintero had to learn what he must forego, but Circle in the Square still made mistakes. If *The Iceman Cometh*, that rumbling juggernaut of impotent glory, could be triumphantly staged there (May 1956–February 1958), why should Brendan Behan's *The Quare Fellow* (November 1958–March 1959), also rambling, also self-consuming and finally impotent, fail to succeed? The answer in part

ESSAYS

is that the brilliant counterpoint of speech in *The Iceman Cometh* was perfectly suited to staging in the round. The dialogue skipped and stuttered, swelled and waned; it signaled from table to table in Harry Hope's bar like a flickering swamp fire. Also, the tension of the play builds up steadily to the Homeric jest of Hickey, and the theater's open form was fine for the gyrations of Hickey's *danse macabre*. (The first-row audiences behind little tables were contiguous with the character-patrons of Harry Hope's bar, the show's setting.) Finally, of course, in this case Hickey was played by Jason Robards, Jr.

The Quare Fellow, by contrast, has a more steady, aching pressure of suspense. It gets its effect by piling one vignette on another to a toppling ironic climax of anticlimax. Scene by scene, the production had fine moments at Circle in the Square, but it never took shape. As a matter of fact, the script was defective in its own structure and would have profited from the formal shape and order that the modern box stage imposes. Another, quite different, example was Fergusson's experiment adapted from *Huckleberry Finn*. *The King and the Duke*, a dramatic square dance with charades, was a warm and ingratiating theater diversion. But it did not succeed—partly because the audience found itself for once almost embarrassingly implicated in the proceedings, partly because the music and dances seemed to ask for more spacious and formal accommodations.

When Mr. Quintero was asked about the stage on which he had worked for ten years, he smiled a little grimly and remarked that Off-Broadway had certainly proved the adage that all the drama needs is two boards and a passion. Two boards are about what most of them can afford. But when he was asked whether he would prefer a conventional, proscenium theater, he said, "No." What Mr. Quintero is trying to approach in his new working place on Bleecker Street is something like the Stratford, Ontario, Shakespearean auditorium, though obviously on a much smaller scale. The Ontario theater is a platform stage almost surrounded by the audience area, but elevated and with a back or inner stage for "closet" scenes. This arrangement is akin to having your cake and eating it.

Now as to money, Messrs. Quintero, Mann, and Connell consider themselves professionals, and a basic professional obligation is to stay in business. At the beginning, Circle in the Square played virtuoso gymnastics on a shoestring and stayed open, quite simply, through a generous camaraderie that is always heart-warming—and always certain to collapse if a spark of success does not catch somewhere. For the Circle, the spark was *Summer and Smoke*, which brought fame to Geraldine Page and for the first time a perceptible reserve in the bank

24

"CIRCLE IN THE SQUARE" (1960)

account. Two plays later (Victor Wolfson's *American Gothic* failed; Truman Capote's *The Grass Harp* was financially a stand-off, though it earned a good deal of prestige, which it had failed to do on Broadway), Fire Commissioner Cavanaugh padlocked the premises at the start of what looked like an almost indefinite run for *The Girl on the Via Flaminia*.

Reluctantly, the management ventured to move *Via Flaminia* uptown, but it failed to take hold in the harsh commercial soil of Broadway. For a time this threatened to put an end to Circle in the Square. Mr. Quintero was engaged to direct a Broadway production of Henry James's *Portrait of a Lady*; Mr. Mann took a job as assistant stage manager with Maxwell Anderson's *The Bad Seed*; Mr. Connell set off exploring new theatrical ventures, in new areas. But none was happy, and soon they decided to try independent production once more. Mr. Mann came back to New York to find a theater (and some rehearsal money). But the old Greenwich Village Inn was still empty and still the only possibility in sight; this time they were able to convince the Fire Department that they could operate it within the safety laws. The institution was running again, after only a broken stride; Mr. Quintero was again its director; and old colleague Connell hurried to rejoin it.

In its second materialization, Circle in the Square has operated with more conventional bookkeeping, but still within limits that would not please an accountant. Accountants admire a little more reserve fat, and Off-Broadway is a lean world. Here are the basic figures for a typical production at the new Circle. It costs $8,000 to $10,000 to mount a play—rehearsals, costumes, promotion, plant overhead, etc. Once running, the weekly break-even figure is around $3,000 and the maximum gross in the 200-seat house is $4,500. That means the theater must run at 67% capacity to stay even and must do, for example, 90% for ten weeks to accumulate the kitty for the next production.

Such figures suggest this is no business for tycoons, and in fact the Circle-in-the-Square management has survived in recent years by extramural work. After the revival of *The Iceman Cometh* had won grateful cheers from critics and public, O'Neill's widow entrusted *Long Day's Journey into Night* to Mr. Quintero's direction and to the management of Messrs. Quintero, Mann, and Connell for a Broadway presentation. This made what is called real money, and although it contributed nothing directly to the Circle's solvency, it did for a time allow the owners to keep their own fingers from the Circle's till by paying them liberal salaries for their Broadway work.

ESSAYS

Last summer, furthermore, Mr. Quintero staged *Macbeth* with Siobhàn McKenna and Jason Robards, Jr., for the Cambridge Drama Festival, and the Circle triumvirate is hopeful of bringing the produc-tion to Broadway. All last autumn Messrs. Mann, Quintero, and Connell engaged in legal skirmishing to bring Bertolt Brecht's *Mother Courage and Her Children* to Broadway, with Miss McKenna in the title role. Broadway, in short, is where the Circle looks to cultivate its cash crop.

But why accept the limitations of the present set-up; why indeed work Off-Broadway at all? A bigger theater (moderately bigger; the Phoenix is immense and so are its headaches) would seem to be the answer. A house of about 500 seats, says Mr. Mann, would be ideal (the smallest Broadway house holds about 750). But in Mr. Mann's ideal house, the overhead could very easily mount as fast as the gross. Union demands would be stiffer, both in base scale and in the number of technical jobs made obligatory; rent and associated expenses would leap. At this level, financing would become a much more formidable problem, and Off-Broadway might begin to depend on the same kind of speculative money that has dominated the theater uptown in recent years.

Obviously, the directors of Circle in the Square are not refugees from Broadway; on the contrary, Broadway found them in Sheridan Square. But they have only made safaris uptown and they prefer to maintain their explorer role. Up on Broadway they are hired hands, or at best operators of one-shot enterprises. Giddy and exciting as the experience can be, and lucrative when it all goes well, it is for them not as satisfying as running their own theater in their own way. The Circle has moved, but it is still in Greenwich Village, with its special traditions and its hungry audiences.

Actually, the permanence of the house (if not a repertory company, then at least a repertory management) is what principally distinguishes an Off-Broadway theater like Circle in the Square from the uptown business. There is no essential difference in the plays produced; often they are the same plays, but offered in revival for their dramatic rather than their box-office, star-vehicle values. The Circle management is not avant-garde; it is, if anything, conservative and has been criticized for a lack of experimental daring. But Mr. Mann points out that the arcane play, the anti-drama or abstract morality that "couldn't possibly attract an audience uptown," has proved equally incapable of attracting an audience downtown. However that may be, the taste of this management is for solid accomplishment rather than for novelty; the three men would rather put on revivals of neglected

26

classics or restage good plays that stumbled on Broadway than man the artistic barricades.

This may be a shortcoming, but they have not done badly as artists over the past ten years. They brought O'Neill back to his big public; they have offered Jean Anouilh, Federico García Lorca, Jean Giraudoux, Jacinto Benavente, Tennessee Williams, and Truman Capote; they did real service (and made money) by resurrecting Edwin Justus Mayer's forgotten *Children of Darkness*; they backed their convictions to produce *The Quare Fellow* when Broadway wanted no traffic with Behan.

Many of Circle in the Square's friends wish they could find new playwrights, and so do they themselves; in fact they are vehement about it, for they know that they cannot forever feed their theater from the files. In this respect, they are somewhat trapped; their standards are not unlike the best Broadway standards, and Broadway uses a fairly fine sieve. An old playwright who promises to write new plays for the Circle is Thornton Wilder. Impressed with the theater's record even before its revival of *Our Town*, Wilder is writing for the Circle a cycle of one-acters called *The Seven Deadly Sins*. But a living theater cannot be content with the contribution of acceptable, older masters; it demands fresh talent on which to nurture itself.

Perhaps a willingness to experiment, even sacrifice, is the price Circle in the Square will have to pay for new voices, and perhaps the economics of their new theater will permit an occasional bet on promise. The contemporary success and usefulness of the Circle are now more matters of fact than opinion. But the theater's ultimate reputation, its place in the annals, will depend primarily on the writers it brings to public notice. In a sense, Messrs. Mann, Quintero, and Connell are anticipatory members of a partnership; the other is that O'Casey, that O'Neill of our day, who has yet to appear.

"The New York Shakespeare Festival" (1960)

The New York theater in the past several years has become a three-part activity—Broadway, Off-Broadway, and Shakespeare in Central Park. The third is my present subject, and I find it rather tricky. Joseph Papp, founder, producer, and often director of the New York Shakespeare Festival, easily falls into the mold of those plucky heroes who supplied our grandfathers with their inspirational reading. He can't be beaten because he won't be beaten, and as a consequence, he

ESSAYS

has provided the citizens of New York with productions of twelve plays over a period of seven years—and charged not one penny for admission. With no money of his own and no close relationship to money, he has created a meeting place for "a dispossessed audience and dispossessed actors." Meanwhile, he has held a full-time job in television to support his family.

Mr. Papp is no philanthropist; he is an idealist and an optimist, but these are different matters. His idealism consists in believing that every citizen needs and is entitled to a theater—just as he needs and is entitled to schools, libraries, and museums—and that actors deserve an alternative to the "talent-destroying" gamble of Broadway. Mr. Papp's optimism consists in believing that others will share his vision of a theater run for beauty and wisdom, not for money. The Shakespeare Festival is an utterly surprising gift to the people of New York; it is also, for the present, a bold and ingenious solution to a personal quest, worked out by a tough young man of powerful ego and daring imagination.

Thus began a shoestring operation so audacious as to seem almost ludicrous. "Shoestring" is, however, not the word for it because that implies a desperate scramble for solvency, and Mr. Papp has never had the least intention of becoming solvent. He *expects* to be supported and, curiously, his strength is that he has always made that clear: "What is basically needed is the conviction that the arts are vital to our lives. Methods of financing will follow." Mr. Papp's method of financing is to announce each season what plays he proposes to stage and how much they will cost (seasonal budgets have risen from a few hundred dollars in 1955 to $100,000 for 1960), and then to start rehearsals. He has steady nerves and is capable of opening a play when he has no funds beyond the first night. Some seasons have been chopped short, but in the main, Mr. Papp has made good on his announcements. Money has been forthcoming: it has come chiefly from foundations, but a steady small stream has come from the audience. Public funds still elude the Festival, but various city departments have given invaluably of materials, equipment, and services. When the 1960 season ended, the city was committed to building a $250,000 permanent stage for the Festival, and Tyrone Guthrie was scheduled to direct *Hamlet* for the first offering in the spring of 1961.

In addition to bringing Shakespeare to the people, Mr. Papp brings a number of good young actors before a very large audience. Besides George C. Scott and Colleen Dewhurst, this number has included Jerry Stiller and his wife, Anne Meara, both excellent Shakespearean comics; Jack Cannon, who has played Touchstone and Tyrrel, among

28

"THE NEW YORK SHAKESPEARE FESTIVAL" (1960)

other roles; Peggy Bennion, John McLiam, Robert Blackburn, and Robert Geiringer. Mr. Papp's theater is not yet so solid an institution as the Public Library, but it is nevertheless an institution.

Now obviously there is a trick to this. You cannot simply throw yourself from a rooftop, crying "I will fly, I will fly," and expect anyone to express more than momentary interest. You must show some aptitude for flying. The first thing always said of the New York Shakespeare Festival is that it is free, but the more important fact is that it is good. The public is said not to appreciate anything it gets for nothing, but night after night, summer after summer, the long line forms at the gate to the Festival grounds and waits as long as three hours for admission. The present theater holds 2,500; it plays to full capacity six nights a week for approximately ten weeks, and on many nights the fences are lined with spectators who arrived too late to get in. People come in the tens of thousands, not because the seats are free—every bench in Central Park is that—but because they are aroused and instructed by the play. And because they come to be fed, the money comes to nourish them. That quarter-mile queue, stretched out between the lake and the playing fields in the twilight, is a breadline, and Mr. Papp is of a background that teaches the moral force of breadlines.

Excellence has been the trick from the beginning. Back when the Festival was still the Workshop, and *As You Like It* was being performed without sets or salaries, Meyer Levin wrote of "the pace of the direction" and "the precise note of stylization" of this "unadulterated Shakespeare." And in the seasons since then, first at the East River Park amphitheater, later touring the boroughs with a portable stage, now based in Central Park with winter seasons at the Heckscher Theatre on upper Fifth Avenue, the productions have elicited similar comment. The critics do not indulge the Festival (they applaud the idea, but judge the product), and notes of sharp criticism have been directed at this characterization or that interpretation. But the Festival has enjoyed what is known as a "good press," and the phrases of appreciation fall into a pattern: the plays are vivid, they move fast, they are exciting and credible, they are clear, and they seem pertinent. Mr. Levin astutely compared the Workshop to the New York City Ballet—all the classic knowledge is kept, but accumulated "tradition" is stripped away and a freshness gets into the material.

Mr. Papp finds himself, he says, at odds with the subjective muddiness of the contemporary realistic theater and seeks a style that rests initially on the words of the play, not on the acting. What an actor does should follow necessarily from what he says; he makes his bearing

ESSAYS

congruous with his lines and does not seek readings of the text that support a "characterization." From this stem several corollaries for Shakespeare: the manner to be sought is heroic—in gesture and clarity, bigger than life—but based on a respect for the characters as real people (even in the Festival's Forest of Arden, the people were extraordinarily real); the action should be *on* the lines, not between them; scenes should move at such a pace that one actually pushes another off the stage; and speech must not only be clear but sufficiently rapid so that the long line of Shakespeare's ideas does not falter.

The ideal is a poetic theater, based on a conviction that the matter in hand is important and relevant to the audience. None of this is easy, and I would not wish to give the impression that it is perfectly achieved. But the program gives a method of approach; it offers the actors—often inexperienced ones—a rational basis for building their parts, and it produces a particular Festival quality. Shakespeare is in vogue at the moment, and on various stages we are offered a variety of brilliant, painstaking productions. But often they tend to be elegant museum pieces or are "translated" into our times and concerns. I know of no company that is as successful as the New York Shakespeare Festival at finding the eternally contemporary in Shakespeare and presenting it, without strain, in its Elizabethan idiom. You get the eeriest feeling, in the Park sometimes, that Shakespeare is alive and among us.

A good way to find out how strong an idea has become is to try to stop it. Robert Moses tried to stop free Shakespeare early in 1959 (he was then New York Parks Commissioner), announcing that he would not renew the Festival's license unless tickets were sold at $1 and $2 with 10% of the gross going to the Parks Department for sundry expenses, including repair of eroded grass. Mr. Papp refused. Mr. Moses, a man of varied talents, has never been a good judge of public opinion and periodically finds himself playing the role of villain to a large and aroused audience. No one has explained why he turned on the Festival after earlier expressions of approval, but it is obvious that he did not foresee a formidable uprising on behalf of Shakespeare. Nonetheless, the uprising occurred and Mr. Papp found a vocal throng of supporters; Mr. Moses received the obloquy of both press and populace for his part in the affair.

Mr. Papp took Mr. Moses into court and was supported by Justice James B. McNally of the Appellate Division, who instructed the Commissioner to reconsider his "arbitrary, capricious, and unreasonable demands." Mr. Moses, now feeling hemmed in, tossed the Festival to another city department, saying in effect, "you can have

30

"THE NEW YORK SHAKESPEARE FESTIVAL" (1960)

your free Shakespeare if the Board of Estimate will give me $20,000 for my erosion." Two private citizens, Edward Bernays and Mrs. Florence Anspecher, offered the money. By June 24th, the Festival was back in Central Park, but with time left for only one play, *Julius Caesar*. It was acclaimed on all sides.

Last summer, Mr. Papp opened the season by directing *Henry V*, Alan Schneider followed with *Measure for Measure*, and Gerald Freedman completed the schedule with *The Taming of the Shrew*. Looking at the first two productions together, one can see what constitutes the Festival style. Young Harry's conquest of King Charles's realm and his daughter's hand was, of course, a happy choice for the Park. The Festival's "wooden O" rang with the clash of personalities and the implied collision of armies. At the same time, Mr. Papp's emphasis made it perfectly clear that the subject of the play is less the struggle between France and England (about which no one now desperately cares) than the determination of the fledgling and notorious Hal to show himself a king of mettle and the legitimate leader of his land. Youth has come into power—the king and his handsome brothers—and though it is disposed to honor and heed the experienced guardians of the state (as shown most sweetly in a fine rendering of the scene with Sir Thomas Erpingham, that valorous old knight), it will not tolerate ambiguity of authority. Thus the moment is one of great uneasiness until Henry demonstrates that he is strong enough to grasp his realm with grace and honor.

Henry V is a drama that never loses relevance, and Mr. Papp found in James Ray an actor able to express the quiet, intelligent force that Shakespeare implied below the surface of Harry's neophyte swagger and youthful heroics. The staging itself was gallant with light and rich cloth and the flash of armor. But every embellishment functioned— every torch lit a dark corner, every brazier warmed a cold soldier, every banner was there to lift the hearts of a ragged band of commandos. And certainly no one moved but to a purpose: this *Henry V* plunged ahead as though caught in a flood, and indeed it is a story of men caught in the flood of events.

By comparison, *Measure for Measure* vacillated, cast about, and lost its momentum. The comparison, I know, is unfair to Mr. Schneider, for not only was he directing his first play in the Park— he is the first director other than Stuart Vaughan or Joseph Papp to work there—but he was engaged with a play that can only with the greatest difficulty be made credible to modern audiences. (The Festival, though, scored one of its early successes with *Two Gentlemen of Verona*, a play you would have thought no one could reanimate

31

ESSAYS

today.) There were good things about this *Measure for Measure*: in particular, Philip Bosco created a convincing Angelo, making of him a shocking but somehow touching man, and the play pulled itself together for a resolute and meaningful conclusion.

But Mr. Schneider let his worries show. They showed in the heavy earnestness with which the cast spoke its lines—arguing, as it were, with the audience instead of one another (the actors often were players I knew to be excellent from earlier productions). And the worries showed in a kind of fussiness of staging (though this was the most handsome of all the Festival productions I have seen) that seemed to be trying to assist Shakespeare. A procession of nuns was beautiful, and beautifully killed the action; a chess game was introduced, served no purpose, and was sheepishly put away; the Duke stepped on a high platform to deliver a soliloquy (why should a man get up on a box to talk to himself?); Angelo sanded his papers so industriously during the first encounter with Isabella that the scene looked more like a lesson in penmanship than a plea for mercy. Busyness is the death of action.

And the characters strained. Lucio is really at the heart of *Measure for Measure*; if you make him credible, you have gone a long way toward making the play credible. Frederic Warriner was encouraged to turn him into a kind of lewd puppet, winking, smacking his lips, playing *glissando* with his voice, hopping about like a beset blue jay. Lucio is, in fact, almost a comic Iago, a man of wit and malice, a good fellow and rotten. Of all the sins in the play, his calumny alone is unforgivable. True, he is extravagant, but no more so than the Dauphin in *Henry V*, with his tennis racket and his apostrophe to his horse. Thomas Aldredge made sense of that fantastical young man; he showed us a youth of precocious promise, spoiled by his elders and bored by them, and overcome by Aubrey Beardsley. Every campus sports a few—and about half grow up to their talents.

I could go on—the comics of *Henry V* were off the streets, the comics of *Measure for Measure* were out of some theory of acting—but I don't want to carry the comparison further than the point requires. The point is that Shakespeare rewards only those who trust him. It is no good saying "they will never take that scene if we play it straight," because it is certain that "they" will not take it if you try to apologize for it. The Festival's quality rests on the fact that it has always assumed that Shakespeare is good enough; that he created people, not characters; that values and behavior change, but motive and impulse do not. The Festival has drawn its pictures with the largest, simplest, fastest strokes it could devise, working outdoors in

32

"THE NEW YORK SHAKESPEARE FESTIVAL" (1960)

the Park as though on a mural, with strong design, bright color, and sure motion.

This year, Mr. Papp gave up his job in television. He has instituted a subscription program whereby patrons contributing $7.50 are invited to previews of the Festival productions. The anticipated 10,000 subscribers will not only add to the annual budget but will also be an active support to the Festival. So Mr. Papp's ingenious scheme for a rewarding life in the theater for himself and his actors, and a theater for the joy of all comers, approaches reality; but its inventor is still not satisfied. For one thing, he wants to be granted a continuing appropriation by New York State's Department of Education. He thinks he has proved that he is an educator, and he does not fear government control: "There can be no guarantee of freedom in the theater or any place else. It is a condition that must be constantly fought for."

He does not plan to restrict himself indefinitely to Shakespeare ("I'm no crazy Bardophile," he once said) and is even now looking speculatively at Bernard Shaw's *Saint Joan*. And he does not intend to confine himself forever to Central Park. It is a superb site; it will be better still with the permanent installations. But for Mr. Papp it has the drawback that, in the center of Manhattan, it attracts too high a proportion of the regular theater public. He recalls nostalgically evenings on the East River when men and women cried out in protest or approval as the unknown drama unfolded, when children ran down to the rim of the stage to menace or support the players. This still happens in Central Park, but not often enough to suit the producer.

Consequently, Mr. Papp wants to tour the neighborhoods where at present the only drama is delinquency. This was his early plan, but it broke down in 1957 because it took eighteen hours to set up and dismantle the equipment and because the mobile stage was falling to pieces. With the Park base now reasonably secure, Mr. Papp is scheming for a better truck stage on which he can take Shakespeare to people who do not know whether Macbeth will live to enjoy his throne or what fate awaits Juliet.

The New York Shakespeare Festival is an astonishing success, but it does not seem to astonish its founder. He said some time ago: "You start with the philosophy that theater is important to people's lives. If you don't believe this, then you might as well give up. Of course it's true. A spirit handed down for 2,000 years and more can't be ignored."

ESSAYS

"Persistent Ibsenism" (1962)

Are we to have an Ibsen revival? In the theater one does not ask such questions—it is like inquiring which way the cat will jump—and I shall venture no more than to say that the idea is plausible and desirable. There are a few signs: David Ross, whose 4th Street Theatre in New York (Off-Broadway) first won acclaim as a Chekhov home, last season presented *Hedda Gabler* in a production that was well praised and well patronized; and he followed it last September with a fine presentation of *Ghosts*. During August, CBS televised scenes from *Brand* on a Sunday morning religious show, and in Provincetown, Massachusetts, over the Labor Day weekend I watched a young company grapple with the mystic desperations of *When We Dead Awaken*.

Mr. Ross's second Ibsen presentation is much surer than his first. There were good scenes in *Hedda Gabler*, but the play was made somewhat shallow by a disposition to see Hedda as an ambitious bitch, rather than as the manifestation of perverse romanticism posing as a higher sensibility, about which Ibsen was concerned. The production of *Ghosts*, with Leureen MacGrath (Mrs. Alving), Staats Cotsworth (Pastor Manders), and Joseph Marino (Oswald), is staged with taut nerves, painful clarity, and a fine particularity of character. The point that a wife should not be obliged to cleave to a man who pursues the parlor maid is no longer controversial. Still, Miss MacGrath acts to make the play pivot on Mrs. Alving's sense of duty; she understands herself very clearly and very much too late. Mr. Ross will surely continue with the Ibsen cycle, for the reception of the first two plays has been good; and New York will thus be shown, in a converted cold-water flat on the lower East Side, something of the range of the greatest theater mind of the nineteenth century.

But the evidence of a revival is not conclusive, for we have always given sporadic attention to Ibsen. In the past ten years New York has seen twelve productions of seven Ibsen plays, better than one a season. The effort, though, has been scattered, the achievement uneven, the attention minimal: we seem to put on Ibsen when we have nothing more pressing to do. Respect for Ibsen is such that his name is never omitted from the shortest list of theater immortals, but this honor comes close to being one of those hollow forms that so roused Ibsen's own savagery as a playwright. He may be part of our tradition, but he is scarcely part of our life.

I do not suppose, however, that the American theater will be so quixotic as to stage an Ibsen renaissance for the sake of the public's

34

"PERSISTENT IBSENISM" (1962)

intellectual honesty. On the contrary, and practically speaking, I think the time is ripe. In particular, it is ripe for Ibsen to stand clear of the protecting cloak Bernard Shaw threw around him. No artist under attack of ignorance ever enjoyed a more brilliant defense, but Shaw's eloquence now stands between Ibsen and the contemporary audience. Younger than Ibsen, Shaw was nevertheless more specifically, like Ibsen, a man of the nineteenth century; if you will, though, he was a narrower man. Further, he was disposed to admire people for their ability to agree with him, and he saw in Ibsen the virtues he knew himself to possess—principally social reason and hot indignation.

In those days—1891 and after—Ibsen was being vilified (in the immoderate terms that only the moderate Victorians could employ without embarrassment) for his immorality, and Shaw proved conclusively and repeatedly in *The Quintessence of Ibsenism* that his subject was the most moral of preceptors. Today the suggestion that there is anything wicked in Ibsen can only make us smile. Indeed, it is hard to find in his work anything we would call unconventional. Even more damaging, perhaps, to our interest in the plays was Shaw's relish for his elder's iconoclasm. It is certainly true that Ibsen was a formidable dynamiter who seriously weakened, if he did not finally shatter, a number of revealed truths. But it is fatal today to celebrate him for having challenged the sanctity of marriage, the omniscience of the church, the efficacy of idealism, the probity of constituted authority, the problem of the "compact majority." These issues brought out the intellectual militia in the 1890s, but Ibsen fairly disposed of them and Shaw mopped up the pockets of resistance. And insofar as they won their battles, that aspect of their work became dated propaganda.

Shaw has become more dated than Ibsen (he now survives principally though his wit) because he was more exclusively a propagandist. His disservice to his hero was that he did not see, or did not sufficiently value, the further depths of the man. The rational, free-thinking socialism, the utopia of the syllogism, that so preoccupied Shaw was not the only wind of promise flowing across Europe in the latter half of the nineteenth century. Ibsen was born in 1828, Freud in 1856 (like Shaw). During the span of Ibsen's playwriting career, from 1848 to 1900, the psyche was coming ever more sharply under the microscope, and though there is not, so far as I know, a single psychoanalytic reference in the plays, they are all of them—and increasingly as the work accumulates—concerned with the functions and maladies of the ego. In that respect, Ibsen is as much our contemporary as Shaw.

Today, of course, the theater steams with psychology: whole scenes are devoted to group analysis, and one can almost detect which of the

ESSAYS

Freudian sects a playwright's analyst adheres to by listening to the prattle of the characters. I doubt that this tendency is good for the stage, or for any other form of narrative in which it takes strong hold. It acts to reduce people to case histories and turns drama into a clinical monograph. We no longer concern ourselves with good and evil, but instead with putting the right tag on a neurosis. This not only vulgarizes Freud: it also pitifully diminishes the human experience.

No one in Ibsen sports a neurosis. His characters struggle against Fortune as though they were men and women of free will and sound mind, assumptions that must be made if we are to struggle at all. But, strictly speaking, Ibsen did not portray a single victim: one and all, his people bring their own wrath down upon themselves. Sometimes they know it, as does Mrs. Alving in *Ghosts* by the time Oswald asks her for the sun; sometimes, as in *The Master Builder*, the revelation is itself fatal; and sometimes, as in *An Enemy of the People*, the curtain falls with the hero plunging still deeper into the delusions of his private night.

An Enemy of the People is an apt example of the persistence of Ibsenism. It scorches alike the wickedness of entrenched commercial power and the prudence of popular opposition. Shaw hailed it in those terms, but who today would cross the street to see a play teaching that bureaucrats will behave monstrously to save their shirts and that their opposition can be routed by the cry of higher taxes?

Consider, however, the personal behavior of the protagonist. Why should Dr. Stockmann, that high-minded and public-spirited man, fall into such a merry humor when he discovers that the medicinal waters on which his town depends for its prosperity are dangerously polluted? Why does he hasten to a newspaper with the sad facts; why does he rub his hands and talk excitedly of smiting, crushing, and beating to the ground those responsible? The fact is, he hates his older brother and is overjoyed to surprise him with his hand in the cookie jar. Dr. Stockmann was not looking to improve matters; he was looking to provoke a fight, and his tragedy was that he no longer had a mother to run to. *An Enemy of the People* fascinates today, long after its social message has been absorbed, because its hero is not only the play's voice of conscience but also its principal villain. It answers a question that we ask ourselves with almost every morning's newspaper: Why are reformers so often more unappetizing than the rascals they pursue?

Shaw commends *Rosmersholm* to us as a demonstration of love's evolution from a lower (animal) to a higher (rational) form, but since the play ends with a suicide pact in the mill race, I suspect that a modern director could define more precisely the relationship between

"PERSISTENT IBSENISM" (1962)

Rebecca West and John Rosmer. Similarly, Shaw praises *A Doll's House* for contributing to the emancipation of wives from domestic tyranny. It certainly does that, but it also comes to the aid of husbands whose wives insist on pretending that the marriage bed is a playpen. Nora not only permits such endearments as "twittering lark" and "bustling squirrel," she gives the impression of encouraging them as part of the Helmers' mating rites. If so, the ensuing intimacies must take a form that does Torvald no good at all. This, however, is not the sort of speculation that would have occurred to Shaw.

I could, I think, show similarly that the psychological aberrations of relatively normal men and women lie at the base of every Ibsen play, and I feel sure that the way to deliver them alive to the stage today is to ask, not what social institution is here under attack, but what is eating the characters. A fault, perhaps, in Ibsen's psychological insights is that he sometimes failed to appreciate how stubborn a neurosis can really be—he lacked, after all, the clinical reports of those long years on the couch. Thus, in *The Pillars of Society*, it is more surprising than convincing that Karsten Bernick, after a lifetime of rationalization so extreme that he can evade the guilt of sending a ship to almost certain death, should in the last scene make an open and healing confession of his lies.

But that, relatively, was an early play. Contrast it with *Little Eyolf*, a much later work, which offers perhaps the most poignant happy ending in modern drama. Alfred and Rita Allmers seek reconciliation and tranquility in a philanthropy dedicated to the memory of their dead son, not realizing that the dagger between them is not guilt for the little boy's lameness (he was injured when they left him unattended to embrace each other) but Alfred's unacknowledged realization that his wife's physical vitality is more significant than his own creative energy. Ibsen's whole work is permeated with the torments occasioned by the illusions and frustrations of the creative process.

And Ibsen's whole work is what should now concern us—not a play this season to fill out a repertory and another next season because an actress would like to try her hand at playing Rebecca West in *Rosmersholm*. We should not pick about among his works to find something that suits us, but should trust Ibsen to be the genius we so glibly proclaim him and give this dramatist the freedom of our stage.

I would not be taken too literally: even Shakespeare does not survive wholly intact. Ibsen wrote ten plays before *Brand* brought him fame in 1866, and I doubt that those early works, based for the most part on sagas and Norse history, could be reanimated. *Brand* is possibly too single-minded and too demonic for our domestic stage in

ESSAYS

America (although it would make a compelling opera); and *Emperor and Galilean*, that gargantuan double drama that sprawls across the Roman Empire and spends whole armies in the search for a Caesar's soul, might overtax our physical resources as well as our philosophic energies. It could be made into the greatest of all Biblical screen extravaganzas, but at what cost to its meaning I will not attempt to estimate.

Beginning, however, with *Peer Gynt* (that terrible portrait of the charming, talent, half-baked man) and skipping the sanguinary pilgrimage of the Emperor Julian, there are fourteen plays for an Ibsen theater. They range from the farce of *The League of Youth* to the tragic dirge of *John Gabriel Borkman*; they are in prose or poetry. Ibsen's job as scourge of nineteenth-century European society is finished, but there is no time limit to his role as guide to the human situation. Except, perhaps, that our time is peculiarly apt for his view of it. We have been dismayed by the discovery that man is the only animal in which the fact of being crippled is almost a mark of the species. Ibsen was pointing this out a hundred years ago—and adding that the battle for survival would still go on.

"The Living Theatre" (1962)

I hesitate to open with a tautology, but the great fact about The Living Theatre is that it is alive. If Broadway is sick, as I am assured by all experts that it is, the malady may stem from excessive traffic in handsome corpses. However, the subject is not the morbidity of Broadway, but the vitality of an enterprise at Fourteenth Street and Sixth Avenue (up one narrow flight in a renovated neighborhood department store). Being alive, The Living Theatre is assertive, sometimes misguided, full of ego, insistent in its demands upon an audience, and given to making statements about itself. For it is a political theater, and it exists, not to beguile, but to influence its audience.

Politics is the art of governing, and governing our understanding is the objective of Julian Beck and Judith Malina, founders, producers, directors, designers, and frequently actors in The Living Theatre repertory. Their most famous production, the play that has given the company a national and international reputation, is Jack Gelber's *The Connection*. It is notorious by now that nothing happens in *The Connection*. Indeed, its central point is that, in the world of narcotic addiction, nothing ever does happen; that the seduction of dope is its capacity to make events superfluous. Verisimilitude is what holds attention at *The Connection*, an immediacy so tangible that only by a conscious

38

"THE LIVING THEATRE" (1962)

appeal to common sense can one be assured that these are actors and not junkies. Therefore, if one thinks of the play in the context of entertainment, it becomes unseemly, a pandering to curiosity no more edifying than a tour of Chinatown. A good many people have thought of it in that way, but it is obtuse of them; the whole force of the writing and staging is to break down the distinction between actor and viewer and to make everyone present aware that, to a degree, he is hooked by an addictive society. That is political, as opposed to commercial or *voyeuristic*, theater.

Since their purpose is to influence, the Becks (they are husband and wife) concern themselves a good deal with the enigmatic relationship of illusion and reality. "We believe in the theater as a place of intense experience, half dream, half ritual, in which the spectator approaches something of a vision of self-understanding. . . . To achieve a full synthesis of experience, he must become totally involved, as in a dream or a religious ritual. It is in order to accomplish this that the avant-garde theater today uses techniques developed by Brecht, Piscator, Copeau, Meyerhold, Cocteau, etc." This statement, made by Mr. Beck in a *New York Times* article of several years ago, well defines the aims, methods, and preoccupations of his theater. Over a period of ten years, he and his wife have drawn their repertory from Luigi Pirandello, Jean Racine, August Strindberg, Sophocles, Jean Cocteau, Bertolt Brecht, Gertrude Stein, Alfred Jarry, W. H. Auden, and Paul Goodman. It is a literature, in the main, of poetry and legend directed to social and political ends, and it lends itself frequently to productions in which such terms as "stage" and "play" and "actor" become ambiguous, in which one cannot be certain where the line has been drawn between actuality and contrivance—or, indeed, exactly when the performance began or ended.

When the public arrives for William Carlos Williams's *Many Loves*, the curtain is open, scenery and props are being set, actors are working in groups upon details of the scenes to come. Gradually, more figures assemble, movement becomes livelier; then the lights black out momentarily (someone calls that a fuse has blown), and at this moment, presumably, the play begins. And during the intermission of *The Connection*, out in the spacious, elegantly impoverished lobby, where coffee and avant-garde publications are sold and where pacifist appeals are given out free, a member of the cast will panhandle you for money to finance his next injection. The Becks (between them they direct all the productions) look in the scripts for lines that can be flung like knives into the audience. Gelber once remarked, at a time when an English production of his play had provoked real riots at the Duke of York Theatre in London: "The conflict of attitudes between audience and players—rather than the conflict on stage—is the focal point." It is the recurring focal point in

39

ESSAYS

Living Theatre productions, and by concentrating on it, the Becks have found that they can operate, in a state of approximate solvency, the only true repertory theater New York has known in many years.

Preoccupation with the mirror bafflements of illusion and reality stems in part from the political orientation of the company; it stems also from the Becks' involvement in the artistic currents of their era. Henry Miller writes autobiographies that are probably fiction; Jean Genet writes fiction that is almost certainly autobiography; John Cage composes music that is governed by chance; painters in every contemporary exhibition offer canvases whose subject is the paint on the canvas. The Museum of Modern Art has recently mounted a major show of "constructions"—works in which the objects of domestic and industrial life become the materials of art, and in which the materials tend to comprise their own subject matter.

It has become good form to explain this eating away of the distinction between creation and occurrence by referring to the world situation: reality has become so fantastic and so fateful that the artist recoils from tempting fate by the exercise or his own fantasy. But the breaking of forms can readily be elevated to the importance of a theory; it then becomes self-defeating, since it depends for its dramatic, poetic, or ethical effect on an expectation of the very forms it is transgressing. Shock is not a theory; it too soon becomes habit.

Because of *The Connection,* and because of their location on Fourteenth Street (the Boulevard Saint-Michel of the pad dweller), it is sometimes ignorantly said that the Becks are spokesmen for the hip and the beat. This suggests a dishevelment of demeanor and a modesty of ambition made ludicrous by the couple's elegance and boldness. They have always been bold. Fifteen years ago, just out of college, they decided that the theater was to be their life and that, in the absence of a company that attracted them, they would have to start one of their own. They started it in their own apartment (the enterprise was originally called The Living Room Theatre), which is modest enough; but they enlisted among their first sponsors and mentors Robert Edmond Jones and Jean Cocteau, and that was not modest at all.

Last year they were invited to participate in the annual *Théâtre des Nations Festival* in Paris and applied to the State Department's cultural exchange bureau for travel funds. Unhappily for them, money bad been previously assigned to a Helen Hayes troupe that was also headed for Europe, and the cupboard was bare. The Becks may have suspected, too, that the State Department preferred Miss Hayes's unobjectionable repertory of Thornton Wilder's *The Skin of Our Teeth,* Tennessee Williams's *The Glass Menagerie,* and William Gibson's *The Miracle Worker* to The Living Theatre's package of controversy: *The Connection, Many Loves,*

40

"THE LIVING THEATRE" (1962)

and Brecht's *In the Jungle of Cities*. By coincidence, the larger foundations also found themselves to be short of funds.

In this predicament the Becks staged a "champagne gala" at the studio of Larry Rivers, charging twenty-five dollars a couple and auctioning donated works by Franz Kline, Grace Hartigan, Willem de Kooning, Richard Lippold, Theodoros Stamos, I. Rice Pereira, and others. In an evening they raised more than half the money needed for what proved a triumphant barnstorming of Italy, France, and West Germany. The company won all three of the important awards at the Paris Festival.

As participants, then, in the contemporary sleight-of-illusion, the Becks share the hazards of the preoccupation. Having granted that they may take such liberties with theater custom as advance their purpose, I yet wonder whether some of their more celebrated exploits really do advance it. Thus, the rather elaborate device of the play-within-the play of *The Connection*—the pretense that this is not a stage performance but the filming of a documentary, and that the actors are really junkies who have been hired with dope to exhibit themselves before the cameras—is intended to make us feel we are "there." But in practice the cast on stage creates a mesmerically terrifying intimacy with the audience; whereas the periodic sallies of "director" and "author," down the aisle and up onto the stage, reassure everyone that the whole business is make-believe.

Similarly, the frame of "dress rehearsal" that surrounds the three very uneven sketches comprising Dr. Williams's *Many Loves* may interest those who have always wondered how one goes about staging a play. Possibly it was also thought that the spectacle of a young "playwright" trying to bring his vision to birth despite the blindness and jealousy of the "world" (his former homosexual lover, now a potential backer) gave sufficient point in Living-Theatre terms to material that was not otherwise strikingly relevant. But the machinery only underscores the dramatic skimpiness of the author's reflections on love (though as quick sketches, two of the pieces are vivid and provocative), and the justifications in his alter ego's anxious monologues draw attention to the fact that there is reason for Dr. Williams's anxiety.

The Living Theatre is a small house (162 seats); the stage is elevated so little as to suggest that one might be looking from one room into another; there is no proscenium arch; there are no wings. More important, Julian Beck, who designs all the sets, has developed a style that, very close to the methods of "assemblage," seems to take canny advantage of discarded objects, scrap lumber, allusive mementoes, and decorations of the sort that clutter the attics of houses long lived in. His sets evoke precisely the atmosphere he intends; they satisfy the eye without unduly stimulating it (audiences, thank God, do not applaud Beck sets, as has become the

ESSAYS

stultifying custom uptown), and they efficiently support a clear, vigorous, and often complicated action in a tiny playing area. For all these reasons, then, communication flows with no hindrance between stage and spectator in this house. It does not need tricky machines to pump it.

Just how excellently it flows may be tested in the production of Brecht's *In the Jungle of Cities*, which Miss Malina introduced last season (it was the American premiere of a play Brecht wrote in 1921–24) into the current repertory. The *Jungle* is a melodrama whose subject is easily stated—it is about a fight to the death between a Malayan lumber dealer and a poor boy from the countryside, in an imaginary Chicago of 1912—but it is almost impossible to know what is happening at any given moment. Having advised us in a preface to "judge without prejudice the fighting form of the contenders and keep your eye fixed on the outcome," Brecht proceeds to hurl so much dramatic debris at our heads that we should hardly keep our eye on an elephant, were one on stage. The play, permeated with nihilism, celebrates the decay of society at its urban centers and is contemptuous of aspiration as well as dubious of virtue. It is written in a tone of high good humor by a young man who had respect for very few and very little, and who certainly did not include the audience in his select minority. You should find yourself ill-used by the play, defrauded perhaps; but Miss Malina so skillfully envelops cast and customers in the play's one human predicament that you feel caught up in a wry and universal vaudeville. Yet the production is marked by no newsworthy departures from theatrical deportment.

The Becks are right that participation is the key to life in the theater. There must be an encounter, perhaps even a skirmish, between actors and audience. But I think The Living Theatre gets its skirmish most clearly when the performers reach for it least elaborately. There is nothing new about living theater: it was alive for the Greeks, it was alive for the Elizabethans, and it was alive for that mythical gold miner in Colorado who leapt from the stage box to save the heroine's flaxen head from the buzz saw.

However, it is clear from Jack Gelber's new play, *The Apple,* that The Living Theatre will continue at least for a time to scout the no man's land between illusion and reality. This play, the company's major work for the 1961–62 season, was originally announced for October and opened, after a series of delays, on December 7th. The postponement of openings has become part of The Living Theatre's personality. The Becks do too much: they act in the current repertory, direct and design the new productions, plan the future; they promote the theater on the air, raise money for an operation that is always a little in the red, support the causes that make demands on their

42

"THE LIVING THEATRE" (1962)

consciences (I first talked to Miss Malina on a picket line). On Monday nights, when there is no repertory performance, the house is host to concerts, movies, poetry readings, one-act-play series, lectures. The Becks also teach in The Living Theatre Studio, an important adjunct to the theater. And next summer the company will again be abroad. It is too much—people can work as shock troops while a company is building, but this company has now been built. Pretty soon the Becks will have to stop answering every alarm bell.

In *The Apple* Mr. Gelber takes his preoccupation with the audience—his conviction that each member of it carries his own play on his back, like the addict's monkey—to the point where he has perhaps invented a new form, therapeutic theater. On stage, the therapy is overt: a group of actors meets regularly in a Greenwich Village coffee shop (coffee is served by the cast from a counter on stage before the performance) to act impromptu scenes that well up from their ids. These provide scope for a number of political and social jibes of varying sharpness and rather tenuous cohesion. *The Apple* is not acted *ad lib*, but I suspect that much of it was written that way, and the top of Mr. Gelber's head is not infallible. On the evening in question, a paranoid (he is that chap who was making a nuisance of himself in the lobby before the show) erupts from the audience and injects himself into the playmaking. This results in a good deal of melodrama and further scrambling of fact and fancy, since the madman performs in earnest the fantasies the others conjure up within the bounds of their art. He also dies and is reanimated, with mystic results. The scenes jump rapidly from a replay of an old silent movie to a parody on the "good jungle doctor" to a domestic spat *à la* television to a moment of Old Southern decay. The actors move in and out of their roles like quick-change artists, and the only rule of association is that it must be free.

Despite the chaotic activity on stage, the cast finds time to maintain a running exhortation to the spectators that they drop whatever they are doing and "come over to our side." Since no one does—since indeed it is not literally intended that anyone should—the effect is a little like a Billy Graham rally at which not a single soul is saved. The theater as a gymnasium for stretching the psyche may be a useful idea, but as conceived here it is a little too stridently frolicsome and not sufficiently developed. Gelber's play is wildly inventive, but that is not to say that it is consistently interesting. There is something a little half-baked about it—as when one of the girls announces that she would like to take on the whole audience by herself, a remark of the sort that produces titters in high school circles. One of the best actors in the

43

ESSAYS

troupe spends three-quarters of the evening pretending that he is a spastic. It was, he says, "an incredible opportunity for an actor," and that is precisely what I think it was not. Much too easy for a talented mimic. *The Apple* both sparkles and wavers; it ends up by asking a rhetorical question—"Isn't our stage more real than your life?"—the answer to which is probably no.

But misgivings about *The Apple* do not necessarily imply misgivings about The Living Theatre. The Becks run a house of experimentation, and by definition they will not always succeed. They are not selling packaged hits; they offer the excitement of work in progress and the satisfaction of a company that works from a consistent point of view toward a style that is both flexible and tough.

Repertory is the only situation in the theater that nourishes style. The style developing at The Living Theatre is very close to that of the Becks themselves. Miss Malina displays a candor that is uncommon, if not unique, in this era of veiled intentions. It is a candor that disarms less than it challenges—even pacifists go armed in our world, and that is her weapon. Julian Beck looks like Amedeo Modigliani, and one feels he has pitched his resolve to a point of asceticism and then fleshed it out with a quiet buffoonery. He is a very funny man, with whom one might hesitate to get funny.

So the plays come at you from the stage with a shocking directness; they are cut lean and move efficiently to their conclusions. (They don't always do so; I am talking of the vision and the successes.) There is no "go for broke" hysteria in the theater. A hit cannot make the Becks rich (not with 162 seats and a $4.50 weekend top), and a flop cannot sink them. They are bound to fail from time to time because success is not primarily what interests them. But the chopping block does not operate here as it does on Broadway. *The Connection* opened in the middle of summer to terrible notices from the second-string critics; it was weeks before the periodical reviews, the belated cheers of the first-desk daily reviewers, and word-of-mouth enthusiasm attracted an audience. Uptown the show would have closed in a week, but the Becks carried it on the shoulders of their going repertory until it took on the main weight itself.

At The Living Theatre no play fails until the Becks decide it has failed. That is repertory, the life in the theater the Becks knew they wanted for themselves fifteen years ago. What goes on uptown is merely show business.

44

"John Arden" (1962)

Astute medicine men win reputations for chumminess with the gods by authorizing rain dances when the direction of the wind, the season of the year, and, if possible, a phone call to the weather bureau suggest that the ceremony will be effective. I shall try to gain a similar reputation for influence within the high councils of the American theater by calling for an early production of the plays of John Arden, only one of which has been staged professionally in the United States, in San Francisco. In this case, there is no bureau to check, but my plea should have a good chance: our producers are not so burdened with golden opportunities that they can overlook for long a talent as strong and varied as this.

John Arden—aged thirty-two—is a young English dramatist whose plays, like those of so many of his contemporaries, have been staged in London at the Royal Court Theatre. No one writing about the contemporary theater can avoid an appearance of Anglophilia. Americans are writing good plays, but talent does not flourish here in a concentration comparable to what prevails in England. John Osborne, Arnold Wesker, Harold Pinter, Shelagh Delaney, Brendan Behan, N. F. Simpson, John Mortimer, Willis Hall, John Arden—the roster proves the point, and this does not exhaust the names. I don't know why this fecundity has come about, but the Royal Court and Joan Littlewood's Theatre Workshop (at present suspended) may have something to do with it. If you let it be known that you respect new ideas and fresh approaches, that you are willing to take a chance on long shots, you are at least more likely to get them. Aside from that, the stage has always been the Englishman's castle, and there is nothing inherently surprising about its current vitality there.

The Arden plays thus far are *Live Like Pigs*, *Serjeant Musgrave's Dance*, and *The Happy Haven*. (There is a still earlier work, *The Waters of Babylon*, but it was shown only in a single special performance.) The first thing that almost everyone says of these plays is that they could very plausibly be the writings of three different men. *Live Like Pigs* is an earthy, raucous comic strip in seventeen scenes; *Serjeant Musgrave's Dance* is a somber historical drama in three acts; *The Happy Haven* is a two-act fantasy with overtones of surrealist horror. This diversity of attack is quite deliberate. Arden has a gift for looking at his career objectively. For example, he has known since the age of sixteen that he wanted to write, but he spent his years at Cambridge and Edinburgh training himself as an architect and thereafter worked two years in an

ESSAYS

architect's office. He says he didn't "know any *way* of becoming a writer," and he did know the way to become an architect. If the writing succeeded, he could always get out of the building profession; if it did not, he had a calling that would support his family. Arden is a poet and a dreamer, but a prudent one: there is something peculiarly Anglo-Saxon about that.

Part of his prudence, evidently, is to serve his theater apprenticeship by writing as many kinds of plays as he can devise. In this he is quite unlike many of his colleagues—especially Wesker and Pinter, whose signatures are very strong on their plays—and he is paying a price for the experience gained. Arden's critical reputation far exceeds his commercial success: the major applause for each of his plays has come after the production closed, with only a moderate run. If he had picked a "number" and stuck to it, he would probably have profited from the momentum of acclaim; that is how his fellows have built such large followings so quickly. But Arden has come on stage each time with a "first" play.

Despite this calculated eclecticism, there is consistency in Arden's work if you look for it. There is, first, the matter of his language. His characters speak a stylized vernacular; that is, the dialogue is much sharper and more allusive than real speech, but it sounds "fitting" in the mouths for which it is designed. For example, this speech from Act I of *Serjeant Musgrave's Dance*:

> Musgrave: There was talk about danger. Well, I never heard of no danger yet that wasn't comparative. Compare it against your purposes. And compare it against my strategy. Remember: the roads are closed, the water's frozen, the telegraph wires are weighted down with snow, they haven't *built* the railway. We came here safe, and here we are, safe here. The winter's giving us one day, two days, three days even—that's clear safe for us to hold our time, take count of the corruption, then stand before this people with our white shining word, and let it dance! It's a hot coal, this town, despite that it's freezing—choose your minute and blow: and whoosh, she's flamed your roof off!

At the same time, however, Arden uses song (in the manner of Bertolt Brecht, though I should think by way of Brendan Behan), and he uses verse. When the emotional content of a scene exceeds a certain intensity, or when he wants a detail pulled forward, as though sharpened by a lens, Arden turns to poetry. It is an effective device, for it is a frank avowal that the theater is art and not life. By going

46

"JOHN ARDEN" (1962)

directly into poetry, Arden spares himself the incongruous "fine sentiments" that result when an author tries to speak for himself through the normal accents of his characters, and that so often ring like lead on the realistic stage. Most of the scenes in *Live Like Pigs* are introduced by songs or spoken quatrains, which state the theme for what is to follow. The song at the opening of Scene V is:

They build a wall to keep you in,
It serves to keep them out.
So when they set their feet on the wall
Beware what you're about.

In subject matter, too, there is congruity beneath Arden's variety. Two of his plays (and possibly the others as well) were touched off by actual events. He wrote *Live Like Pigs* after reading of a riot that occurred in a northern industrial housing development; and *Serjeant Musgrave's Dance*, though set in the 1860s, was inspired by a massacre that took place one night during the terror on Cyprus. An Arden plot is characteristically a specific moral or social dilemma, and what marks it as his work is that he respects dilemmas too much to solve them by some theatrical presto chango. It takes unusual maturity, particularly in this age of social manipulation and psychological rehabilitation, to recognize that cutting the Gordian knot is always a cheap dramatic trick. It also requires great technical skill to bring a play to a satisfactory end without pretending to dispose of the problem it raises. Arden's plays do not offer the last word—which may be another reason why they have not set box-office records. Audiences must accustom themselves to the fact that he promises no revelations and guarantees no cures; he is a dramatist of the intractability of life.

If I were sponsoring Arden in this country (offering unsolicited advice is great fun), I should open with *Serjeant Musgrave's Dance* (recently published by Grove Press). It is not the easiest of his plays, but it is the most substantial and the one that can exert the greatest impact on an audience. The time is the Crimean War. Serjeant Musgrave and three troopers under his spell have deserted after participating in a peculiarly pointless massacre, and have returned to England—posing as a recruiting unit—to let their countrymen know the reality of war. They make for a particular mining town because, as we eventually discover, they carry with them the skeleton of one of their mates who was a youth from that town. It is their plan to display this relic as a symbol of the road to glory—and Musgrave has in mind

47

ESSAYS

other devices of direct and terrible logic (scarcely guessed at by his henchmen) to drive the lesson home. What gives the play its power and its present relevance is that Musgrave is a *religious* man. He is akin to those Cromwellian troopers who carried Bibles in their knapsacks and worshiped a God of Wrath. Musgrave wants peace, but he wants to impose it by the sword; and of course he is a man accursed, one who carries violence like a contagion.

Serjeant Musgrave's Dance is built as a sculptor builds in clay: handful by handful the material is laid up, and gradually the composition takes on mass and shape and the tension that gives it life. Plot, character, background—all parts of the play grow simultaneously, and it is perhaps at its greatest power as it comes to its conclusion. It is a play that must be directed plastically, in space rather than in time, and with each moment exploited for its own quality as much as for its contribution to the total object. Arden provides good clay— he is lavish with humor, violence, suspense, vivid personalities, high jinks, and deviltry. But the play carries, thus, a good deal of baggage and, since it is not hauled forward by an urgent narrative, it could bog down. If its details are relished, however, and if it is staged with a material richness (the costumes should be vivid, the furniture solid) and a vigor of motion to match its stature, it will build tremendous momentum. It needs the money and the professional polish of a Broadway production.

Live Like Pigs (published by Penguin but not yet distributed in the U.S.), on the contrary, would float like a breeze Off-Broadway. It demands quick wits and a rough agility, but not much in the way of appointments. If *Serjeant Musgrave* is heroic clay, *Live Like Pigs* is ironic cartooning. Its central character is the Sawney family, described thus by Arden in an introduction:

> The Sawneys are an anachronism. They are the direct descendants of the "sturdy beggars" of the sixteenth century, and the apparent chaos of their lives becomes an ordered pattern when seen in terms of a wild, empty countryside and a nomadic existence. Put out of their fields by enclosing landlords, they found such an existence possible for four hundred years. Today, quite simply, there are too many buildings in England, and there is just no room for nomads. The family in this play fails to understand this, and becomes educated in what is known as the 'hard way,' but which might also be called the "inefficient way."

As the play opens, Sailor Sawney, his wife Big Rachel, her son Col,

"JOHN ARDEN" (1962)

his daughter Rosie, and Rosie's daughter Sally have been evicted from the derelict tramcar in which they resided and have been installed by the authorities in a housing project. They are shortly joined by Blackmouth, a half-mad half-Gypsy who is the father of Rosie's children; by The Old Croaker, a crone of senile craftiness; and by Daffodil, her deformed but avid daughter. Next door live the Jacksons—husband, wife, and salesclerk-daughter—a family self-intoxicated with lower-middle-class respectability. One gathers that the neighborhood is rife with such as they.

The Sawney tribe of thieves, whores, drunks, and roisterers did not choose to be housed in genteel digs; they do not propose to moderate their old manners to their new surroundings. And the smallest, the oldest, the feeblest, or the dottiest of the Sawneys is more than a match for the best the Jacksons can put forward. Four hundred years of quick jabs and billingsgate are not wiped out by a fortnight in a "model" home. But the Jacksons have a terrible weapon unknown to the Sawneys: they can organize, and having done so, they can roll over nonconformity and crush it flat. And they do.

One could milk a good deal of pathos out of this situation—natural exuberance at bay, the end of romance, the juggernaut of propriety grinding out the last sparks of individuality. It is clear, however, that Arden intends no such sniveling. The Sawneys are scarcely to be equated with the noble savage; they are sadly, if also comically, neurotic victims of injustice that dates back four centuries. Their roaring and lusting look attractive only in juxtaposition to the mealy pretensions of Jacksonian aridity, and in fact they are half-starved, wholly ignorant, a plague to themselves and to anyone they encounter. Their life of dreams is pulled down by people no better than they—only more modern. It may not be progress (though a little crossbreeding between the Sawneys and the Jacksons *could* be enlivening), but it is certainly inevitable.

Live Like Pigs is a lark, bitter but uproarious, to commemorate the passing of a breed that never did more than make a virtue of adversity. It should be staged as a burlesque show—hard, fast, rancid, knowing, essentially innocent, with complete sympathy and no pity at all.

About *The Happy Haven* (unpublished as yet) I am less certain—perhaps because it is a kind of play I do not find congenial, but also because it is a little slippery as to content. It is a dark fantasy, a cautionary fairy tale for adults. Happy Haven is an old folks' home, run by a doctor (half mad-scientist, half super-salesman) who has discovered an elixir of youth. His inmates are to be his guinea pigs. Now you might suppose that these octogenarian ladies and gents

ESSAYS

would snap at a chance to sample the doctor's brew, but it turns out that they want no part of it; and when a test draught works with spectacular success on an invisible dog that has been cavorting around the stage all evening, they turn on the calculating humanitarian and dose him with his own medicine.

The style of the play is modified Grand Guignol, with the decent façades of the aged pensioners slipping from time to time to allow a glimpse of monstrosities within. It is quite brilliant in tone (in a way, it is virtuoso dialogue, but not always in a good way); the point, however, seems to me to blur. One of the old crocks, himself excluded from rejuvenation because of a physical impediment, convinces the others that their lives have been far too miserable to be lived over again. That does not persuade me, on the other hand, for Arden has given his aged crew such a determined grasp on life that they would obviously leap at the prospect of running the course again.

What could have enraged them, and urged them to turn the tables on the doctor, is the discovery that they are not being cared for but used. No man grows so old, so feeble, so useless, that he will consent to being regarded as an object—it is a sin against the soul and not to be tolerated even in exchange for life everlasting. But that is only what one supposes from meeting Arden's company—there is no support for this thesis in the text.

The Happy Haven was played in London in masks. Arden felt that it would be cruel to ask actors of an age comparable to those of the characters to play such parts (but aren't elderly actors accustomed to taking parts beset by age?); at any event, the action is so athletic that genuinely old people could not possibly sustain it, and so he puts masks on youngsters. He would have profited from seeing Sudie Bond play Grandma in Edward Albee's *The American Dream*. That play is also a fantasy: it puts no value on realistic illusion, and Miss Bond did not pretend to be Dame Sybil Thorndike. She played a caricature, as did everyone in *The American Dream*, and as everyone must in *The Happy Haven*. But if you add the exaggeration of masks to what are already caricatures, you must double the stimulus in a confusing way. Some such confusion evidently did bedevil the London production.

I keep my fingers crossed, then, about *The Happy Haven*—at least, I'd be in no great rush to import it. But *Serjeant Musgrave's Dance* would lend stature and *Live Like Pigs* would lend effervescence to any season in which they appeared. They are not easy to stage, but the theater is not an exercise in rolling off a log. They would repay the labor and brains that were invested in them—and of how many new plays can that be said?

50

"Upstaging Scenery" (1962)

The theater in the 1960s is the heir to so many inventions and traditions of stage design—expressionism, constructivism, the box set, the unit set, the apron stage, theater-in-the-round, Max Reinhardt's flyspecks, Gordon Craig's screens, Adolphe Appia's expectant emptiness—that any orderly review of their evolution and intertwined influence is a task for the historian, not the essayist. But it has been, speaking very broadly, a two-edged inheritance. We are the beneficiaries of the Greek amphitheater and Shakespeare's "wooden O"; we have also incurred a guilty knowledge of those architectural splendors and natural stupefactions (Vesuvius in spate, great seas in uproar) that in centuries past threatened to efface the drama in the cause of spectacle. True, it has been a generation or more since Eliza skipped across the tumbling ice in Harriet Beecher Stowe's *Uncle Tom's Cabin*; large and exotic animals are at present out of stage-fashion; and I cannot remember the last time a performer made his entrance upon a cloud. Still, the temptation to confuse the magic of the theater with the trickery of the stage is in our blood, and our sets today fall roughly into two categories: they offer a picture or they offer a playing space.

Obviously, these alternatives are almost never presented in pure form—the most picture-oriented set must still provide the actors with the physical essentials of their trade, and only the most dedicated theorist will sweep his stage as naked as a laboratory table. Nevertheless, you can usually tell whether the stage was set primarily to flatter the eye or to facilitate the actor's assignment. I can illustrate the difference by describing an experiment that was unaccountably abandoned in 1957 at the Shakespeare Festival in Stratford, Connecticut.

The Stratford theater, a remote descendant of Shakespeare's Globe, is a house of inviting proportions, admirable acoustics, and great technical versatility. But its stage is vast in all its dimensions, and sets scaled to fill it place the action in jeopardy. I well remember the dress rehearsal of *Julius Caesar* in 1955, the company's first season, when shortly after midnight it was decided to scrap Horace Armistead's breathtaking panorama of Rome because it was diminishing the affairs of Cassius and Brutus to triviality.

For the second season, Rouben Ter-Arutunian designed a stage that seemed to me an ideal frame for Shakespeare. It consisted of tremendous panels of lattice, walling the entire playing area; neutral in tone, these took light and shadow beautifully. Moreover, they were infinitely flexible: openings could be made almost at will; sections could be thrust forward to provide balconies, rostrums, battlements;

ESSAYS

inner stages, dungeons, grottoes, private doors, or ceremonial gateways could be conjured out of the pliant slatwork. Since the lattice was ambiguous—interior or exterior, nature or fabrication—any object added to it was vividly suggestive, and a very few props—a tapestry, a throne chair, stacked arms, a glowing brazier—would sharply focus the scene. The space was as great as ever, but it was space undefined by perspective or scale, and in that limpid element the actors took on the heightened presence that is part of what makes theater magic. I don't know why the Shakespeare Festival shelved this exemplary scene for the pastel and *papier-mâché* agitation that became its style in later seasons. This theater does business primarily with the summer colonies along the shore; perhaps such an audience does not appreciate self-effacement raised to an art.

The question of whether the stage is to be a vision or an instrument is linked to equivalent theories as to the relationship between the audience and the occasion; it has been given particular relevance in our time by the proliferation of theaters in accommodations never meant for the drama. If the playwright is the manufacturer of more or less intelligent pastimes for a market that can pay well to be amused, then everything possible should be done to present a beguiling package. I have considerable admiration for the professional efficiency of Robert Bolt's *A Man for All Seasons*, but it falls, I think, into the category of entertainment. And its eye-catching unit set, dominated by a magnificently proportioned spiral ramp, its scene changes wittily engineered into the action, suits the intentions of the work and contributes to its popular success.

Such decorative virtuosity, however, makes an almost tangible barrier of the proscenium frame; the audience feels itself in exile from fairyland. I recall still the elegant sensuality of Christian Bérard's set for the production of Molière's *L'École des Femmes*, which Louis Jouvet brought to America a good many years ago. The insolently aristocratic chandeliers, the exquisitely scaled street arches, the garden walls that parted on silken hinges to disclose the most perfect of formal gardens—these blandishments of texture and proportion made the audience purr. But I also remember that I watched Molière through flawless plate glass: one looked in rapture, but one was not touched.

The playgoer who forsakes such luxury of the senses for the opportunism of Off-Broadway may feel himself curtly received, unless at the same time he shifts his view of himself from pampered guest to committed participant. No one perched on the bleachers of the 4th Street Theatre (founder, David Ross)—that railroad flat bisected by a card-table stage—deluded himself that the theater is a spectator sport.

"UPSTAGING SCENERY" (1962)

If a play took life in those surroundings, it was because audience and cast willed that it should do so; and perhaps because the challenge was so obvious, the miracle occurred there with dependable regularity. I don't pretend that this former American home of Chekhov and Ibsen was ideal for its purposes: I was disconcerted by spying a second audience, a kind of mirror image, dimly across the lighted playing area; the little stage was so crabbed that one ground plan had to be used, play after play.

The Off-Broadway definition of a theater is any room that can seat one hundred or more persons without incurring the instant hostility of the fire department. Sometimes these unlikely warrens are brilliantly suited to the material at hand. José Quintero's production of Eugene O'Neill's *The Iceman Cometh* at the original Circle in the Square (since torn down to make way for an apartment house) fit with almost no artifice at all into the long, bleak room, broken by pillars supporting the low ceiling. And the Provincetown Playhouse, mean in dimensions, grimy, threadbare, neglected, was a den ready-made for Krapp's prowlings in Beckett's play. I recall, finally, the throatconstricting expectancy of that operating table of a stage deep below the tiered seats where Jean Genet's *The Blacks* was played. It was made a place of ritual merely by the vertiginous pitch of its sight lines.

There are evident limitations to the lucky compatibility between house and play. These absurd theaters of Greenwich Village and the East Side have proved excellent frames for the Theater of the Absurd that now dominates our avant-garde; but their idiosyncrasies and raffish squalor do not always suit: William Congreve's *The Way of the World* stepped its minuet bravely at the Cherry Lane, but it seemed to be slumming. Despite an almost continual ululation in the profession, poverty can be a tonic in the theater, but I would not therefore prescribe it as the principal diet.

What is so inspiriting about these makeshift stages, however, is that the room for a play often seems to have been created by main force. The audience feels itself a crowd of witnesses on the verge of trespassing upon the minimal arena where the performers are getting on with their imperative task. At The Living Theatre it has be come almost a matter of style that the actors exhort patrons to join the act. The revivalist appeal is hardly necessary, for the house itself throws everyone into the melee.

Uptown in the more decorous houses, formalized by their curtains and proscenium stages, it is not so easy to mount a performance that takes on the quality of a communal ceremony. The distinction between

ESSAYS

picture-scape and playing space still operates. A set, when it is first revealed, should make you inch forward in your seat; too often, it urges you to lean back after perfunctory applause. The designers, members of one of the few real guilds left in the world, work with such authority, so fill the stage with their strong personalities, that there often seems no opening for author or actors.

Tennessee Williams's *The Night of the Iguana* is a case in point. The play impressed me as the most relevant, most humane, dramatically most engrossing work that Williams has done in some time. But I was aware that the playwright was fighting the set for my attention. This fully conceived hotel of dubious propriety, deep in the Mexican jungle, projected so much personality of its own, its cunning angles and subtle imbalances were so diverting, its vegetation so feverishly rich, that the cross-purposes, precarious sanity, and rampant vitality of the play's personnel were gentled by the visual boisterousness. The performances, though good, were perhaps a little too consistently strident. That could be accounted for by the presence of Bette Davis, whose professional aura does not encourage reticence in her colleagues, but the steaming jungle must take a share of the blame.

I dislike a set that stands on its own feet: it should be like a bicycle—functional only in motion. Thus the sets for Terence Rattigan's *Ross*, a play I did not much admire, seemed to me excellent. They were so shallow, sometimes so perfunctory, as to be disagreeably saltless in repose. But they keyed the action and stood well aside to let the actors get everything humanly possible out of the script. Of course *Ross* is a play in innumerable scenes, and the budget for individual tableaux must have been spartan. A writer these days who constructs a one-set play invites the designer to paint him off the stage.

Box sets are out of favor just now, but they have a great virtue: they allow the performance to build emotion under the pressure of confinement. Still, the emphasis of these boxes should be on the space they enclose and not on the furnishings the designer can plausibly pack them with to "heighten" the illusion. Nothing so deflates illusion as *bric-à-brac* that upstages the actor. Such sets invariably draw applause as the curtain rises on a parlor maid dusting the armor; in my view, any set that draws applause should instantly be scrapped for a plain backdrop. Stage design is like editing or undertaking—no trade for *prima donnas*.

I say that, realizing that the two greatest figures of modern stage design—Adolphe Appia and Gordon Craig—were *prima donnas* of the first rank. But they were also seers, men transfixed by all-embracing visions. Appia decreed a stage of neutral emptiness to be

54

transformed by light; Craig appealed to the theater world to be saved by his "thousand scenes in one scene"—a distillation of the total human environment that, translated, became: "flat floor—flat walls—flat roof." The stage structures imagined by these men were noble, expectant, almost religious, and fairly crying out for great deeds and inexorable decisions. But in both cases they also bore a strong resemblance to England's Stonehenge or the Giant's Causeway in Ireland; had they prevailed, they could have restricted the repertory to Richard Wagner, *King Lear*, and Henrik Ibsen's *When We Dead Awaken*.

However, the theater has never been in danger of succumbing to the high-minded rigors of Craig and Appia. The kind of threat it does have to be on guard against is the staircase that is more beautiful than the heroine, the living room that is busier than the villain, and the forest of Arden in which you cannot see Touchstone for the trees.

"The Actors' Studio" (1962)

For the past fifteen years the Actors' Studio has been the dominant school in the American theater and possibly the most controversial organization in the theatrical world. Therefore the decision, made definite over the summer, to expand the Studio's activities to include a producing company is of more significance than the not uncommon announcement that still another theater is in hopeful gestation. Two million dollars will be raised, a house in the Broadway area will be secured on a long lease, a large roster of actors (many of them Studio graduates) will be placed under contract for services as needed, plays will be optioned, directors will be assigned, and we shall see what we shall see.

Without quite knowing it, perhaps, we have been awaiting this sight for a long time. The Actors' Studio has been a force without a face since its inception. Institutions with comparable authority in the theater have almost invariably combined instruction with performance in an ascending curriculum—one graduates from class to stage. The most obvious example is the Moscow Art Theatre and its associated school, both under the direction of Konstantin Stanislavsky, whose much-bandied Method provided the framework for instruction at the Studio and has given the name of Method actors to its alumni. Similarly, the School of the American Ballet is the nursery for the New York City ballet, and influential schools are built into the Comédie Française, the Old Vic, and Sadler's Wells.

ESSAYS

Lee Strasberg, who came into the Actors' Studio a year after it was founded by Cheryl Crawford, Elian Kazan, and Robert Lewis, and who almost at once became its dominant personality, is a man of the professional theater. As a youth he acted in Theatre Guild productions and was stage manager of the second *Garrick Gaieties*. But it was as a director of the Group Theatre in the 1930s that he made a permanent impression on the New York scene with productions of Paul Green's *The House of Connelly* and *Johnny Johnson*, Sidney Kingsley's *Men in White*, and Melvin Levy's *Gold Eagle Guy*. Strasberg has not worked in public for many years, however, and there has never been an acting company into which the students of the Studio could graduate. As a consequence, the procedures of this school have assumed some of the aura of a secret brotherhood, and the influence of the Method has been almost as widely suspected as it has been widely acknowledged.

One hears, for example, that the Studio spoils actors in every sense of the word, and it is notorious for some of its more famous pupils, who display on occasion idiosyncrasies of headline proportions. One hears that Method actors resist directors, that they are preoccupied with the cultivation of their own emotional lives to the detriment of the emotions specified by the playwright, and that they are given to quoting their revered teacher in disputes with directors under whom they are rehearsing. If all this is true, then Method manners must be infuriating.

Even more widespread is the notion that the Actors' Studio propagates a mystique akin to some introspective religious experience. This view causes a *New York Times* writer, in a generally sympathetic article, to refer to Strasberg as the "resident guru"; it moves Paul Scofield, the elegantly disciplined star of Robert Bolt's *A Man for All Seasons*, to say in an interview published by *Show* magazine that, unlike the "Method people," he prefers technique to spontaneous emotion. "They have to be lucky to hit the bull's-eye without technique. What happens to them on an off-night? . . . They have nothing to fill the vacuum with." Outside observers are not encouraged at Studio classes; the few who do penetrate come back with anecdotes about young performers being encouraged to "let themselves go" in spontaneous outbursts of intimate melodrama.

It all sounds unpleasantly visceral and professionally unpromising. It also sounds a little unlikely—unlikely, that is, that the Method is no more than a warm bath of psychological release. Lee Strasberg was working with Stanislavsky's directorial principles back in the days of the Group Theatre; in fact, the Group introduced the celebrated

"THE ACTORS' STUDIO" (1962)

Russian's ideas to the American stage—where, acknowledged or not, they have been influential ever since. The productions credited to the Group in the annals of the American stage—not only Strasberg's productions cited above, but also the plays directed by Harold Clurman (Irwin Shaw's *The Gentle People*, Clifford Odets's *Awake and Sing!* and *Golden Boy*)—were scrupulously disciplined and in some cases markedly poetic. Retrospective reports on the Group fall into the old trap of confusing the players with their parts: the 1930s nurtured the so-called theater of protest in the United States, and the plays written were earthy and filled with social agitation. But the Group Theatre was not a proletarian workshop: on the contrary, it was an artistic utopia run by tough disciplinarians.

It is known that Strasberg has modified the Stanislavsky Method for use in America, but is not plausible that, as the persistent rumors suggest, he has thrown away half of it. Stanislavsky, who was a gifted writer as well as an actor, director, and teacher of legendary prowess, conveyed his system to future generations in two now-classic books: *An Actor Prepares* and *Building a Character*. He had a highly organized, almost mathematical mind, and he broke his curriculum down into a set of hierarchies as intricate as a royal family tree. The basic division was between the interior mental and emotional condition of the actor and the exterior communication of the play.

The first subject, discussed in *An Actor Prepares*, is an investigation into the ways by which an actor may find, within his own resources and experiences, intellectual and emotional correspondences to his stage role, and a description of the exercises that will enable him to evoke these states of mind and spirit in their original vividness for as many nights as the run continues. That is, few actors who are chosen to play Othello will in fact have strangled their brides, but almost every man and woman has suffered jealousy to some degree. Stanislavsky discovered that he could develop in himself, and train others to develop, a facility for recalling such experiences of pain or joy and adapting them to the given circumstances of the play.

"Always and forever, when you are on the stage, you must play yourself." That famous sentence from *An Actor Prepares* has caused much of the confusion about Method acting, it being supposed that Stanislavsky meant the stage to be a platform for enacted autobiography. But the "self" he had in mind is an imaginary being created from the "smelting furnace" of the actor's life and re-created in the role he has to play.

Building a Character, on the other hand, is a handbook of stage presence that begins with such fundamentals as walking and sitting

ESSAYS

(which must be re-learned before they can be undertaken in front of an audience) and moves on to voice, placement, phrasing, and timing; the discovery of the play's essential theme (not to be confused with its overt plot); and the relating of characters to this unifying idea. Thus Stanislavsky struck the balance between interior motivation and exterior craft that is implicit in every art.

But, as Robert Lewis pointed out several years ago (in a series of professional lectures published under the title *Method—or Madness?*), the curriculum did not reach America in that balanced form: *An Actor Prepares* was published in the United States in 1936; *Building a Character* did not appear here until 1949. Students and practitioners of the theater in America were thus for thirteen years in possession of a Stanislavsky system that seemed to concentrate on the state of an actor's soul and to concern itself not at all with how he should place his feet, move his arms, deliver his lines, or in general make himself an instrument of the playwright's designs. Even the half of the system that was generally available was soon vulgarized by readers who reported, for example, that Stanislavsky held that to play a wanton one must be a wanton, and who overlooked in an eagerness for sensation his insistence on "as if" (Stanislavsky himself called it "the magic if") as the basis of the actor's imagination.

Strasberg and his Group colleagues had been to Moscow and seen at first hand the whole of Stanislavsky's curriculum. Nevertheless, the Method acquired early in its career a reputation for psychological egocentricity, and the Actors' Studio has regularly been the butt of jokes and the victim of disparagement. How do we know, it is asked, whether Geraldine Page, Marlon Brando, Joanne Woodward, Paul Newman, Eli Wallach, Tom Ewell, and Ben Gazzara are accomplished actors because of what they have been taught in Strasberg's classes, or whether what Strasberg teaches has become solemn doctrine because, necessarily, a handful of the many aspiring actors who pass through his classes have been talented? In all honesty, the questions have been hard to answer in the absence of a theater operating in accordance with the pedagogy.

Another service the Actors' Studio Theatre can be expected to perform will be to focus attention once more on the performances actually taking place on our stages. In the lifetime of most contemporary playgoers, these stages have been dominated by texts. Anyone reading in the history of the theater will discover that not so long ago the stage was ruled by its great performers—by Edwin Booth, Sarah Bernhardt, Minnie Maddern Fiske, Eleonora Duse, William Macready, and the Barrymores (Lionel, Ethel, John), to name at

"THE ACTORS' STUDIO" (1962)

random a very few from a regal roster. We have stars—indeed our commercial theater is hobbled by the start system—but for the most part these are monetary attractions, plums in highly touted entertainment packages. Except for the Lunts—Alfred Lunt and Lynn Fontanne (who now appear seldom, and still less frequently in material of consequence)—what actor today stamps his art on the theater?

Reviewers seem to devote such acumen as they possess to discussions of the intellectual stature, ethical content, and entertainment quotient of the playwright's work. They make judgments, typically of a convenient generality, as to the "style" of a production. But when it comes to the work of the actors they resort to personal epithets—so-and-so was manly, such-and-such a miss was winning, a certain beldam was poignant. (So, for that matter, are your postman, the girl who rings up your order at the supermarket, and your grandmother.) The darlings of the critics nowadays are for the most part these professional applause-stimulators who conduct love affairs with the audience and leave their stage partners to the unproductive exercise of delivering their lines in a vacuum. Actors who play to the audience remind the audience of its own wit and charm; actors who play to the play draw the audience into a world of imagination, beauty, and virtue that the stage can offer with a vividness unrivaled in the arts. Stanislavsky said this almost every day of his life—it is at the heart of his Method.

In fairness, actors themselves are hardly responsible for the decline of their authority in the theater. With the straitening of opportunity, with the increasingly hectic commerce of the theater, they have become hired hands—and frequently not hired. One of the unceasing problems of the contemporary actor is that of finding a place to work—if not before an audience, then at least in a practice hall. Dancers must take classes every day, prizefighters avoid the gymnasium at their peril. The Actors' Studio has been called a theatrical gym, and in that capacity it has preserved the techniques of many actors who might otherwise have been driven from the profession by the atrophy of their skill. Membership in the Studio is for life, and there are no fees; experienced players can be found there every day, sparring with one another to keep their hands in. Whatever arguments there may be about the efficacy of the Method, there are none in the profession about the value of the Studio as a gym.

Early in 1963, when the Studio Theatre opens, public attention will almost perforce be redirected to the art of live performance. I expect a period of wild and irresponsible comment as the critics and the audience grasp for standards of evaluation that have long been out

ESSAYS

of use. But discrimination will come with practice. There are no small parts, Stanislavsky once observed, only small actors. Now perhaps we shall see who is small and who is large.

Ironically, the immediate motive for expanding the activities of the Actors' Studio into public productions is not related to the craft considerations I have been discussing. It is being done because the Lincoln Center for the Performing Arts did not invite the Studio to become a part of its theatrical empire, and Lee Strasberg was made angry by what he took as an obvious snub to the most influential stage school of the modern era. To make the wound even more painful, Elia Kazan has resigned from the Studio, pleading apprehension that his new directorial and administrative duties at Lincoln Center might produce a conflict of interest. It remains to be seen whether pique is a sound impulse for the Studio's new venture.

Other aspects of the plans raise misgivings. In the first place, Strasberg is apparently unwilling to direct any of the Studio productions himself. His last foray in the theater (Henrik Ibsen's *Peer Gynt*, with the late John Garfield) was badly received, and he is reluctant to expose himself again. Instead, guest directors—a good many of whom have worked in the Studio's directors' unit—will stage the plays.

The Actors' Studio has always been ruled by committee. Stanislavsky ran his theater and he ran his school. George Balanchine is the master of his ballet company and of his school of ballet. Such control is not as democratic as committee government, but it may be closer to the nature of art. The recently reorganized directorate of the Studio consists of Lee Strasberg, Cheryl Crawford, Geraldine Page, Rip Torn, and John Stuart Dudley. Under them will serve a production board consisting of Anne Bancroft, Frank Corsaro, Paul Newman, Arthur Penn, Fred Stewart, Michael Wager, and Edward Albee. In addition, Roger L. Stevens, the celebrated producer and real-estate operator, will act as general administrator (i.e., he will watch the money); and Max E. Youngstein, the president of Cinemiracle International, is being prominently mentioned as the man who will raise one half of the requisite two million dollars. This mixed group of actors, directors, playwrights, administrators, and tycoons will have to serve with singular unanimity and selflessness if the project is not to founder on cross-purposes and hurt feelings.

The plays known to be under consideration by the Studio Theatre are by Tennessee Williams, William Inge, and June Havoc. Havoc's script is said to be autobiographical and that raises a flicker of interest, but the other names seem wrong for the venture. This is not said in disparagement of the writers: on the contrary. Williams and Inge are discouraging in this context because they are so sure-fire. The responsible heads of the Actors' Studio are all professionals and they naturally go about their business in a professional way; the danger is that they will achieve no more than a professional success.

Despite a lifetime fanatically dedicated to the theater, Stanislavsky was never entirely professional, and perhaps the fanaticism was proof of his amateur heart. Stanislavsky was, of course, a wealthy man (incredible though it may seem, he ran a lucrative family business on the side), and of course there was Chekhov. I will not ask that the Actors' Studio Theatre find a Chekhov between now and January 1st, but I would be more sanguine for its future if the playwrights it sponsored were not so little in need of sponsorship. (What can anyone do now for Inge or Williams?! It is rather a question of what they can do for the Studio, and the relationship is uneasy.) And especially I would look forward to the new theater with great expectation if Lee Strasberg would take responsibility for one of the scripts under contract and demonstrate in public what he has for so many years been teaching in private.

"Repertory Defended" (1963)

The Metropolitan Opera is perhaps less venturesome than it need be, the New York Philharmonic is said to be suffering from excessive personal showmanship, the Museum of Modern Art has been accused of manipulating taste. Reforms are ever being urged on these and similar establishments, both in the United States and abroad. But there is no dissenter so passionate that he would urge their abolition. The public knows instinctively that such institutions preserve the heritage of the arts they embody and provide standards to be met, excelled, or on occasion, rebelled against.

In Europe the dramatic theater also maintains, and is sustained by, institutions—the Comédie Française, the Moscow Art Theatre, the Abbey Theatre, the national and regional companies of almost every European country. At the apex of the American theater is Broadway. Broadway, however, is not an institution: it is a phoenix. It dies on Memorial Day every year and is born anew on Labor Day. This may sound romantic and admirably indomitable, but in fact our theater lacks the energy for this annual rebirth. Year by year, it becomes harder to break out of the egg, and Broadway grows more anxious, more opportunistic, more expensive. It cannot build a following

ESSAYS

because it provides no entity to which loyalty can be pledged. As a result, the New York theater has no audience in a meaningful sense; it survives on consumers for whom it packages hits.

Where this leads can be seen in the forecast published by the *New York Times* last fall: "With a new season getting under way next month, Broadway is talking about musicals and money. The musical picture is clear; the money situation is cloudy. The trend toward musical theater grows. . . . Recent Wall Street activities have not been ignored by theatrical investors. Producers are finding it more difficult to raise money." The kind of money here in question is venture capital; it is available—when it is available—for the enrichment of its owners, not for the enrichment of the theater. Art and cultural philanthropy do not come into the picture. Venture capital wants quick and handsome returns, and the best chance for that lies in the closest feasible replica of Meredith Wilson's *The Music Man*.

It is thus against the background of Broadway's steady debasement that one should heed the current revival of interest in that perennial word of hope: Repertory. Minneapolis is building for Sir Tyrone Guthrie the Guthrie Repertory Theatre; it will open this spring. For the past three seasons U.C.L.A. has had its own Theatre Group, run by John Houseman. Last fall the University of Michigan engaged a repertory group, the Association of Producing Artists, as "company in residence." Also in the fall, the Ford Foundation announced grants totaling $6,100,000 to its nine repertory theaters now operating in various parts of the country. In 1961–62 the National Repertory Theatre, its cast headed by Eva Le Gallienne, Faye Emerson, Scott Forbes, and Frederic Worlock, toured fifty cities and eight college campuses and played to a total of more than 250,000. It is seeking funds to augment its repertory—an ambition that earned it a pat on the back in the *Congressional Record* but no public funds. There are now, according to a recent *Life* magazine survey, an astounding 5,000 regional theater groups in America; a great many of them operate on a repertory basis.

For better or worse, however, the nerve center of American theater is still New York, and one awaits with greatest anticipation the completion of the Vivian Beaumont Theater—described, in the words of its principal donor, as a house "designed with primary emphasis on the needs of the company presenting repertory"—now in construction under the great cultural umbrella of Lincoln Center. The anticipation is somewhat chilled by anxiety, for the theater will be in the hands of Robert Whitehead and Elia Kazan, two of the most spectacularly successful operators of the Broadway gamble.

"REPERTORY DEFENDED" (1963)

Mr. Kazan's preliminary announcements have raised fears and hackles. The director has talked, for example, of making the classics vital in contemporary terms and avoiding the smell of the library; this sounds depressingly defensive. He hopes each year to offer two new plays by leading American playwrights, which would be snatching the bread right out of Broadway's mouth. He advocates the dramatization of novels, an idea that smells, not of the library, but of Hollywood, and is preposterous when set against the list of immortal plays that have not been seen in New York within living memory. He would use stars, would test his productions out of town, and promises a box-office scale not so much below the Broadway norm as to be awkwardly competitive. Since Broadway has priced itself out of the reach of its natural audience, this last resolve is particularly dismaying. However, Mr. Kazan is being given ample time for second thoughts.

It is as though repertory were an unknown experiment. What it can do and the problems it presents (some of them peculiarly American problems) are known from many admirable and a few noble ventures. In the first place, however, what exactly is repertory? It is not stock, though both normally work with a resident company in a permanent house. Stock is the system whereby three, four, or five plays are offered in successive runs of a week or more each. Joseph Papp's New York Shakespeare Festival is a season of stock. Repertory offers several productions simultaneously, playing a different work at each performance and varying the fare from week to week as new productions are added and as the public makes known its relative interest in the offerings. The Metropolitan Opera and the New York City Ballet are repertory companies. At present the only dramatic repertory in New York is the Off-Broadway Living Theatre. It is a doctrinaire group and very uneven; it also shows a vitality and a parity of intention found nowhere else in town.

Stock is in many ways the easier system. The proprietors can concentrate on one play at a time. By hiring one or two actors specifically for each production, they can get along with a relatively small permanent cast. The storage of sets and costumes is not formidable, since only one physical production need be in the house. Finally, the public knows what is being offered in a given segment of the season. The one drawback—the great hazard—is that if a play does not succeed, the company is stuck with it for the duration of its run. And, unlike the situation on Broadway, a hit cannot turn into a bonanza because previous commitments limit its run. Stock theater is necessarily cautious theater—Brandon Thomas's *Charley's Aunt* always seems a good idea.

ESSAYS

Repertory requires a larger and more versatile company; it involves a constant handling of sets, costumes, and props, and considerable space for storing them; it demands an audience sufficiently interested to keep abreast of the program (the Metropolitan Opera and Balanchine's New York City Ballet seem not to suffer much on this score). At the same time, repertory offers an organic season—steadily growing, continually responsive to public interest—that is unmatched for excitement and usefulness in any other form of theater. It is the only system by which a play that makes a strong appeal to a limited audience can be allowed to reach that audience. Provided that the manager has some knowledge of and respect for the stage, there need never be a failure in repertory. A play that is shown only once in ten days can be as successful (and, in the end, can be shown as many times) as one that plays three performances out of seven—each fills its house. Eva Le Gallienne, who from 1926 to 1933 ran the Civic Repertory Company and gave New York the most consistently splendid theater it has ever known, reports that in the first two seasons her house drew 45% of capacity, in the third season it drew 75%, and in the last two seasons, 95%.

From time to time an editor made ingenious by laziness will concoct a feature story by asking a group of theater notables for lists of an ideal repertory. These can be entertaining for the light they throw on the contributors. *Theatre Arts* completed such a symposium for an anniversary issue back in 1941. Eugene O'Neill produced a list that looked like the curriculum for a postgraduate course in tragic drama; Laurence Olivier submitted one that seemed to promise attractive roles for all his friends. Thornton Wilder fired back a furious paragraph in which he denounced American directors for their inability to handle great plays of the past without "veiled condescension." William Saroyan, unable to find just what he wanted in the accumulated wealth of centuries, asked that plays be composed for the mythical occasion from Walt Whitman's *Leaves of Grass*; Mark Twain's *Tom Sawyer* and *Huckleberry Finn*; Chicago's intellectual life of the period 1905–25; the slapstick movie comedies of Mack Sennett, Hal Roach, Harry Langdon, and Co.; newsreels; and sports (particularly baseball, football, and track). At that, his instinct may have been right, for all such lists are basically frivolous: they assume something called the ten—or twelve or twenty—greatest, most appropriate, or most successful plays, whereas the essence of repertory is not a list but a process.

Repertory is not intended to supplant stock; certainly it is not meant to supplant the long-run commercial production. What it is intended to do is give the theater the continuity, the depth of history, and the

64

"REPERTORY DEFENDED" (1963)

standards of invention and performance that every other public art derives from its institutions. What this means in a specific case can be impressive: from 1921 to 1929 the Cleveland Playhouse under the direction of Frederic McConnell offered its audience eighty-nine productions, including such diverse works of genius or enduring talent as *The Importance of Being Earnest*, thirteen plays by Shaw and five by Shakespeare, O'Neill's *The Great God Brown*, Ibsen's *The Wild Duck*, Pirandello's *Six Characters in Search of an Author*, Synge's *The Playboy of the Western World*, Čapek's *R.U.R.*, Gozzi's *Turandot*, Sheridan's *The School for Scandal*, Euripides' *Hippolytus*, and Andreyev's *He Who Gets Slapped*, to say nothing of such lighter fare as A. A. Milne's *The Truth about Blayds*, Langdon Mitchell's *The New York Idea*, and Claire Kummer's *Rollo's Wild Oat*. I do not know what the quality of these productions was, but the very list inclines me to believe it was high. When you are told that a diver has executed a full gainer with a half twist, you do not ask whether he did it well: there is no other way to do it.

Let us skip, as obvious, the joy of living within reach of such a cornucopia of theater wealth, and consider it from a more specialized viewpoint. What would one think of a young writer who set out to be a novelist without having read, to pick at random, Tolstoy's *War and Peace*, Thackeray's *Vanity Fair*, Balzac's *Père Goriot*, and Melville's *Moby Dick*? Yet how many who launch themselves as playwrights have seen Shakespeare's *Coriolanus*, Aeschylus's *The Eumenides*, Chekhov's *The Seagull*, or Ibsen's *Peer Gynt*? They will have read them, perhaps, but in the case of plays, reading is a pale approximation of the live creation. It is like encountering masterworks of painting in reproduction.

One of the difficulties confronting an American repertory company, one of the reasons why it is harder to found and maintain one here than in Europe, is that the United States has no national heritage of drama to provide a proud base of operations. Consider what lies at hand for a French, English, Russian, or Irish producer who may want to appeal to the patriotism of his audience, and compare these legacies with what the American producer can draw upon. When the point comes up here, everyone instantly mentions Eugene O'Neill and then babel ensues. Thornton Wilder, Maxwell Anderson, Lillian Hellman, Elmer Rice, Robert Sherwood, Arthur Miller, Tennessee Williams? Yes, all these and others who come perhaps less quickly to mind are suitable. Indeed, a function of repertory should be to keep the more enduring work of such craftsmen alive. Nonetheless, the planners are haunted by a suspicion that these names hardly qualify

ESSAYS

for Olympus: Where is the Shakespeare, the Molière, the Chekhov, the Ibsen? An all-American repertory would be composed entirely of excellent side dishes and no main course. With the possible exception of O'Neill, we have produced no dramatists of absolute rank—none to stand with the European immortals; none, for that matter, to stand with our own novelists: Herman Melville, Henry James, Nathaniel Hawthorne, James Fenimore Cooper, Mark Twain, Theodore Dreiser, Ernest Hemingway, William Faulkner.

Is that, perhaps, because we have provided no institutional theater? It is a chicken-or-egg question, but at least it may be noted that Shakespeare had the Globe, Chekhov had the Moscow Art, John Millington Synge had the Abbey, and O'Neill himself had Provincetown. It is probably safe enough to say that until we provide a great repertory house, endowed for and dedicated to excellence, a house in which playwrights can learn the language, history, and magic of their art, we shall produce no drama of the stature that gives a nation its place among other nations. We have a great deal of talent, but I am not speaking of that. Genius is another thing, and if O'Neill is a genius, as I think time may show he is, he is to date our only one.

Repertory in America, therefore, must acknowledge its native poverty and offer itself as a world stage. It must hope to develop a style that is at once receptive to a wide variety of sources and yet has a cohesive American texture. This in itself will require a kind of genius: Joseph Papp's seasons in Central Park and the New York City Ballet suggest that it is possible. The productions of these companies could have been created only in the United States. They are marked by a lucidity, a colloquialism, a lean energy and youthful expression of delighted discovery that are essentially American. At the same time, they serve well their great European sources.

Lacking an obvious backing of plays, the native repertory producer also lacks an obvious backing of players. And here there is no question of the chicken or the egg. Our actors are not educated through apprenticeship; they are tuned up by competition in a commercial atmosphere where getting across is the goal. American actors learn to project themselves on an audience before they learn to propel themselves through a door. They become personalities before they become professionals— if, indeed, they ever become that. I generalize unfairly, I know, for there are many fine actors on the American stage (though the best-trained, it seems to me, are usually in support of the glorious stars). But as a generalization the charge is accurate; our actors, deprived of the training of many seasons of steady and varied work, become set in narrow frames that exploit their natural gifts and do not expose their

"REPERTORY DEFENDED" (1963)

ignorance and inexperience. Guthrie once said that it is profitless to discuss an actor's ability until he has played a great classic role. How many of ours ever get the chance? Our star system, rigid and self-aggrandizing, is at the opposite pole from the virtues of repertory.

I would, however, expect the problem of actors to solve itself relatively quickly. As a class, actors show themselves eager students: you have only to note the alacrity with which young players desert opportunities on Broadway and in the acting studios to play in Off-Broadway cupboards that offer instruction in the trade. By quickly, though, I do not mean instantly. Mr. Kazan, or anyone else who wants to assemble a group of players as accomplished, flexible, and harmoniously attuned to one another as the musicians in any first-class orchestra, will have to count on slow progress through a good many seasons. A director who lacks the patience or nerve for such a course, who wants or needs early applause, will shop for stars and shape his repertory to the names for hire. The result will be something like the American Shakespeare Festival in Stratford, Connecticut—opulent mediocrity.

Patience not only implies nerve, it implies money—a subject I have left to the last because I know little about it. Writing for *Theatre Arts* back in 1958, Oliver M. Sayler, a man who learned his trade with the Moscow Art Theatre and Max Reinhardt, warned that no one should attempt a full-scale repertory in an urban center until he had $3-to-$5 million for the company alone, safely stored in blue-chip investments. Ongoing subsidy he rejected as much too chancy—it is the nature of angels that they lose their fervor after a time or after they suffer a clipping of their wings. Miss Le Gallienne, writing a few months later in the same magazine, endorsed Sayler's views from personal experience. The Civic Repertory died in 1933 because its private Croesus was not exempt from the Depression that then gripped the whole country.

Another warning from old repertory hands is that the management must never succumb to the temptation of sending a hit to Broadway for a straight run. It may look like quick and easy money, but the effect is to deprive the rest of the repertory of the support it must have. The company back in the home theater collapses while the prodigal riots among the fleshpots. The kind of money we are talking about now is not venture capital, but benevolent capital. It troubles some people that a theater of high resolve should need to be endowed, but that is only because they have been conditioned by the finances of show business, where the only resolve is to make a killing. All orchestras are endowed, as are all opera and ballet companies, museums, libraries, colleges, and hospitals. So, in their own ways, are the U.S. Postal

67

ESSAYS

Service and the New York Rapid Transit System. Any facility set up for the benefit of society at large must depend on resources beyond its immediate income.

Lincoln Center is budgeted at present at $132-to-$140 million for construction and land, $10 million for "education and artistic achievement." That works out at a ratio of fourteen to one for body and soul. I hope the soul is not being shortchanged. Particularly, I hope that Messrs. Whitehead and Kazan get a sum close enough to $5 million that they are not constrained to the jackdaw practices of Broadway.

The Metropolitan Opera and the New York Philharmonic come to Lincoln Center with an old tradition to sustain them; the repertory theater must create a new image among all the new marble and plaster. Right now, the Vivian Beaumont Theater is the best chance for the survival of noble repertory in New York. But I should not like to think that it is the last or only chance.

"Orson Welles" (1963)

The most disconcerting thing about Orson Welles's screen version of *The Trial* is that in retrospect it doesn't seem to matter. At the moment, it is entertaining; at times its ingenuity and insight are admirable; it commits (except for a grotesquely inappropriate final shot) no factual offense against Franz Kafka's novel. Yet a few days after I had seen the movie, it had slipped off my mind and left the book just as it was.

The same thing, I find, can be said of the pictures Welles made of *Macbeth* and *Othello*. They had great cinematic vigor; they were clearly intended as shocks to entrenched attitudes toward both the plays themselves and the suitability of the screen for the transmission of Shakespeare. But whereas I have had to work at erasing Laurence Olivier's movie-Hamlet from memory, Welles's Macbeth and Othello have obligingly bleached away. How does it happen that someone of Welles's stature in the theater can work to such impermanent ends? And, if I am right in this, how does it happen that he continues to be a figure of international fascination? The answer may lie in the fact that Welles is a quite unusual species of man—he is an adult prodigy. And to explain what that implies I must digress a bit.

A child prodigy, and Orson Welles was almost the archetype, differs from a child in that he never plays with things: he *uses* them. Give him a typewriter and he will publish a newspaper; give him an easel and he will paint your portrait; give him blocks and he will design a model city; give him a gun—no, don't give him a gun. Some children display

68

"ORSON WELLES" (1963)

specific talents—for music, mathematics, poker; the true child prodigy is born with the gift for instant accomplishment. Welles, for example, was staging his own adaptations of Shakespeare (he had been given a model theater) before he could read. And he taught himself to read at the age of three by using *A Midsummer Night's Dream* as a primer. At ten, when he was examined by a group of psychologists assembled in Madison, Wisconsin, he was described in the local paper as a poet, painter, cartoonist, and actor; the reporter did not know, apparently, that he was also a pianist, an accomplished magician, and a critic of Nietzsche. At that meeting, by the way, he routed the brain probers by replying to their questions with erudite pronouncements of complete irrelevance. In short, instant accomplishment.

The prognosis for children who show this gift for handling the adult world as though it were their rattle is statistically not very promising. The child of single and singular talent often develops into a talented adult; the way is much harder for the generally prodigious child. A few become excellent men and women, but in more cases they are eventually overtaken by their contemporaries and find themselves ill-prepared to compete on equal terms. It is only rarely that the child prodigy converts into an adult prodigy. After adolescence the difference between the prodigy and the talented is not so easily defined. The most reliable guide, perhaps, is that in the former case public attention tends to focus more on the remarkable circumstances surrounding an accomplishment than on the accomplishment itself. And it can therefore happen that the prodigy's reputation is not integrally associated with his achievements.

If it is good luck to be Orson Welles—and I think it must be one of the most exciting experiences a man could have—then Welles has been lucky all his life. He was born in 1915 in Kenosha, Wisconsin, which is on Lake Michigan. As a child, he was surrounded by precisely the sort of adults a prodigy should cultivate. His mother, Beatrice Ives, a beauty and a concert pianist, introduced him to artistic society in Chicago when he was little more than a baby. Like most prodigies, he was much in the company of grownups, and he attributes his disconcerting knack for being able to carry on one conversation while absorbing two or three others going on in his vicinity to the early habit of eavesdropping at the vivacious gatherings he attended with his mother.

She died when the boy was nine, and he returned to his father (the parents had separated), a retired manufacturer and inventor—an improved bicycle lamp, a mess kit used by the U.S. Army in World War I—who was to devote the rest of his life to travel and good living.

ESSAYS

He was named Richard H. Welles, and a race horse, as well as a restaurant and a cigar, was named after him. Young Welles had seen Europe and the Far East by the time he was in his early teens; he had become accustomed to champagne suppers and the laughter of beautiful women.

Then there was Dr. Maurice Bernstein, who visited the family professionally, and who guessed that Welles was a prodigy at the age of one-and-a-half. It was Dr. Bernstein who provided the model theater, the paints and brushes, the magic kit, which the child seized with infallible hands. It was Dr. Bernstein who, as legal guardian of the teenager when he became an orphan (at thirteen), allowed Welles to declare Harvard superfluous and to go off instead on a sketching jaunt through Ireland, which within a year had brought him to Dublin and to leading parts in the repertory of the Gate Theatre.

Welles was not uneducated; he spent five years, from eleven to fifteen, in school. Again he was lucky, for the Todd School of Woodstock, Illinois, was very possibly the only educational institution in the country that would have tolerated Welles or that Welles himself would have tolerated. Roger Hill, the headmaster, was undismayed on being told that Welles was devoting his energies in history to exposing the ignorance of the eminent Egyptologist James H. Breasted; and Hill was able to adjust the curriculum so that his unusually energetic student could produce, direct, and act in an average of eight plays per school year. The Todd School has ever since rather specialized in dramatics, and Welles has maintained an interest in his only alma mater.

After the season at Gate, which Welles got by telling Hilton Edwards, its director, a wholly preposterous and little credited yarn of stellar performances at the Theatre Guild, he returned to New York, aged seventeen, and was offended by the city's failure to take any formal notice of his presence. He thereupon retired to Morocco, where, as the guest of the local prince, he worked on a school edition of Shakespeare that he and Roger Hill brought out together and that has sold 100,000 copies over the years.

On his next trip home Welles met Thornton Wilder, who sent him to Alexander Woollcott, who introduced him to Katharine Cornell, who engaged him as a juvenile for a repertory tour on which she was then starting. He was eighteen, and we may say that his status as a child prodigy was over. Welles's career now begins to accelerate, and no attempt will be made to touch on every event.

In the mid-thirties, America was still far down in the Depression; as a time for launching oneself in the theater, it had only one thing to

70

"ORSON WELLES" (1963)

recommend it—relatively few vessels were being launched and you could make a relatively big splash. In 1935 Welles was offered the lead in *Panic*, an experimental verse play by Archibald MacLeish that derived its title from the Wall Street collapse of 1933, and in which the banker (Welles) was named McGafferty. This in itself was not much of a splash; the play was scheduled for only three performances, with the critics invited, prudently, on the second night. But John Houseman was a member of the sponsoring group, and he and Welles were soon to become a memorable theater team.

In 1936 the Federal Theatre Project (of the Works Progress Administration, or WPA) engaged Welles and Houseman to produce an all-black, "Voodoo" *Macbeth* in Harlem. (It was set in Haiti and employed witch doctors instead of witches.) In addition to its dubious artistic premise, this enterprise involved some very trick racial diplomacy. Welles survived both the events on stage and the agitation along 125th Street, and went on to direct for the WPA a production of Marlowe's *Dr. Faustus* that was presented on a bare stage and organized by the use of great sheets of light beamed from banks of overhead spots.

He then set to work on Marc Blitzstein's *The Cradle Will Rock*, and at that point the WPA panicked. It smelled subversion in the script and locked the theater. Welles and John Houseman found another theater, and on their own opened *The Cradle Will Rock* without scenery or costumes and with Blitzstein himself at the piano. That was the beginning of the Mercury Theatre, which, in the next two years, 1937–1938, produced the famous anti-fascist *Julius Caesar* (Welles played Brutus in a shabby overcoat and a slouch hat); *The Shoemaker's Holiday*, an Elizabethan romp by Thomas Dekker that galloped irresistibly through a set composed entirely of unpainted lath lattice-work; and Shaw's *Heartbreak House*, in which Welles, now twenty-three, played the octogenarian Captain Shotover. This is perhaps the most unplayable of Shaw's works, but it was seen to foretell the fall of England's house—which made it a tract for the times.

Those plays, in those money-tight days, were not profitable, but by 1938 Welles was also a veteran radio actor. He played innumerable real-life public figures for "The March of Time"; he was "The Shadow"; he was hired for so many dramatic programs that he some-times arrived in the studio as the show was going on the air and grabbed a script with no advance notice of whether he was playing hero, villain, or idiot bystander. There were times when he hired an ambulance to get himself rapidly through the midtown traffic; it was

ESSAYS

an expense he could well afford, since his fees were running to $17,000 a year. Much of that money went to support the Mercury Theatre.

We come now to 8 p.m. on the evening of October 30, 1938 (Halloween), when the Mercury Theatre of the Air, directed by and starring Orson Welles, was to give its regular weekly entertainment in the series called "First Person Singular." The idea was to adapt famous stories—Charlotte Brontë's *Jane Eyre*, Robert Louis Stevenson's *Treasure Island*, Charles Dickens' *Oliver Twist*, and John Buchan's *The 39 Steps* were some that had been used—to a formula precisely suitable to radio. As Welles explained it: "When someone comes on the air and says, 'This happened to me,' you've got to listen." They certainly listened to the offering of October 30th: *The War of the Worlds*, by H. G. Wells.

The narrative method used on this particular evening was as simple it proved devastating. Welles created a fake newscast (a form of entertainment subsequently avoided by all the networks). He updated the original story to the night in question and set its critical episode in Grovers Mill, New Jersey, a remote town that was yet not far from New York and within easy reach of a very large segment of the listening audience. After the customary station introduction and a brief "foreword" by Welles, both of which made it crystal-clear that this was fiction and both of which were as clearly missed by millions of late-tuners, the "show" started with a weather forecast, followed by dance music from the Hotel Park Plaza (there was no such hotel) in New York. There came shortly an interruption: Intercontinental Radio News (no such agency) had just issued a bulletin about several large explosions on Mars that had been detected on the earth a half-hour earlier. Then more music, then additional explosion details, followed by a "background" interview with Professor Pierson (Welles) of the Princeton Observatory. This was in turn interrupted by a flash: "a huge flaming object" had fallen in a farmer's field near Grovers Mill.

No one should have been fooled. There was the standard station opening, there was a mid-hour identification, and no other station on the air was "reacting" to the ghastly events. Further, the events took place at ludicrous speeds. (For example, Dr. Pierson would have had to drive from Princeton to Grovers Mill over the back roads of New Jersey at several hundred miles an hour to arrive at the moment when he was heard to say, from observations made at a distance of some thirty yards, that "the metal casing is definitely extraterrestrial.") Finally, one would have thought that a "meteor" with a screw top was a sufficiently trite hobgoblin to disabuse the most gullible. One would have thought wrong.

72

"ORSON WELLES" (1963)

America, or a significant segment of America, panicked as Welles spun the old Martian thriller out over the CBS network. The worst disorders occurred in New Jersey, near the place where "the monsters had landed." Highways were blocked with refugees fleeing the lethal gas of the invading octopi; the telephone system broke down, police stations were jammed, and at least one of them advised hysterical questioners to follow precisely the advice coming from their radios. It all lasted only an hour or so, but the anguish induced across the whole country is entirely incalculable. I am not going to discuss the reasons for this extraordinary response to a yarn so shopworn that Welles had hesitated to use it. The incident is analyzed in detail in Hadley Cantril's sociological study titled *The Invasion from Mars*. In defense of the American public (and it is hardly a sufficient defense), it should be recalled that the capitulation of Neville Chamberlain at Munich had occurred only a month earlier, and terror was epidemic in the world.

The relevant point is that, as a prodigy, Orson Welles was lucky again. He hadn't meant to cause suffering with his Halloween charade; he hadn't schemed to become a national focus of mixed admiration and anger. Nevertheless, events had shown in the most dramatic way conceivable that the touch of Welles was unlike the touch of other men. And the proof continued to pile up. Hollywood signed him to one of the richest, most open contracts ever offered a newcomer. (That and a beard grown for a production of Joseph Conrad's *The Heart of Darkness*, which was never made, earned Welles the instant and virulent hatred of the film colony.)

His first big picture was *Citizen Kane*; it is the best picture he has ever made and probably the most notorious one ever made in the United States. We may safely ignore the disclaimers—*Citizen Kane* was indeed based on the life of William Randolph Hearst. It held that life up to scorn and pity; worse, the film envisioned its end, and Hearst, who had a morbid fear of death, trained the fire of the most powerful and ruthless newspaper empire in America on Welles, on RKO Pictures, and on Hollywood. There was no battle: RKO made a few bold statements; Hedda Hopper fired some girlish grapeshot at Hearst's Louella Parsons; Welles tried quite futilely to get hold of his own creation. RKO, and certainly Hollywood, had no intention of fighting for anything as abstract as a principle. To this day, *Citizen Kane* has never had a wide circulation. One of Welles's holds on fame, then, is that he made a great movie that has had fewer viewers than any of similar renown.

Citizen Kane opens with a fake "March of Time" newsreel on the death of "the great man" that is as brilliant as the Martian broadcast.

ESSAYS

At its conclusion the lights come up on what is seen to be a preview studio, where the editor is expressing dissatisfaction because the picture does not get to the central "truth" about Charles Foster Kane. This is not entirely likely—it being no function of newsreels to provide such pinpoint analysis—but it does provide a splendid narrative device. A reporter is assigned to track down the meaning of Kane's last word—"Rosebud"—and the film proper is a series of flashbacks showing the public and private Kane as he is remembered by the men and women who were closest to him. These portraits are alike—but not quite; and the real portrait is the sum of the discrepancies.

What makes *Citizen Kane* so good is not the rather thin psychological thread that ends in "Rosebud." It is rather that Welles drew a character of genuine stature, and through the reporting device showed his man with depth, clarity, anger, understanding, and compassion. Welles himself was superb in the role of Kane. I doubt that there is much autobiography in the characterization—at least conscious autobiography, though Welles did name Kane's lifelong friend and advisor after Dr. Bernstein. But Kane also was more prodigy than giant, and Welles understood his subject. The unforgettable scene in which Kane-the-young-publisher dances and clowns in front of the distinguished staff he has just bought away from a rival paper is curiously like a report I have recently read of Welles fooling around, telling wild stories, and being the life of the party on the set of *The Trial*. Kane lived his whole life in front of an audience; so does Welles.

Every discussion of *Citizen Kane*, or of any other Welles movie, is sure to bring up his camera sense. In *Kane* there is, as noted, the brilliant pseudo-newsreel of the great man's death; the Senate investigation scene that is modeled on the inquisition of J. P. Morgan; the wide-angle lens that is supposed to approximate the eye's normal scope (and which for the first time required ceilings to close off the sets); the bold cutting that snaps the picture from one perspective to the next; the persistent low-angle shots that make Kane seem to tower above lesser men—and above the audience. All such matters are handled with a sureness that is astonishing in a man making his first motion picture. We are back again to the gift of instant accomplishment—like knowing how to invest a bare stage with the highest dramatic tension, or how to use the mechanics of radio with such deftness as to turn a stock thriller into an hour of public terror. Such a gift constitutes an instant feel for the nature of the vehicle; the effect is dazzling virtuosity.

There is a price to be paid, however. Welles has said that anyone can learn the whole of movie technique in four hours. That is not

74

"ORSON WELLES" (1963)

true—though it may be approximately true for Welles. But if he learned the technique in something like four days, he has never quite assimilated it, in the sense that he is no longer self-conscious or self-deprecating about the tool at his command. A child prodigy is applauded for his improbable skill with adult equipment; no one asks whether he is achieving adult results. But an adult should not go on indefinitely parading dexterity.

Yet it is characteristic of Welles that one is repeatedly aware of the effects he is creating. Whether it is the deliberately unreal sleigh party in *The Magnificent Ambersons*; the studied irony of the Lucullan picnic and the eerie horror of the house of mirrors in *The Lady from Shanghai* (there were a fake snowfall, a grotesque picnic, and an infinity of mirrors in *Citizen Kane*, too, as Welles's tricks repeat themselves); the architectural kaleidoscope of *Othello*; or the 900 desks stretching to infinity in *The Trial*—however effective such devices may be technically, they divert the audience from *what* is being done to *who* is doing it. "Welles is at it again," we note indulgently, and thus he wins attention for himself at the expense of his creation.

I do not think that Welles means to do this, but then I do not think he meant to be an adult prodigy. Events like the necessity to defy the United States government over *The Cradle Will Rock*; like discovering in *Julius Caesar* a knife to use against Hitler; like being called a broadcasting menace to the sanity of the entire nation for *The War of the Worlds*; like incurring the senile rage of William Randolph Hearst, the world's most phobic publisher—all of these froze Welles in the role of prodigy. And it is the nature of prodigy to be the master magician of whatever art he enters; only occasionally is he a master artist. Welles *was* that in *Citizen Kane*, though even that picture, for all its bravura screen effects, is not essentially a movie. It could be a novel, or a play; it lacks the cumulative power of an ongoing visual flow that occurs when someone really exploits the genius of the camera—when, for example, John Huston makes *The Treasure of the Sierra Madre*.

Orson Welles created his best stage productions back in the thirties, and he made his best picture in 1941. *The Magnificent Ambersons*, which followed *Citizen Kane*, seems curiously implausible and uncertain today, but Welles claimed that the film's point was edited out of it in his absence, and he broke with RKO over its release in truncated form. His other Hollywood pictures are superior Hollywood products; indeed, they often look like Hollywood outdoing itself. *Macbeth* and *Othello*, both filmed abroad, contain gimmicks designed to make Shakespeare work on the screen.

75

ESSAYS

The gimmicks in *Macbeth* are the removal of the scene to the barbaric era of the original legend and the portrayal of Lady Macbeth as a priestess of blood and lust. The results are striking, but the poetry does not transport as readily as the setting and the Elizabethan preoccupations come oddly from half-savage lips. The gimmicks in *Othello*, in addition to the aforementioned architectural dazzle, were to choreograph the action like a ballet and to suppose that Iago is motivated by impotence. The effect is sadly diminished tragedy. There was a lot of Welles in these two films; it is a question whether there was enough Shakespeare.

Over the years Welles has been acting a great deal, at home and abroad. He can play any part that is slightly bigger than life. He was the famous Harry Lime in *The Third Man* (1949, Carol Reed); an aging Southern gentleman in that curious transmogrification of Faulkner, *The Long, Hot Summer* (1958, Martin Ritt); a fictional version of Clarence Darrow in *Compulsion* (1959, Richard Fleischer); Benjamin Franklin in *A Royal Affair at Versailles* (1954, Sacha Guitry). He directed and took the title role in *Mr. Arkadin* (from his only novel, or in any event from several of his combined radio scripts), and it is the one Welles film I have seen that I would call a clear failure—pretentious, obscure, and unamusing (which last is a fault almost unknown in Welles's work).

There have been other parts. By chance I came upon a recent paragraph from Italy reporting the suppression of a short film and the imprisonment of its director (Pier Paolo Pasolini) on the ominously inquisitorial ground of defamation of the state religion. This was *La Ricotta*, a movie-within-a-movie about the Crucifixion, in which Welles plays a film director. He has said that his next picture will be about an aging film director, once great, now in eclipse: a romantic who cannot adapt to the narrow and canny realism of the "cool" generation. Kane was not Welles, nor will this old man be—but Welles has been a director most of his life and a romantic since birth.

Which, finally, brings the subject back to *The Trial*. The opportunities it afforded Welles to behave like a prodigy are obvious and legion. Kafka's nightmare world is a magic box for camera trickery and visual surprises, for baroque décor and bizarre characterizations. There have been complaints that Welles woefully over-visualizes a book that was visually almost barren. But I have always thought that I "saw" a good deal in the novel, and by and large the scenes evoked by Welles seem to me to do no violence to Kafka's intent. The picture goes astray because Welles is a romantic—and, I think, an optimist.

He cast Anthony Perkins, a yearning juvenile, in the lead, as though he thought that Josef K. were a romantic hero. And he got from Mr. Perkins a remarkably solid performance. Nevertheless, Kafka's story of a man who is the law's victim because he is the utterly lawful man becomes the tale of a student rebel, the sort of young man who looks as though he couldn't care less about the law and its institutions. In the book the law devours its most ardent disciple; in the film the totalitarian police pick up a potential dissent (and quite properly, given the viewpoint). That is an idea for a picture, but it is not Kafka's idea. Nor did Kafka have in mind to warn his public against the imminence of atomic war—he was dealing with a horror of the soul. The mushroom cloud at the end of the movie is another example of the boy scout in Welles; he has never been able to pass a soapbox without jumping up for a brief exhortation.

Still, the failure of *The Trial* comes much more from a gulf between the temperaments of author and director than it does from a prodigy's self-bemusement with the dexterity of his technique. If Welles does make that movie about the romantic director in a "cool" world, he will have a subject that corresponds to his own instincts. It could mark the end of the adult prodigy and the début of the full-grown artist. The magic creations of his youth may seem very far in the past, but, after all, Orson Welles is only forty-eight years old.

"Tyrone Guthrie" (1963)

It is accurate to say that Sir Tyrone Guthrie is the most renowned and probably most controversial of contemporary British stage directors (in compliance with a venerable English theater tradition, he is of Irish stock); but this identification does not explain why last summer the much gratified and more than a little astonished citizens of Minneapolis discovered that their city had become, for a season, the most exciting theater town in America. A superb new playhouse named for Guthrie had been built, a repertory company that combined magnetic stars with group versatility had been assembled, a season of four world-famous plays had been sumptuously mounted, and Minneapolis found itself playing theater host not only to the Middle West but to pilgrims from every state of the Union and points abroad.

To understand how this happy and almost ludicrously unlikely bolt of drama hit the Middle West, it is necessary to describe Guthrie, not merely as a director (he could as well be a producer or an actor), but as a man of the theater—using that term as one says man of letters, to

ESSAYS

designate someone who is concerned for the standards, creative vigor, and public recognition of the art to which he has dedicated his life.

As a young man, just after World War I, Guthrie seems to have recognized in himself unusual resources of creative energy; at any rate, he decided quite soberly to become a celebrated artist. He thought first of being a singer, but his voice, though large, was not entirely pleasing. He turned then to acting, but the stage does not offer a great variety of roles to a man six-feet-five and amply framed for his height. Radio had just been born and Guthrie, pending the arrival of fame, took a job with the Belfast station of the B.B.C. There, putting an occasional dramatic half-hour on the air, he found in himself a knack for making rehearsals "go with a swing." A gentleman from Scotland observed him one day exercising this talent and invited him to present himself to the board of the Scottish National Players. He got the job, though his new employers were not conspicuously gracious in bestowing it— they made clear their total inability to find anyone else.

Guthrie did not awaken the next morning in Glasgow to find himself famous. Indeed, reading his autobiography *A Life in the Theatre*, it is not possible to say just when fame caught him in its current; and the most probable reason is that all his life Guthrie has worked as much for the theater as in it. You can see this in the choices he made, when he was far enough along to have a choice: he habitually elected to associate himself with institutions. True, he has worked in the West End and on Broadway; he knows the intoxication of a hit and the hangover of a flop; he has respect for the commercial theater and harsh words for colleagues who find its calculations and vulgarities offensive to their talents. He has said that a director who cannot make a stab at "staging anything from *Hamlet* to striptease does not know his job."

Nevertheless—from the National Players in Scotland, back to the B.B.C. in London, to the Festival Theatre in Cambridge, to the Canadian Broadcasting Company (as director of a serial called *The Romance of Canada*, sponsored by the Canadian National Railways), to a converted London movie house named the Westminster Theatre, to the Old Vic (where fame *did* catch up with him), to the Phoenix on Second Avenue in New York, to Habimah in Tel Aviv, to the Edinburgh International Festival, to the Festival Theatre in Stratford, Ontario, and now to the Tyrone Guthrie Theatre in Minneapolis—the mainstream of his career has been channeled into long-term organizations based on convictions rather than into short-term ventures based on risk capital. And in that world one is not "made" by a first night; fame does not rocket, it accumulates.

"TYRONE GUTHRIE" (1963)

At any rate, Guthrie had become a celebrated figure by the end of World War II, and today his name is almost certain to head any popular list of "great" directors. The audience is aware of Guthrie, perhaps, because he is so very much aware of the audience. He likes it and understands it; he knows that it is a crowd and has pointed out that the way to a crowd is not through its mind but through its emotions.

Guthrie is also on record as deploring the pinch-mouthed view of the theater that attempts to "elevate" it by pretending that it is a school, a church, a political forum—it is, he insists, a place of entertainment. This is not frivolous, for Guthrie takes seriously the need for entertainment—recreation—in men's lives; but it is light-hearted and, together with his conviction that there can be no such thing as a definitive production of a great play, evokes a gusto, and daring enterprise on the stage, that the audience now recognizes as his mark.

His affinity for crowds, moreover, applies not only to the audience but to the stage itself: Guthrie is probably the most brilliant ensemble director of our era. Of course, every good director must be conscious of the broad stage picture, but Guthrie more than others seems to revel in the moments when the scene bursts out in flashing jewels and swirling capes, with trumpets sounding, armies passing, and fortune on the wing. Unlike most dramatic directors, he admires opera (but not its customary staging) and has mounted productions of *The Barber of Seville*, *Carmen*, *Falstaff*, and *La Traviata* at Sadler's Wells and the Metropolitan. He has staged every kind of play available to a modern director, from Ibsen to Sophocles, from J. B. Priestley to William Congreve, from Wilder's *The Matchmaker* to Shakespeare's *Tamburlaine*, but he will be remembered, I think, as the director who pounded the dust out of the classic spectacles and brought them roaring back to life. As the Canadian critic Robertson Davies has said: "What is realistic or small in scale is not for him; indeed, it does not easily survive his sort of treatment."

In the past ten or fifteen years the tangible evidence of Guthrie's activity is that wherever he applies himself, you may expect to find that a new theater of a particular design has been built and in it a company is playing a repertory of world classics. This was true at Edinburgh and at Stratford; last summer it became true at Minneapolis; and it is unlikely that the list will end there. As a man of the theater Guthrie has developed a set of interlocking convictions, a philosophy, about the virtue and prosperity of his art; as a famous director he has a skill and a name to contribute to whatever enterprise

ESSAYS

will implement his convictions. Fame probably concerns him very little anymore; he cannot, in any case, avoid it.

I would not give the impression that Guthrie is a latter-day Kubla Khan who goes about the world decreeing pleasure domes; a creation like the new theater in Minneapolis rises from impulses much more complex than that. It began when two New York producers, Oliver Rea and Peter Zeisler, discovered that they were tired of the hit-and-run opportunism of Broadway and began to scan the country for some community that wanted a theater rather than show business. They chose Minneapolis—or Minneapolis chose them—because it was a rich town, a proud town, the site of the second largest university in America (Minnesota), and the gateway to one of the country's largest resort areas. And Guthrie, with whom Rea and Zeisler had baited their hook, liked Minneapolis—probably because it is the most American of cities and as far as you can possibly get from anything recognizable as organized theater. If his theories worked there, they would work almost anywhere.

The Guthrie credo begins with the proposition that the essential magic of the theater is not illusion but ritual. From this it follows that the classics are the plays in which men have found, not an imitation of life, but an occasion for the ceremonies that give life its shape and abstract its significance. And further it follows that the theater in which such plays are to be mounted should provide a platform stage with the audience disposed in an encompassing arena—first, because the greatest of the classic playwrights, the Greeks and the Elizabethans, wrote for such a stage, and second, because this design, in which the audience is aware of itself wrapped about the playing area, supporting, or as in French, "assisting at," the performance, most enhances the atmosphere of ritual. The commercial theater can be relied upon to support a contemporary body of work (the unrecognized masterpiece is so rare as to be a myth), but it will not keep the classics alive. Therefore, a second, institutional theater must be maintained, by subsidy if necessary. This should consist of repertory houses because repertory provides the richest public experience with the means available, and because it affords actors the variety of assignment and familiarity with the basic literature of their art without which they cannot become craftsmen. (Guthrie's most serious charges against the commercial theater are that it offers the actors no goal beyond their own success, and that it forces them either to jump rapidly from one failure to the next or to bury themselves for months, perhaps years, in a single role.)

80

"TYRONE GUTHRIE" (1963)

That is Guthrie's credo; it is the program that was accepted at Minneapolis.

The theater, adjoining the Walker Art Center and standing on land donated by that institution, has a frivolous exterior: a non-functional plywood molded screen of unconvincing abstract design that cost some $60,000—a sum that could have been better spent, I was somewhat bitterly informed by everyone in the company with whom I brought up the point, on backstage facilities and amenities. But the first impression is the only bad one: inside, the public spaces are large, functional, and relaxing; the auditorium, seating 1,437, is an arc sweeping 200 degrees around a platform stage of dark, lustrously polished wood. This playing area is said to be a septagon, but when you are in the theater its shape is inviting and elusive. Nothing in the Tyrone Guthrie auditorium is symmetrical. For two thirds of the arc, the rows of seats are arranged in orchestra and balcony, but very steeply raked; in the remaining third, the seats plunge uninterruptedly from ceiling to floor (the company calls this the ski jump, and club ladies have been seen to freeze when entering from above). The ceiling is baffled with a complex of acoustic "clouds," and the stage does not center upon any axis of the house. This ambiguity of design sets up a tension of expectancy in the audience; from the viewpoint of the productions, it makes relatively easy the creation of fluid stage patterns: the left-right, back-front *rigor mortis* that too often overcomes plays set within a proscenium is almost impossible on this enigmatic and versatile platform. At stage rear is a two-story "house" with windows and platforms, a functional structure in the Elizabethan pattern; it is mounted on two trucks and can be replaced by more specific "sets." Two broad ramps run from the stage under the audience; they allow almost instantaneous mobbing or evacuation of the stage.

The company, this first season, was headed by Hume Cronyn, his wife Jessica Tandy, George Grizzard, Rita Gam, and Zoe Caldwell. The assistant director, responsible for half the productions, was Douglas Campbell; Tanya Moiseiwitsch was the principal designer. Here, in a coldly practical way, the necessity of someone like Tyrone Guthrie to the project is evident. Theater people are the servants of their own reputations; they cannot afford to move far or for long outside the strongest current of their profession. But Guthrie diverts the current to wherever he sets up headquarters; and last summer it was not only artistically rewarding, it was professionally useful, to be working in Minneapolis. I cannot take the space to list the extensive supporting cast; it was clearly of a caliber that could not possibly have been attracted to a typical summer season.

ESSAYS

The plays in the maiden year were *Hamlet*, Molière's *The Miser*, Chekhov's *The Three Sisters*, and Arthur Miller's *Death of a Salesman*. (The Medici-like largesse provided by a well-designed repertory season is shown, I think, by the fact that I arrived in Minneapolis on a Saturday noon, left on Monday morning, and in that span of less than forty-eight hours saw productions of Shakespeare, Molière, and Chekhov. I did not see the Miller play because it had not yet come into the season.)

And what of the quality of these productions? They have been widely discussed, and I shall not review them systematically here; but, given Guthrie's reputation, they contained surprises. The recurring charge made by his detractors is that Guthrie, for all his loudly avowed dedication to the classics, shows a lack of respect, verging on contempt, for the texts and intentions of his revered masters. It is implied that his main interest as a director is to prove what a bold, ingenious, and witty showman he can be with familiar material; and the English critic T. C. Worsley has accused him of founding the "Wouldn't It Be Fun (Just for a Change) School of Production." There are horror stories of occasions when whole scenes had to be dropped from a Guthrie production because the willful director had led his cast so far from the true path that the sections in question would be patent absurdities. There is so much smoke of this sort in the theatrical archives that I will not say there is no fire, but I did not find it at Minneapolis.

The two plays staged by Guthrie were *Hamlet* and *The Three Sisters*, and the quality that struck me about both of them was their surpassing legibility. I have seen performances of these works that I thought, in the one case, rose to higher grandeur and, in the other, evoked a more searching poignancy; but I have never seen performances in which the author's design for the structure, the shifting relationships, or the course of the action was more limpidly set forth.

For one thing, *Hamlet* was staged in its entirety, and it became clear that the "versions" of this play when it is trimmed to what is conventionally deemed a full evening in the theater are never skillful enough to avoid distortion. To give just one example: when the lines of Claudius are not cropped—as usually they are—it can be seen that, however he acquired the crown, he is a competent king and deeply preoccupied with running his country. Hamlet's obstinate gloom is at first no more than a nuisance to this busy man—it upsets his wife: notice how he keeps the youth waiting until he has disposed of more urgent business. But it is not long before the astute older man senses danger as well as bother in that quarter. Hamlet, after all, is heir to

82

"TYRONE GUTHRIE" (1963)

the throne, and murder has a way of begetting murder. If you wonder why Hamlet "hesitates," why he feigns madness, why he runs about so much and buttonholes everyone he meets, consider that he may be trying to kill his uncle without being killed himself. As for Rosencrantz and Guildenstern, who are they but the first and second murderers from *Richard III*? (In Guthrie's sharp business suits, they bear a passing resemblance to Roy Cohn and G. David Schine.)

Those who worry that Guthrie is not respectful enough make a good deal of his enthusiasm for mounting costume plays in modern dress. He defends it on the grounds that the Elizabethans saw their productions so dressed (Shakespeare, after all, was for the most part writing historical plays), and that costumes more familiar than capes and furbelows convey quickly to the audience such relevant information as time, place, and the social position of the wearer. Probably so, though modern dress is a manner of speaking; in *Hamlet*, as in other Guthrie productions I have seen, the style is scarcely what you would expect to meet with in Mamaroneck, New York. It is exceedingly elegant, uniforms of Ruritanian bravura abound, formal dress is observed in almost all scenes, and the general atmosphere is certainly elevated, if no longer antiquated. The occasional suitcase, tennis racket, set of binoculars, or pearl-handled revolver probably calls more attention to itself than its function in the scene is worth.

As for the title role, George Grizzard played with an impressive sense of what it means to be a handsome, rich, and powerful young man with the burden of a considerable tradition resting on his shoulders. His manners were excellent, his wit was quick, he was graceful, tough, daring, and honest—a formidable youth, as his foster father was only too well aware. With Grizzard at the focus, the production became a descriptive *Hamlet* rather than a soaring one, and Guthrie told me later that he worked consciously for an expository quality—an emphasis on what the play is *about*—for playgoers, many of whom would be seeing a Shakespeare text come to life for the first time. Grizzard's voice has not much range and some of the poetry escaped him, but his speech was decent and it was wonderfully clear. Most important for a young man playing the part for the first time, there was nothing in his interpretation of Hamlet to block its continuing growth—provided, of course, that he ever gets the chance to play it again.

With *The Three Sisters* one comes upon the other side of the open stage versus proscenium argument. Chekhov wrote for the box set; he can be staged on an open platform, but he does not profit thereby. Guthrie admits the problem, but thinks that such plays are not harmed

ESSAYS

as much as the older classics are helped by his architecture; that to the degree that open staging shifts the feel from realism toward ritual there is a gain. The argument will not become acute until such time as the platform gains the near monopoly that the proscenium has held for two hundred years.

The atmosphere of Chekhov is not dissipated in the arena theater. The isolation, the taut futility, the closeness of minds and bodies, can be expressed as well on a platform as behind a frame. It is a matter of furniture (in this case ringing the edges and facing into the center), lighting, and the attitudes of the players—hunched shoulders bring the claustrophobia close in. What bothered me was a seeming confusion in the crosscurrents of the play. With Shakespeare the structure of intercourse is relatively formal and simple. You have mob scenes or you have duets, trios, sometimes quartets. An actor is in the action or out of it, and the lines guide the eye. But with Chekhov everyone is constantly involved, currents are moving simultaneously in many directions, and it is not safe to assume that the lines define the action. In that situation a proscenium stage offers the audience a better chance to keep its eye on the whole tableau. The possibilities of grouping and movement are certainly limited, sometimes awkward, and for that reason theater people get very weary of their box sets. But I found in *The Three Sisters* a tendency for the stage to begin swirling in a slow whirlpool, and I do not think Chekhov wanted any such vertigo. I sometimes lost track of a character important to me; I could not be sure that a quick glance hadn't been masked. Guthrie says that it is a much more relaxed and natural production than could be put onto a conventional stage. Very likely, but the price, I think, is that a new, and unmeant, strain is put on the audience.

It was a lovely, gentle performance, and in this third offering of the first season, Guthrie began to evoke a "company" flavor. It is a quality as elusive as the bouquet of wine; the audience feels it as a sense of well-being: these players know and trust one another, and each dares to give what is within him without reserve. Guthrie defines a great director as a great audience—an audience of one for whom the players will unfold themselves to the maximum. One felt that *The Three Sisters* was being played for that audience.

Chekhov's humor came through like a chime; the tragedy was perhaps a little conventional, lacking the bittersweet quality of Chekhov's disillusioned compassion. The play can cut deeper into one's heart, but it was nevertheless performed here with exemplary style and feeling. It showed what Chekhov thought of his people, even if it may not have shown everything he felt about them.

84

"TYRONE GUTHRIE" (1963)

The third production of my weekend in Minneapolis was directed by Douglas Campbell: it was the one that, with some justice, might have been criticized on grounds usually used against Guthrie. *The Miser* was handsome to the point of being gorgeous (styled, it is said, after Picasso's *Three Musicians*), pitched in a key of unflagging hilarity, and run off at the speed of a patter song. It was also excessively busy, a little strident, and apparently determined, by inventive stage business and an incipient hysteria, to make up for Molière's inadequacies as a writer of farce. This is not entirely fair to Campbell; he had a difficult problem in that *The Miser* as written does not quite fill an evening, and there were probably not the resources this first season to polish up a curtain-raiser. Padding was needed, and once you start padding Molière with dances, dumb shows, and double-takes, it is hard to draw the line.

Nevertheless, the tone seemed to me unnecessarily sweet and creamy. Molière was a satirist, not a confectioner. The cast was campaigning for laughter; whereas a more confident farce group will fend it off, knowing from the bitter experience of clowns that the laughs will not be denied. Thus Hume Cronyn, who can move with a virtuoso cunning unmatched on the American stage, appeared at times to be racing around the platform in imitation of young Bobby Clark chasing his own tail. He was great fun to watch, but the cast seemed to be watching him, too.

It must be said, though, that Campbell knows his audience: *The Miser* was the hit of the season. To be accurate, the Tyrone Guthrie Theatre was the hit of Minnesota and the states bordering thereon. How could these heartland Americans have guessed that anything so sumptuous, so intelligent, so overwhelmingly alive would spring up in their midst? Someone who wasn't born yesterday decided that for the preview performances of *Hamlet* and *The Miser* the invited audience should be composed of the carpenters, plumbers, electricians, and truck drivers who had worked on the building, plus their wives, and as many local bellhops, desk clerks, and taxi drivers as the premises would hold. I talked to no plumbers or carpenters but spent a good deal of time in hotels and taxis. The word "Guthrie" seemed to work faster than a tip.

Guthrie had left before I arrived; he was, in fact, off to Ireland to preside at a meeting of a jam factory he had been instrumental in starting in County Monaghan as a device for slowing the sad migration of rural youth to the scant promise of the Irish cities. (The jam, he promises, will be excellent and hideously expensive.) However, I caught up with him in New York. It was early on a very

ESSAYS

hot morning, and Sir Tyrone received me in a cotton wrapper. In this pseudo-Roman garb, and with his height and near-Cyrano profile, he gave me a vivid, if incongruous, flash of Charles de Gaulle. I wondered how many of his Minneapolis associates, who refer to him so cozily as Tony, call him that to his face. He is an easy man to like, but I should not find it easy to get friendly with him.

I asked Guthrie some obvious questions and got better answers than I deserved. How had he decided upon the plays for the first season? The first consideration was not to patronize. You don't ask people to build you a $2,000,000 playhouse in order to give them *Three Men on a Horse* (not, he added hastily, that it isn't a dandy play). At the same time the people of Minneapolis are intelligent but not theatrically knowing—they would probably not accept avant-garde work. In that situation the safe choice is the very best. Therefore, *Hamlet*. And once you have chosen *Hamlet* you need relief; therefore (also the very best) *The Miser*. Then it becomes a question of seeing what other works of excellence, preferably from different periods, your cast of the first two plays would fit most efficiently. In this case the jigsaw worked best with *The Three Sisters* and *Death of a Salesman*.

I asked him why for the role of Hamlet he had chosen George Grizzard, an actor known previously for his roles in such contemporary plays as Joseph Hayes's *The Desperate Hours*, Hugh Wheeler's *Big Fish, Little Fish*, and Edward Albee's *Who's Afraid of Virginia Woolf?*. Guthrie replied: he has a quick wit and he wanted to do it. I had not thought of it before, but what sets Hamlet apart from his associates at Elsinore is not that he is gloomier than anyone else but that he can think circles around the lot of them. Grizzard's fast mind is the key to his interpretation.

Then I asked Guthrie what he would like to show Minneapolis next. Something by Ibsen (Minnesota is Scandinavian country); Ben Jonson's *Volpone*; one or another of the Restoration comedies (all fine for the open stage, he says, because basically ritual and entirely without illusion); and something from the 1930s in the style of that period—maybe George S. Kaufman's *Dinner at Eight* with elaborate sets rolling in on trucks.

Would he hire the same company next year? Not necessarily. Guthrie's idea of repertory is something between the pure hazard of the commercial theater and the utter security (boredom) of a resident company. He believes in yearly contracts, to be renewed at the pleasure of actor or management. That way you have a nucleus to start each season, and there are enough new faces to keep things bright. He

"TYRONE GUTHRIE" (1963)

doubted that the Cronyns would be back next season, though he very much hoped to see them in Minneapolis four or five years from now.

But of course four or five years from now Guthrie himself will not be in Minneapolis. Will the theater survive without him? I didn't ask him that question; what could he say? No one is indispensable; but Guthrie is a large man, and he designs on a very large scale. His theaters do not grow to maturity; they are born full-grown, and their roots are not deep enough for their spreading aspirations. Guthrie is clearly aware of the danger; he worries about the vitality of the monuments of which he has been the master builder. On the occasion of the Canadian Stratford's tenth anniversary, last summer, he was worrying to this effect in the *New York Times Magazine*, and in that instance he threw the challenge to the audience. Is it self-generating, is it serious (not snobbish but committed), will it open itself to the sort of training in the great past that a repertory company can offer, and must offer, if it is to extend and deepen its range?

The festival theater, Guthrie pointed out, is the successor to the road company. The players once came to the people; now the people come to the players. The switch occurred because we have become an incredibly mobile society—it is much easier these days to draw an audience from five states than it is to move a stage production through those five states. And a festival can offer a level of performance and an elegance of occasion quite beyond the expectations of the "national companies" of Broadway hits.

Given the decade at Stratford, and the combination of local civic pride and country-wide applause that made the first Minneapolis season glow, Guthrie is carefully optimistic. "If the theater is to survive," he says, "it can only be as something more serious and interesting than Showbiz. . . . This presupposes some responsibility—maybe not even that, maybe no more than common sense on the part of both feeders and fed, in order that the diet be both agreeable and nourishing." Theater stars are said to be arrogant, but there is modesty as well as generosity in that statement. Guthrie is more than a star; perhaps he is what he set out to be—an artist.

88

REVIEWS

REVIEWS

A Phoenix Too Frequent, by Christopher Fry, & *Freight,* by Kenneth White (1950)

A Phoenix Too Frequent and *Freight,* two long one-acters presented jointly (Fulton Theatre, Broadway) to make up an evening, opened on a Wednesday and closed the same Saturday. It would be interesting to know why. There is much that could be said against these plays and their manner of presentation, but the thing to be said for them is that both, according to their violently opposed moods, projected their striking, self-reliant, and fully developed personalities into an audience that was impressed and clearly appreciative. Is this such a common feat in the contemporary theater that, because of cool reviews and perhaps a small advance sale, the production could be forfeited before a single word of mouth had time to be spoken?

A Phoenix Too Frequent is by the currently fabulous Englishman, Christopher Fry, and is admittedly one of the slighter efforts of a man who deals in effervescence. The story, from Petronius, is of a Roman lady who at midnight lies inviting death by her husband's tomb and at dawn is joyfully offering his corpse to relieve the embarrassment of her new lover, a member of the night guard from whom the body of a gibbeted felon has been stolen. The play suffers in its own right because the content does not support the verbosity, because the tongue-in-cheek extravagance bursts of over-inflation.

In this production the play suffered also because the cast of three (Nina Foch, Richard Derr, and Vicki Cummings) seemed aware of the flaws and inclined to kid the kidding. Nevertheless, it was graceful, elegant, and pretty, and the laughter was still there in the morning. Overnight laughter is a commodity that I, for one, am always ready to buy.

Freight, a race battle in a boxcar, is an editorial drama—attributed to Kenneth White—of the kind seen a good deal in the years of the WPA (Works Progress Administration). It could be dismissed perhaps for overstating its case, for trafficking in hysteria, for being written not for the stage but the pulpit. The performance of *Freight* could not so easily be booted into an alley.

After a slack but emotionally shrill opening, the cast settled down to a drumming upon the nerves and understanding of the spectators that effectively blotted out the knowledge that you had been through all this before. Dots Johnson (the black G.I. in Rossellini's *Paisan*) and Maxwell Glanville dominated and drew sparks from a company of admirable actors enlisted from the American Negro Theatre; Glen

90

Gordon, the only white man in the cast and the symbol of lynching, sank himself into a role of pitiless degradation. A rickety body and a rickety mind are not easily assumed, but there was no pretense or mock madness in Mr. Gordon's frightening performance.

Though I can't pretend that there was any great originality to *Freight*, a production that coerces participation in, and thus knowledge of, an extreme and terrible situation is worth at least some run for its money.

Julius Caesar, by William Shakespeare (1950)

One thing is now known for certain about the arena theater: it is no place for Shakespeare. Some plays may profit from the intimacy and spatial realism of theater-in-the-round (to a degree, George Kelly's *The Show-Off* did, and it would be useful now for some dramatist to aim directly for this central staging), but almost everything is wrong with the current production of *Julius Caesar* (Edison Theatre, Broadway).

It is not appropriate to play heroic tragedy at such close quarters; no company of actors should be asked to take on work "most bloody, fiery, and most terrible" while the audience squats around the pit like yokels at a cockfight. Again and again, the performers had to be marched from the arena's stage in a disciplined fire drill, the last pairs of the procession staring with morbid fascination at their fingernails as they waited their turn to pass out quietly. The action was more than confused; it induced an eye-exhausted vertigo. And when Brutus and Antony, haranguing the Roman cattle, must revolve slowly on the rostrum like models at a Paris opening, the jig is clearly up.

Under these circumstances, there is little profit in examining the interpretation or the acting, but in this *Julius Caesar* they are certainly not commendable. The play was pitched at a vulgar level, performed with broad superficiality. Shakespeare's lines obliged the actors to apostrophize one another's proud birth and noble spirit, but the proof was wanting. Caesar (Horace Braham) was crotchety and gone womanish with age, Antony (Alfred Ryder) was a strutting bully-boy, Brutus (Joseph Holland) was a prig of wood, and Basil Rathbone's Cassius belonged behind the coal-oil footlights of a Tom show. Rathbone is demonstrably better than that and, at least by implication, so are the others.

Shakespeare is not such a complaisant playwright that he can be whipped together on a weekend and displayed in someone's attic.

REVIEWS

Billy Budd, by Herman Melville (1951)

On Sunday, March 4th, the day after it was scheduled to close, *Billy Budd* was granted a two-week extension of its unseemly short run (Lenox Hill Theatre, Off-Broadway). The reprieve was made possible less by a show of interest on the part of theatergoers than by the extraordinary operating economies agreed to by all concerned in the enterprise. From authors and stars to stagehands and electricians, everybody connected with *Billy Budd* was reluctant to let it die, and anyone who has seen it should be able to understand why. It is a real play, serious, engrossing, and provocative of meaningful discussion; if the public now fails to come to its support, the public deserves the succession of smartly packaged devices that are rapidly becoming its staple fare. It isn't only in government that we get what we have coming to us.

There are some things wrong with *Billy Budd* as translated to the stage by Louis O. Coxe and Robert Chapman. I think almost anyone would agree with me that the text at times becomes too wordy, that the development of character is sometimes stifled by the flow of eloquence. And I think a good many people would accept my view that, in an effort to make sure their text would "play," the playwrights have gone too far in clothing Herman Melville's austere argument in warm particularity. Melville was discussing absolutes—good as such and evil as such, and authority in the abstract—while the play concerns an innocent boy, a wicked man, and a sadly troubled captain. The two sets of elements are not readily transposed, and thus it happens that the events of *Billy Budd* on the stage raise a number of questions about the probability of human behavior that are quite irrelevant to *Billy Budd* as its author conceived it.

But the fact that Messrs. Coxe and Chapman resolved their problem in one way, whereas some spectators might wish they had met it in another, is part of what is meant by the excitement of the theater. Whatever its faults, *Billy Budd* is a demonstration of disciplined imagination vigorously carried out; the performances by Dennis King, Torin Thatcher, and Charles Nolte in the pivotal roles are full-bodied and challenging; Norris Houghton's direction is strong and explicit; the sets by Paul Morrison are in line with the spirit of the play, vivid and specific without being irritatingly eye-catching, and they are spacious, workmanlike platforms for action.

This *Billy Budd* is material for a real theater audience to get its teeth into, something to be attended closely, thought about, and criticized for the benefit of one's own understanding. Of course, if there is no

Stalag 17, by Donald Bevan & Edmund Trzcinski; *Dream Girl*, by Elmer Rice (1951)

After a profitable summer and fall run at the 48th Street Theatre (Broadway), the comedy-thriller *Stalag 17* will be taken to Hollywood and turned into a pleasant, low-budget picture. It is the kind of entertainment that—on stage or screen—is better done in America than anywhere else. There is no depth to it, but the surface is a miracle of theater craft. *Stalag 17* is written, directed, and played with a perfect ear and sense of timing, an instinct for the outward evidence of American personalities that is exact to the nicest detail of accent and gesture. Its ambitions are modest but its workmanship is exceedingly canny; quite properly, it takes the audience to camp.

The co-authors, Donald Bevan and Edmund Trzcinski, were in such a POW stockade in Germany as they describe; their melodramatic, raffish heightening of this experience has been staged by José Ferrer with a large and busy cast that he nevertheless controls with crisp discipline. He might, however, have a word one of these days with Robert Strauss and Harvey Lembeck; they are superb clowns and they carry the show, but they have taken to snapping at flies a little early in the run. The serious aspect of the play (who is the spy in the *Stalag?*) is carried to a high tension by John Ericson, Laurence Hugo, Frank Maxwell, and Lothar Rewalt. The background G.I.s have little to do dramatically, but they contribute a sense of furious speed to the action. *Stalag 17* gets you nowhere but it gives you a wonderful night out—not a bad thing for the theater to do.

For its part, the revival of Elmer Rice's *Dream Girl* was apparently a great success in the New York City Theatre Company's production (City Center, Broadway). I doubt that it will do much for the lasting reputation of the Maurice Evans repertory; I'm sure it will do nothing for Judy Holliday. If this play seemed fresh when it was first presented six years ago, it has wilted astonishingly in the interval. Its tale of a female Walter Mitty, a less sophisticated lady in the dark, now seems labored, obvious, and wretchedly unfunny. That would not matter, of course, if Miss Holliday were in top form, but she seems unable to get

REVIEWS

a grasp on the part. She made the mistake, I think, of trying to get away, but not far enough away, from Garson Kanin's *Born Yesterday*; if she had never played Billie Dawn she might have thrown herself into *Dream Girl*. As it is, Miss Holliday seemed baffled and annoyed by a milksop girl whom Billie would have scuttled with a flick of her stole.

Mademoiselle Colombe, by Jean Anouilh (1954)

Jean Anouilh, a repeatedly successful playwright in Paris, has been spurned four times running in New York. He has implied that if the local market proves cold to *Mademoiselle Colombe* (Longacre Theatre, Broadway), he will drop America from his future plans. The ultimatum is only sensible, and the play is a good test case. It offers showy parts for Julie Harris and Edna Best, two talented entertainers with high Broadway ratings; its tone is often naughty but often edifying; it is extremely busy, which gives one the feeling of having been amply regaled. This, obviously, is theater.

The busyness springs from the fact that Anouilh has had the dexterous notion of presenting simultaneously a domestic tragi-comedy (Miss Harris) and a backstage farce (Miss Best). The Siamese device, besides encouraging liveliness, clouds the fact that neither of the twins has anything very pressing to say. Miss Harris's play tells how Colombe, when still too young to know that she is a realist, marries a boy who has known from the cradle that he is an idealist. He wants to love her for her virtue; she wants to be loved for her lovableness and has no trouble finding someone—her husband's brother—who will do just that.

Miss Best's farce sketches the personality of an aging star who, having once been worshipped as Venus in the flesh, continues to play the role after years and hard experience—eight husbands—have shaped her into a dame with the voice, figure, and manners of a regimental sergeant. The joke is that she gets away with it. The narratives are spliced together by the fact that the old girl is the young girl's mother-in-law and stage sponsor.

Since this is good boulevard fare, Colombe has the last moral word. Her husband is seen as a man who earns his horns, and one must admire the ingenuity of an erring wife who vindicates herself on the ground that her impulse to appear naked at bedroom windows has been repressed.

The Harris yarn descends straight from the Courts of Love by which lords and ladies once sped the tedium of the plague; it is the old game of showing how many lovers can dance on the head of a pin. Miss Best's caricature touches the great theme of life's capitulation to art, reduced to a vaudeville that amuses everybody and disturbs no one. In the present context, it is also a parodic refutation of the argument in the love story that the real body must prevail over the ideal spirit. Thus the author not only fills his stage but hedges his philosophy: the play is so full of loopholes as to be impregnable.

Mademoiselle Colombe is set in Paris about 1900, but I never felt very far from Broadway, 1954. The New York adaptation, by Louis Kronenberger, is written in a spruce American vernacular that flows easily but seems a little flat, considering the French reputation for *bon mots*. Miss Harris, Eli Wallach, her husband, and William Windom, her lover, are as specifically modern American as Ohio State University; Miss Best's rich performance is based on an honest vulgarity that suggests the opera houses of the Midwest more than it does the *Comédie Française*. Therefore, the genuinely European demeanor of the main supporting actors—Sam Jaffe, as an embittered and poisonous secretary to Venus, and Mikhail Rasumny, as her private playwright and poet-toady—makes the principals seem like American tourists aping Continental manners.

Since Harold Clurman was working with performers who are much better at projecting their own attractive faces than at assuming unexperienced masks, he might have done better to settle for a light suggestion of time and place. His decision to try for exotic flavor results in an air more Frenchy than French. On the other hand, his direction gives the play the great merits of speed and clarity. *Mademoiselle Colombe* romps through the evening under his expert jockeying, and his stage planning has kept in perfect order a structure so cunning that it could have been a shambles in less painstaking hands. Mr. Clurman is helped in this by Boris Aronson sets that are both fetchingly tricky and entirely workable.

The Desperate Hours, by Joseph Hayes (1955)

A little profundity is a dangerous thing. Melodrama is a surface affair, a net of thrills and terrors mechanically spun for momentary amusement; it is a mock battle of life, and since nothing in it is real we can be entertained without being engaged. But it seems now that our melodramatists have lost their innocence and become ashamed of their station in life. Not content to be showmen, they aspire to engage our hearts and minds as well as our nerves. This happens, no doubt,

REVIEWS

because they feel the real shock and terror of the day; but it often appears that they have nothing to say to the heart and mind, and then their pretensions are exposed.

You see this all the time in the movies and you can see it now in Joseph Hayes's *The Desperate Hours* (Barrymore Theatre, Broadway), which is a novel (also by Hayes) passing across the stage on its way to Hollywood. The play is a pretty piece of desperation: a trio of escaped convicts has gone to earth in the suburban house of an average family, and the problem is to flush them out of there so they can be captured or killed without serious damage to their unwilling hosts. Since one of the villains is a lunatic and another a mental deficient with a liquor problem, and since the family includes a pretty girl in her late teens and a boy of twelve with delusions of heroism, the level of excitement can be maintained at a high pitch.

But this is amusement only if the author keeps it on the surface, and Hayes is determined to probe. He must search out motives and psyches; stage touching scenes between father and son, husband and wife; beg compassion for sick and suffering characters. When you respond to this appeal, however, you discover that the purpose of the play is really frivolous. Once you believe in the existence of lunacy and horror and wanton killing, they are no longer fit topics for idle entertainment, yet entertainment is all that Hayes has to offer.

Robert Montgomery has staged *The Desperate Hours* as a tight and lucid production in a pleasant, mechanically efficient set by Howard Bay. Karl Malden, as the head of the beleaguered household, drags the play across its gaping embarrassments by the force of personality. Paul Newman, playing the head hoodlum, works earnestly to add a new portrait to the modern gallery of juvenile delinquents, but he never has a chance. The part is really impossible—a little Freud, a little Marlon Brando, a lot of spitting and bad words. It is too revolting for entertainment, too synthetic for serious attention: being the focal character, it thus epitomizes the play.

The Dark Is Light Enough, by Christopher Fry, & *Silk Stockings*, by George S. Kaufman & Abe Burrows (1955)

After several evenings spent marveling at the dubious merchandise with which the show-business peddlers find they can attract a crowd, I am grateful to Christopher Fry for *The Dark Is Light Enough* (ANTA

THE DARK IS LIGHT ENOUGH   SILK STOCKINGS

Theatre, Broadway). Though unlikely to please an audience as much as it obviously pleases its author, it is a play of sufficient moment to prevent your eyes from straying toward the nearest exit.

Fry calls it a winter comedy, by which he means that, despite a lightness of treatment, the content is serious. So it is—serious and important, though not sufficiently debatable to strike many sparks off the attending minds. His theme is that humanity has a value quite independent of its particular human example, that the champion of humanity must defend it on every occasion and not qualify his allegiance according to the merit of the individual. In short, charity is absolute.

How this might work out in practice the author demonstrates in three acts of very fine talk. His place is a country house not far from Vienna during the Hungarian revolt of 1848–49. The object of charity is one Richard Gettner, an Austrian who, having joined the rebel army, now deserts it in the hour of battle and seeks refuge with a family where he was once son-in-law. His protector is the Countess Rosmarin Ostenburg, a woman whose forbearance has won her a large following of admirers and a wide circle of influence, though not all her admirers are certain that her influence is harmless. A refusal to judge can so readily be interpreted as a failure to accept responsibility.

Gettner is a thoroughly worthless fellow, full of self-importance though quite without pride, intemperate and childish; solicitude for him appears to cause pain in varying degree and in ever-widening circles. But the Countess's position is that we can never be sure of cause and effect; all we can be sure of is the human instance—of which Gettner is an example. There is a small epilogue to suggest that, at least momentarily, Gettner understands what he exemplifies.

Fry develops his thesis with a pleasant modesty, but he couches it in a style that is neither pleasant nor modest. He suffers again, as he always suffers, from a verbal facility that he will not curb. He chatters like a squirrel brought up on Oscar Wilde, never failing to see the epigram, never failing to pop it into some character's mouth, never noticing when the flow of language has broken its banks and become a flood of words. He employs a poetic license too large for his poetic gift. Fry is a moralist, and it is ironical that his lust for rhetoric seduces him into the position that there is nothing good or evil but phrasing makes it so. It is still more ironical that in a time when most dramatists do not write elegantly enough, he makes a vice of elegance.

Katharine Cornell, as the Countess, bears the brunt of Fry's poetry, and she speaks it with astonishing endurance. But she gives me the impression that she is making a stage appearance, not participating in

97

REVIEWS

a play. It is a fault in great figures of the theater to use drama as a personal occasion, to suppose we come to revere a legend rather than to witness a performance. The problem is the director's, but Guthrie McClintic is too much part of the Cornell legend to cope with it.

Tyrone Power plays Gettner overloudly, for which he deserves some sympathy. It is the second principal part in the play, but it could be eliminated entirely and not be much missed. Gettner is what the play is *about*, but he is not really part of its action. The character keeps complaining that no one pays any attention to him, and Mr. Power understandingly feels this to be a disadvantage.

Marian Winters, as the daughter of the house and one-time wife of Gettner, offers the warmest performance; she is the one person of the company who can make her feelings seem more than verse-deep. Arnold Moss, as a Hungarian officer, is one of Shakespeare's innocent soldiers; William Podmore, Donald Harron, and John Williams, who attend the Countess, move about the stage like court gentlemen and handle Fry's verbal beanbags dexterously.

Postscript. After reading Wolcott Gibbs in the *New Yorker*, I see that my statement of Christopher Fry's intention in *The Dark Is Light Enough* was insufficient. It is not just that the countess will not yoke human charity to moral judgment. It is also, as Mr. Gibbs says, that she finds positive merit in the position of the renegade Gettner: he is an uncommitted realist in a world of romantic partisans, and she feels the world has suffered enough from partisanship of the purest motive. Having had this pointed out to me, however, I am even less satisfied by Tyrone Power in the Gettner role. He entirely fails to show a glimpse of integrity beneath the maudlin self-interest; Mr. Gibbs astutely discovered it for himself.

Silk Stockings (Imperial Theatre, Broadway) is the big new musical hit. Many people have been involved in bringing this successful venture into town, and I do not intend to abuse them individually. The product is a cooperative disaster—tuneless, ugly, boring, and without taste. It contains three performers—Leon Belasco, Henry Lascoe, and David Opatoshu—who capably pursue the trade of burlesque comedy and who have been supplied by George S. Kaufman or Abe Burrows with jokes sufficient for their purpose. They are the only hint that converting Ernst Lubitsch's film *Ninotchka* into a musical comedy might have been a good idea.

98

BUS STOP   THE MASTER BUILDER

Bus Stop, by William Inge, & *The Master Builder,* by Henrik Ibsen (1955)

It is the so-so play that makes work. Before the curtain has been up two minutes at *Bus Stop* (Music Box Theatre, Broadway), a reviewer knows he can put his pencil away and lean back. The professionals have come to town.

This is William Inge's third Broadway play (*Come Back, Little Sheba* and *Picnic* preceded it) and his third Broadway success. He is probably not a great playwright (at least, I doubt that anything he has done thus far will be included in the archives of our century), but he is an acute, compassionate, and amused observer who has trained himself to write approximately perfect theater. Like all good craftsmen, he makes it look as easy as instinct.

The people who have brought *Bus Stop* to the stage—Harold Clurman, Boris Aronson, the actors Kim Stanley, Elaine Stritch, Anthony Ross, Albert Salmi, and others—enjoy the same economical authority. This is probably the most easy-going show in town; it can afford to be casual. *Bus Stop* is funny and witty and shrewd. It acknowledges uglier matters but, being in a holiday mood, it steers clear of them.

A small party of travelers is storm-bound for the night in a roadside restaurant thirty miles west of Kansas City. (This antique device is for experts only; others will be crushed by the weight of precedent.) The bus is carrying, in addition to its driver (Patrick McVey) and an unfrocked, tipsy professor (Anthony Ross), two cowboys heading home from a Kansas City rodeo and a singer from a nightspot near the stockyards. The younger of the cowboys (Albert Salmi) has, in fact, abducted the girl (Kim Stanley) because, being very young, he assumes that any female who would bed with him must love him, and the only way he knows to be masterful he learned from roping cows. The young lady is frightened and annoyed by this display of muscular gallantry, and the older cowboy (Crahan Denton), an employee turned foster father, is embarrassed and worried for them both. The locals at the restaurant are its proprietor (Elaine Stritch), her child assistant (Phyllis Love), and the town sheriff (Lou Polan), who functions as both the guardian of order and the voice of experience.

With this assorted group, jailed together for the length of a snow-storm, Mr. Inge rings changes on the definition of love. The bus driver and the restaurant owner begin what will become a weekly seduction, as brief and efficient as the timetable that controls it; the professor

REVIEWS

makes a dead set for the child (he is that sort of professor); the young cowboy and his chick come to an understanding that may work out better than one would expect. That, in fact, is what Mr. Inge is saying about love: all sorts of unlikely solutions do work out. The bus driver and his Grace are not without tenderness; the professor does have a genuine instinct for beauty, and, though his intentions are shocking, they do not shock the intended victim—even when she understands them; the cowboy and the singer are a pair of innocents, whatever the facts may be. Eros is a compassionate and accommodating god and the only man to be pitied is the older cowboy, who has forsworn him altogether.

Yet the play should not be abstracted so. It is no treatise, but a captivating excursion into the joys and comedies of humanity. The script and the performance are so accurately pitched that, though these people are bizarre, they never become grotesque. It is delicate work: the nightclub girl who is vulgar but not cheap; the cowboy who is absurd but not ridiculous; the professor who is pitiable but not maudlin; the restaurant owner who is tough but not callous. This is partly technique, of course, but even more it is the way Messrs. Inge and Clurman see people. We hear so much brave talk these days about the dignity and importance of mankind; therefore, it is exhilarating to encounter men who take human virtue for granted.

Oskar Homolka is a Viennese, and the version of *The Master Builder* that he directed and in which he plays the lead at the Phoenix Theatre (Off-Broadway) is a waltz version of Henrik Ibsen's bitter salute to age. Mr. Homolka's instinct may have been right: Ibsen's misanthropy has become so proverbial that we come to the play discounting the gloom. A *Master Builder* staged as another exercise in Scandinavian pessimism would be "Yes, just what we expected," and we should be armed against it. Stage it in sunshine, therefore, let the often sparkling dialogue shine, and the play may once more fell an audience with its sour but unavoidable truth.

But Mr. Homolka has gone very far. The mood he creates is almost playful—a wry and Gallic commentary on an old man's follies—and the stage seems given over to people so shallow that they cannot perceive the horror surrounding them. The tragedy has been thrown out with the trappings.

Mr. Homolka himself gives a sure performance at the level he has selected and, since he is at the center of the action, he can make the role consistent. But the satellites around him go into strange orbits. Margaret Barker, as his wife, finds it almost impossible to make her

THE MASTER BUILDER   THE THREE SISTERS

near-mad sorrow real; Gene Saks, as the young architect of whom the master builder is jealous, appears shrill and very young indeed. The oddest impersonation is given by Joan Tetzel as Hilda Wangel. Hilda—"youth knocking at the door"—is certainly a symbol of the old man's fear, fascination, hate, and doom. But she is also a person in the play, and I don't believe that Ibsen meant her to be entirely fey and to perch on things like Peter Pan.

For their part, the Boris Aronson sets are brilliant—formidable but not heavy, strong, original—but as ideas unfinished. This is the kind of work, one can believe, by which Halvard Solness made his own great reputation.

The Three Sisters, by Anton Chekhov (1955)

I am very late reporting on *The Three Sisters*, playing in a closet known as the 4th Street Theatre (Off-Broadway). I shall try to make amends for tardiness with enthusiasm. Unfortunately, the production is so miraculously good that it almost defies comment, especially when you have seen no other staging of this Anton Chekhov play. Is it better than Eva Le Gallienne's production? Does it conform to the Stanislavsky interpretation? Did Katharine Cornell have something more penetrating to offer? I don't know—but I do know that the present production carries the magic of a great play greatly personified, and that we have not been shown anything of comparable quality for a long time.

The best-known names in the cast are probably Morris Carnovsky (Andrei), Philip Loeb (Chebutykin), and Roger DeKoven (Vershinin); they play brilliantly but no better than Eileen Ryan as Masha, Peggy Maurer as Irina, Carol Gustafson as Olga, Leonardo Cimino, Shirley Gale, George Ebeling, Frances Chaney, or anyone else in the cast. The director is David Ross; I am in awe of him. He appears to have understood exactly what Chekhov intended, known exactly which actors could best impersonate his people, and been able to fire them with his respect and love for this great play. He works on a stage about the size of my desk in a long, low, and narrow loft never intended for a public gathering, and he sends you home aware once more that the theater is a noble institution.

I am not going to talk about the play. I can scarcely pretend to have discovered its beauty and terror, and I am unlikely to add anything new to what has been said of it. Or perhaps one thing: there is a great deal of suffering in *The Three Sisters* but almost no cruelty. Chekhov

101

REVIEWS

knew as much as we do about human misery and he took no very hopeful view of the race. But he wrote without patronizing his characters and without brutalizing them.

Our writers have been through analysis and have learned all about the corruptions of the psyche. Reserve in sorrow, generosity in pain, gentleness in adversity have almost entirely given place to the single scientific observation that a hurt dog howls and bites. Why then do the tragic men and women of *The Three Sisters* seem so much more important and so much more real than the groveling snappers that occupy the attention of our analyst-moralists? Chekhov was a doctor, too.

Cat on a Hot Tin Roof, by Tennessee Williams (1955)

The hero of *Cat on a Hot Tin Roof* (Morosco Theatre, Broadway) walks with a crutch and refuses to cohabit with his wife—she, in consequence, is the "cat" of the title. This celibacy, supported by an alarming consumption of alcohol, is his gesture of revulsion against being charged by her with incipient homosexuality. However, his father, all-wise but dying of cancer, forces the boy to admit that the pose of dipsomaniac disgust hides in part a fear that there may be some truth to the slander and still more a guilt at having deserted his friend when the charge was first made. The son retaliates by telling the old man the truth about his illness—thus effectively finishing him off— but the self-knowledge is so efficient that, as the final curtain drops, the crutch has been laid aside and husband and wife are settling slowly into the marriage bed.

It is not difficult to understand what Tennessee Williams is up to. He is writing a charade that spells "psychoanalysis," and the people move through the play as in a dream. The heroine walks on stage and removes her dress; the mother points to the bed and says portentously, "This is where the trouble begins"; the father boasts grossly of his virility; monstrous children rush onto the stage and scream "bang, bang"; the dying patriarch tells a very old and not very funny dirty joke; the hero drinks and drinks but gets no drunker; large sections of the dialogue are delivered in a sing-song monotone; members of the family are referred to by such infantile names as "big daddy" and "brother man." I doubt that even on a Mississippi Delta plantation people behave so when they are awake.

All this preoccupation with the symbolism of the consulting room seems to be a little old-fashioned of Mr. Williams, but I want to make

CAT ON A HOT   INHERIT THE WIND   TROUBLE IN TAHITI   27 WAGONS

an even more old-fashioned complaint: I wish his play weren't so disagreeable. I left it feeling that I had spent the evening with a group of corpses that had had little to recommend them when they were alive. Villainy in the theater is a splendid, stimulating force, but this cold second-rateness seems to me the negation of drama. Where is the suspense, if no soul is worth saving? Sex and death and money preoccupy Mr. Williams's characters; in the face of death, the sex is regulated to get the money.

This is bitter, but in itself it does not make a bad plot for a moral fable. What ruins it for me is my inability to care whether anyone in the company sinks or swims. Let them die, let them breed, let them grow fat on the wealth—it is none of my business and I don't have to watch. I put it thus personally because I realize that all around me other observers are cheering.

I think they may be cheering the brutality, in the belief that it expresses a concern for humanity. Certainly the performances that Elia Kazan has extracted from Ben Gazzara, Burl Ives, Barbara Bel Geddes, Mildred Dunnock, and the rest are technically powerful. They snap at and slash one another like dogs, and if you could believe in them as people it would be inexpressibly shocking. Williams is not a trivial man, and it is evident that he wishes to instruct. But he has a diabolical gift for laying bare the crumminess of humanity, and this time I think he has carried it to the point where the humanity disappears. Without love and hope, discussion of vice and virtue becomes academic.

Inherit the Wind, by Jerome Lawrence & Robert E. Lee; *Trouble in Tahiti,* by Leonard Bernstein; & *27 Wagons Full of Cotton,* by Tennessee Williams (1955)

On the face of it, the Scopes trial ought to make an exciting play with a sharp moral for our time. But *Inherit the Wind* (National Theatre, Broadway) is rather leaden business despite the presence of Paul Muni, a notable rabble-rouser; and the epic duel between Clarence Darrow and William Jennings Bryan never becomes more than a remote and innocuous tempest in Tennessee.

The authors, Jerome Lawrence and Robert E. Lee, have meticulously stated the circumstances of the famous monkey trial: how Bryan, defending the Book of Genesis, won the case in the courtroom,

103

REVIEWS

but how Darrow, upholding Charles Darwin, won before the court of public opinion. They are very solemn and prolix about all this, and optimistic to suppose that our hearts will pound as we await the outcome. It requires the tautest writing and most perceptive characterization to build suspense out of an episode that is part of common knowledge, and these authors do not work at that level. Their dialogue is ponderously instructive, and they have caught little more of their two great protagonists than the obvious features of caricature. Of course Mr. Muni and his opposite number, Ed Begley, work prodigiously to look and sound like Darrow and Bryan, but it is all surface trappings and gives an effect of two astonishingly diminutive titans.

As for the moral, I am not sure it would have hit the nail on the head even if it had been more effectively presented. Darrow had no legal case, as he well knew, for John Scopes was obviously breaking the law when he taught evolution in Tennessee. So, relying on his great name and great showmanship, Darrow made a national joke of the law and a national clown of Bryan, who appears to have died of the experience. It happens that I think Darrow was right—that the people of Tennessee were drunk with Fundamentalist fervor—but the technique he used is an uncomfortable one for the champions of democratic process. The moral of Scopes himself might be something else again, but Scopes is a minor figure in the play—as, indeed, he was at the trial.

A miniature opera by Leonard Bernstein called *Trouble in Tahiti* and *27 Wagons Full of Cotton*, a short play by Tennessee Williams, are on the same bill at the Playhouse Theatre, Broadway. Each of these items has a good deal to recommend it, but the sum does not add up to its parts, and one goes home feeling somewhat indigestive and undernourished. A good programmer would presumably know how to put together a program better balanced and more harmonious in flavor.

Mr. Bernstein's opera is a small tragedy of suburban incompatibility and inarticulate ennui. It has two main characters, the husband and the wife, sung by John Tyers and Alice Ghostley; as well as a chorus trio whose job is to close-harmonize a ditty about "that little white house in Scarsdale (or Shaker Heights or Paoli or wherever)" at appropriate intervals in the action. Constance Brigham, John Taliaferro, and James Tushar perform this task with fine satiric understanding of the "intime" style and content.

Satire, in fact, is the salvation of *Trouble in Tahiti*. I am no judge of their singing abilities, but Miss Ghostley and Mr. Tyers are both excellent comics, and they are each given a glorious solo spot in which

104

to display their talent for mockery. When he tries to cope with the subject of middle-class malaise directly, Mr. Bernstein himself gets a little moist.

The performances by Maureen Stapleton and Myron McCormick, with the strong assistance of Felice Orlandi, in *27 Wagons Full of Cotton* are the best acting I have seen this year on Broadway. They create in the small compass allotted to them the illusion of utter and inevitable tragedy. The play itself is a kind of Tennessee Williams synopsis, stripped down to the cruelty, weak meanness, stupidity, and sexual horror that constitute his view of humanity. In this skeleton form the formula is brutally effective theater; the three actors have given it a vitality that is more than theatrical.

The Honeys, by Roald Dahl (1955)

It is astonishing what people will laugh at if they are told it is funny. *The Honeys* (at the Longacre Theatre, Broadway) is advertised as a farcical comedy, and the night I was there people were laughing their heads off at the spectacle of two cruel and empty-headed women murdering their sickly, ill-tempered husbands in the messiest fashion imaginable.

I remember Joseph Kesselring's *Arsenic and Old Lace* and do not maintain that murder is an impossible topic for farce. But certain rules have to be observed. You must move the killing straight out of the world of probability and logical consequences; the victims should be people you do not care about; the killings should be merciful and if possible invisible; and the murderers must in some eccentric way be pure of heart. What goes on in *The Honeys* is as probable and as awful as murder for profit usually is. I didn't care much about the husbands, but I liked them a lot more than their ignorant, pretentious wives: those two silly old girls were as dirty a pair as I've been forced to contemplate for quite a while.

Consider their methods; being stupid as well as heartless, they have to use quite a few: they leave an old man to starve to death in the jammed elevator of an empty house; they feed an old man oysters rotten with ptomaine, and then they chop up something in his medicine that will perforate his bowels. Or, splendid jest, they crush a man's head with a frozen leg of lamb, then cook the weapon and eat it with gloating glee. And all the time they speculate on how much money their husbands will leave and how many young men can be bought with it. I am convulsed, but not with laughter.

REVIEWS

I know I should not get excited—*The Honeys* is a calculated risk, a cold-blooded potboiler. Roald Dahl, who wrote it, figures that if you show the most conventional and boring people engaged in the grossest villainy, the incongruity will seem so deliciously funny that no one will be upset. Unfortunately, I assume that gross villainies are usually perpetrated by otherwise conventional and boring people, and I was upset plenty.

The principal actors in *The Honeys* are Jessica Tandy and Dorothy Stickney as the wives, and Hume Cronyn as both husbands. This is not such a trick, for they are twin brothers. It provides a chance, however, for some of that trapdoor tomfoolery that always gets a big hand. I thought Mr. Cronyn looked remarkably like a comparatively young actor impersonating a couple of old geezers; his tremors were not much more plausible than his wigs. Miss Tandy and Miss Stickney so much resembled each other, not in looks but in quality and address, that I had to keep referring to the program. But that is not really their fault; Mr. Dahl wrote one part for them both.

Mary Finney, the only other member of the cast except Dana Elcar, who plays a stock policeman, takes the part of a breezy, horsey widow who is known to have disposed of her husband by the comparatively decent method of shoving him out a window. She is heartily coarse and jolly—with none of the sickening refinement of the other two—and since we do not meet the late Mr. Fleishman, she seems less foul. I thought Miss Finney was the one point of humor in an evening of pretty ugly fun.

Damn Yankees,
by George Abbott (1955)

Every reviewer has a blind spot. The one of mine that I know of—there may well be others—is musical comedy. All that noise, all those bright lights, all those grinning gymnasts, and the money poured out for those big production numbers throw me into a mean Presbyterian dudgeon. It isn't that I flatly dislike musicals—the way, for example, that I hate sweetbreads—but that my standard for them is absurdly high. I thought Frank Loesser's *Guys and Dolls* was dandy; before that, I liked Oscar Hammerstein's *Show Boat*. (I never saw Rodgers and Hammerstein's *Oklahoma!* or their *South Pacific*, which shows how closely I follow the song-and-dance business.) I once knew a book reviewer whose taste in fiction was so extravagantly elevated that he would praise no novel that fell short of Austen's *Pride and Prejudice*

106

or Dostoevsky's *The Brothers Karamazov*. He rarely had occasion to say a kind word.

This personal note is only fair as a preface to saying that I was fitfully amused but generally depressed by *Damn Yankees* (46th Street Theatre, Broadway). It is probably much better than the average musical, and I can see that the book—taken from a novel by Douglass Wallop—is miles above the run of such literature. A fanatic supporter of the Washington Senators sells his soul to the devil in return for being transformed into a baseball player of such surpassing ability that he can lead his hapless team to victory over the hated champions from the Bronx.

My fits of amusement were caused by the male chorus, which looked like a bunch of ballplayers and danced the way ballplayers might dance, if you can imagine such a thing; by a male quartet that sang with oafish insouciance; by Gwen Verdon, the star, who makes a fine joke of her absurd sexiness; and by Ray Walston, who played the devil in witty style. Mr. Walston is small and moves abruptly; he looked as though he had just had a manicure. For the most part, he dressed in conservative grays, cut sharp and with scarlet accessories, and he spoke in clipped wisecracks. A most successful Mephisto. There was also a good mambo, sung and danced by Miss Verdon and Eddie Phillips.

In general, though, the music and lyrics were spiritless, the big numbers were confused and dowdy, the humor was primitive, the action dragged, and Stephen Douglass, who played the hero, could not sing, dance, kiss a pretty girl, or wrestle with the devil to my satisfaction. I kept wishing I was at a ball game.

The Maids, by Jean Genet (1955)

Jean Genet is a forty-five-year-old Frenchman, a bastard, a homosexual, and a confirmed thief who has spent a good part of his life in prison. Between 1942 and 1948 he wrote extensively—novels, journals, and plays. This incongruous literacy brought him the attention of Jean-Paul Sartre, among other critics, and in the past few years his name has been spreading in Europe and America. One of his plays, *The Maids*, is now being well performed at the Tempo Playhouse on St. Mark's Place (Off-Off Broadway).

There are two maids in the play, Claire and Solange; Madame also appears, but briefly. Monsieur, who has been sent to prison by the false and anonymous accusations of the maids, works unseen on the

REVIEWS

proceedings. The action is largely a ritualistic masquerade, in which Claire and Solange take turns at playing Madame and each other. It is a game of murder symbolizing sex—masochistic, compulsive, never fulfilled. When Madame appears, the maids try to poison her—or at least they tell each other that that is what they are trying to do. When she leaves, the game starts again. This time the "preliminaries" are omitted and they get nearer to a climax, Solange-as-Claire leading Claire-as-Madame offstage to murder. But Claire returns and commits suicide. It will look like murder and Solange will achieve a spurious fulfillment from a meaningless killing she did not commit.

On the surface *The Maids* is slightly disgusting, an unclean fever. Beneath the surface, I suspect, it is a vision of the absolute based on ignorance. Sartre says in his introduction to the published text that Genet was attracted to the theater by "the element of fake, of sham, of artificiality"; that he turned dramatist because "the falsehood of the stage is the most manifest and fascinating of all." This is the poorest possible reason for turning to the stage, and I cannot understand why Sartre is seemingly so impressed by Genet's involvement in the appearance-reality dilemma. He wished, Sartre tells us, that his female characters should be played by adolescent boys, not primarily because he has a taste for boys, but because travesty would add one more level of falsehood to this process of distilling the essence out of the event.

To wit: an actor pretends to be a maid who pretends to be her mistress who pretends to revile her maid who pretends to be herself. Truth thus crumbles at whatever point we grasp it, and the only reliable fact is the lie. This variety of intellectual nihilism very probably exerts a strong pull on a man who sees himself as a multiple outcast. It is also a playing at epistemology by an ambitious mind that is unschooled in metaphysics and does not know it is breaking away down a well-traveled path. The theater is a sham only to those who are so naïve that they do not presuppose its conventions, and educated minds are not willingly seduced by paradox.

In the Tempo production, the maids and Madame are not played by boys but by three talented and well-directed actresses: Claire by Julie Bovasso, Solange by Joyce Henry, and Madame by Fran Malis. To offset this compromising reality, the scene is set so that the audience can see backstage, where the stage manager appears now and then, script in hand, to exchange glances with the players and to signal light changes as well as the ringing of telephone and door bells. The only fault I found in the proceedings is that you know the instant the curtain opens that a masquerade is in progress; I believe Genet means us to be fooled, at least for the first few speeches. The lies, I think, are

108

THE MAIDS   THE TRIAL

supposed to be stripped off one by one, reducing us to a state of nirvana, or vertigo, when we finally realize that the truth will always be the next lie but one.

Is *The Maids* worth doing? I think so. People read Genet and read a lot into him. It is interesting, in the first place, to see how his play will play. Technically, it plays rather well, but it trips its author up. Confusing illusion with falsity, Genet did not foresee that an actor is palpably an identity, however many levels of masquerade he is made to wear. Beneath the quaking ground of Claire-become-Solange-become-Madame are the characters and talents of the three actresses. They cannot prevent themselves from developing independent images on the stage, and the inescapable rationality of the theater forces order on Genet's anarchy of prevarication. If boys were playing the girls, the ultimate effect would be no different: the observer *will* make sense of what he sees, however hard a perverse illusionist tries to bewilder him. Therefore we come out of the theater, decently asking what Genet means, and he has lost the round—for what he means is that we should despair and stop asking.

The Maids is a long one-act play (here presented with one intermission), and Tempo offers as a curtain-raiser *The 13th of March*, which consists of selections from Gertrude Stein's *The First Reader*. This seems to be some rather contrived "automatic" writing in which a group of young actors play at being children on a rainy day in a garret. They go in strongly for murder, not scaring themselves as healthy children should, and I suppose Miss Stein wants us to be scared by the devil-children within us. It was all a little too cute to be edifying, though again I admired the performance. The players cannot help seeming as though they were mentally retarded, but they make no apologies and are as little embarrassing as possible. That's nice.

The Trial, by Franz Kafka (1955)

The adaptation of *The Trial* that is now being shown by Theater 12 at the Provincetown Playhouse (Off-Broadway) is a skillful text, intelligently performed. Aaron Fine and Bert Greene have distilled as much from Franz Kafka's novel as can well be brought to a stage—they fudge a little by supplying a narrator to bridge material they *can't* get on the stage—and the cast, notably Gordon Sterns as Joseph K., comes as close to meeting a reader's expectations as the illustrations in a novel ever do. Anyone in urgent need of a dramatization of *The Trial* will do well to rent this text and if possible engage this company.

REVIEWS

But the question is why anyone should feel such a need, or, to put it another way, why so capable a group as Theater 12 should be impelled to so unpromising an enterprise. It seems to an outsider that the non-commercial theater has an enviable variety of dramatic material to choose from and need not strain to stage work never meant for the purpose. Perhaps *The Trial* has an odd box-office appeal in the sense that readers baffled by the novel will seek out the play in hope of enlightenment. They will be disappointed The play is simpler to the extent that a great deal has been left out. But it is no clearer, and for all I know may be even more obscure.

For all I know, because I have by no means grasped everything that Kafka intends to say in *The Trial*. It seems to me likely that K.'s case is his life, that the verdict he seeks is vindication for having lived, and that the trial persists only because K. persists in asking a kind of spiritual assurance that the world does not at present provide. Also, the novel is a foretaste of bureaucracy gone totalitarian, and it is couched—and couched with surprising brilliance—in the cloud-logic of a dream. But I am only a reader—not a student—of Kafka, and I recognize that there are levels of religious, psychological, and social comment in *The Trial* that elude. I come back to the book because its virtuosity fascinates me and because K. is like a strange, half-familiar brother.

These attractions were dimmed in the play. It is clear, I guess, that the action simulates a dream, but Kafka's alarming insight into the mechanisms of all our dreams is gone. He establishes it in the novel with many precise, small observations, often asides and unexpected juxtapositions that cannot be preserved in direct dialogue and certainly cannot be translated into stage equipment. The novel contains two camps: K. and the people of his waking world—his housekeeper, his uncle, Fräulein Bürstner, the personnel at the bank, and so on—who are "real" even though seen in the askew mirror of a dream; and the officials and familiars of the court, who, though perhaps suggested by K.'s experiences, are not delineated by his familiarity with their daytime deportment. The two groups behave differently, though the difference is often subtle, and this might have been indicated in the play but was not.

K. on the stage seems a particular man fighting for his physical freedom in the cruelest circumstances. The play thus swings toward the drama of protest, a style that dates almost as soon as it is written. The novel concerns deeper dissatisfactions and will not date, at least in our epoch.

The Iceman Cometh, by Eugene O'Neill, at the Circle in the Square Theatre (New York), 1956.

The Connection, by Jack Gelber, at the Living Theatre (New York), 1959.

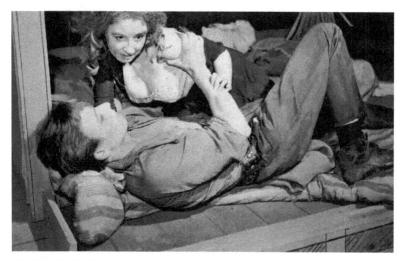

Live Like Pigs, by John Arden, at the Theatre Company of Boston, 1965.

Macbeth, by William Shakespeare, at the Lafayette Theatre (New York), 1936.

The Three Sisters, by Anton Chekhov, at the Guthrie Theatre (Minneapolis), 1963.

The Desperate Hours, by Joseph Hayes, at the Barrymore Theatre (New York), 1955.

Bus Stop, by William Inge, at the Music Box Theatre (New York), 1955.

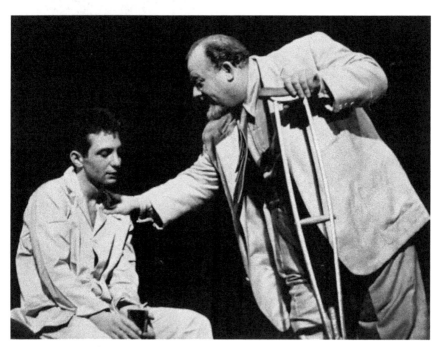

Cat on a Hot Tin Roof, by Tennessee Williams, at the Morosco Theatre (New York), 1955.

Damn Yankees, by George Abbott, at the 46th Street Theatre (New York), 1955.

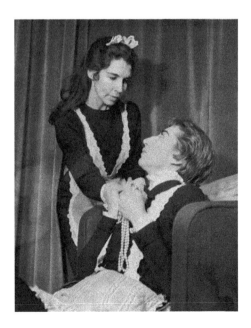

The Maids, by Jean Genet, at the Tempo Playhouse (New York), 1955.

115

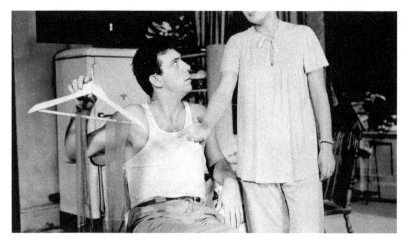

A Hatful of Rain, by Michael Gazzo, at the Lyceum Theatre (New York), 1955.

The Lark, by Jean Anouilh, at the Longacre Theatre (New York), 1955.

The Most Happy Fella, by Frank Loesser, at the Imperial Theatre (New York), 1956.

Johnny Johnson, by Paul Green, at the Carnegie Hall Playhouse (New York), 1956.

Orpheus Descending, by Tennessee Williams, at the Martin Beck Theatre (New York), 1957.

A Moon for the Misbegotten, by Eugene O'Neill, at the Bijou Theatre (New York), 1957.

Endgame, by Samuel Beckett, at the Cherry Lane Theatre (New York), 1958.

The Visit, by Friedrich Dürrenmatt, at the Lunt-Fontanne Theatre (New York), 1958.

Krapp's Last Tape, by Samuel Beckett, at the Provincetown Playhouse (New York), 1960.

Roots, by Arnold Wesker, at the Mayfair Theatre (New York), 1961.

The Blacks, by Jean Genet, at St. Mark's Playhouse (New York), 1961.

The American Dream, by Edward Albee, at the York Playhouse (New York), 1961.

The Caretaker, by Harold Pinter, at the Lyceum Theatre (New York), 1962.

The Merchant of Venice, by William Shakespeare, at the New York Shakespeare Festival, 1962.

Who's Afraid of Virginia Woolf?, by Edward Albee, at the Billy Rose Theatre (New York), 1963.

Dutchman, by LeRoi Jones, at the Cherry Lane Theatre (New York), 1964.

The Memorandum, by Václav Havel, at the Public Theater (New York), 1968.

Promenade, by María Irene Fornés, at the Judson Poets' Theatre (New York), 1969.

The Cherry Orchard, by Anton Chekhov (1955)

Modest productions of fine plays continue to brighten the corners of our city. At the 4ᵗʰ Street Theatre (Off-Broadway), for example, Anton Chekhov's *The Cherry Orchard* may be seen sensitively done by a youngish company. Not all the casting or acting is adequate, although the Trofimov of Gerald Hiken and Nancy Wickwire's Varya are excellent. What is more important is that there is some real feeling for the play in the production, and that the play itself is warm, sweet, humane, understanding, and forever significant. I have seen it in several languages and in many different types of production, but I have never failed to be touched by it.

There would be little point in this limited space in my attempting to interpret the play anew. All that I care to emphasize here is that the recent outcry in some critical quarters about the undramatic nature of plays about frustrated and futile people is founded on a fundamental fallacy. The frustration of Chekhov's people is moving and dramatic because they are deeply perceived, real, and lovable people while the activity of most characters in contemporary shows is meaningless— because the characters are empty stereotypes whose usual goal is to accomplish something about which we care very little. What Chekhov's people desire is greater human contact, love, and an ideal by which to live.

Chekhov's plays, written from the viewpoint of a particular time and place, are at once social and universal. The time and place are no more, but the human condition that his plays express is still with us, even in the America of 1955!

The Bourgeois Gentleman, by Molière, & The Chalk Garden, by Enid Bagnold (1955)

The *Comédie Française* has been playing *The Bourgeois Gentleman* for 285 years. It does not grow stale and it does not lose its cutting edge, but neither does it offer new generations much scope for interpretation. Monsieur Jourdain, the would-be gentleman, is as immortal a comic figure as Falstaff, but he is an explicit figure. He prevails because he was drawn—without shadows or ambiguities—to be true for all time. We cannot discuss what the character of Jourdain means to us—he means exactly what Molière meant.

If you cannot interpret, then you may wish to polish, and the production of *The Bourgeois Gentleman* with which France's national

REVIEWS

theater opened the first American engagement in its history (Broadway Theatre, New York) is polished beyond any pertinent comparison on our contemporary stage. The set is pure and elegant as though carved in ivory; the costumes sing together; the speech is a miracle of precision and styed characterization (and you can know that without knowing much French); every gesture is guided by almost three centuries of unbroken tradition; and the stage movement flows like quicksilver.

The effect is a ravishment of the senses; also a removal from contact—the so-perfect picture is behind glass. I do not say that to object. *The Bourgeois Gentleman* is one of France's most precious state jewels and I am glad to admire it in its case. But Molière, though he wrote for the court, did not write for the museum, and I had expected to meet Monsieur Jourdain on more workaday terms.

Another success of style—or in this case, perhaps, stylishness—is Enid Bagnold's *The Chalk Garden* (Barrymore Theatre, Broadway). The subject matter of the play is wit, or so it emerges from Albert Marre's cut-glass direction. The play has content as well as sparkle, but Marre took the right course. If he had allowed *The Chalk Garden* to ride on its dramatic substance, we should have been depressed by Bagnold's disinclination to look very thoughtfully into the melancholy situation she has invented for a play.

A chalk garden is one in which flowers do not thrive, and Laurel is a young girl who is not thriving in her grandmother's house. Miss Madrigal, engaged as a companion, has seen little of the world (when the judge comes to lunch, we learn why that is so), but she has a knowledge of soil chemistry and an insight into the process of growth. Once she arrives, the flowers and the girl are understood, but the old gardener (Laurel's grandmother) is without an avocation.

That is all. You could play it like Shaw—with bad results. But Marre plays it like Wilde, and though it is not Wilde, it is an evening of gratifying persiflage. The cast beautifully suits the manner. Siobhán McKenna (Miss Madrigal) and Fritz Weaver (the valet Maitland), though young at the game, are quite up to Gladys Cooper's tricks (as Mrs. St. Maugham, Laurel's grandmother), and the three of them bat the lines around with never a time out for missed shots. It is not always possible to catch the meaning as you follow the sport, but the loss of sense is more than made up by the gain in fun.

Miss McKenna comes to America on a wave of unrestrained London enthusiasm for her recent St. Joan. Miss Madrigal is not a test for much more than the surface of acting, but the part shows us a handsome, fleet-witted woman with a sure presence and a deadly accurate delivery. Mr. Weaver is a phenomenon these days—a young actor whose strength lies in a stage craft that he has learned and not in a stage personality that he cultivates. Betsy von Furstenberg, as Laurel, is more the personality, but Laurel is only the object of the play, and it doesn't much matter how she is performed.

A Hatful of Rain, by Michael Gazzo (1955)

One of the most widespread and least agreeable of human traits is the urge to gaze on anguish. Therefore accidents draw crowds and *A Hatful of Rain* (Lyceum Theatre, Broadway) can scarcely fail to be a hit. Those attending it will witness terror and violence, creeping horror and pain so intense that it blots out the mind. They will also see compassion and courage, stupidity and cruelty; but they will not see a play.

A play is a matter of conflict, but *A Hatful of Rain* is a matter of diagnosis. The hero is a drug addict, helplessly caught beyond the appeals of his associates, compelled to make any sacrifice for his hunger, so disabled that he no longer qualifies as sane. He therefore presents an extreme medical problem, but no dramatic problem at all. The action can continue only until someone takes the obvious step of calling for professional help, and his wife does this as soon as she discovers what is wrong. The fact that it takes her three acts to make the discovery does not constitute a plot; this is only an arbitrary—and in the circumstances a not very plausible—decision on the part of the playwright.

Curiously enough, the work contains allusions that could be made into a play if the author had wanted to develop them. The Pope household consists of Johnny, the addict; his wife, Celia; and his brother, Polo, who earns good money as a nightclub bouncer and pays for Johnny's dope. John Pope, Sr., a shallow and selfish man who demands affection from the sons he has always ignored, is visiting at the time. Polo is jealous of his brother, in love with his sister-in-law. Is he perhaps trying to murder his brother under the guise of protecting his secret? This at least is subject matter for a melodrama. But in that case the conflict is between the brother and the wife, there must be a showdown between them, and Johnny is the object of their struggle. The action does not develop so.

Similarly, the pseudo-paternalism of Pope, Sr., the sterile upbringing of the boys in public institutions—these are grounds for a play with a socio-psychological background and the father as villain. But Johnny is an addict, less because of an unloved childhood, than

REVIEWS

because irresponsible army hospital nurses dosed him too heavily with sedatives. The villain is neither the father nor Polo; dope is the villain, and you might as well cast coronary thrombosis in the role.

But if Michael Gazzo has not written a play in his first produced work, he has written some very shrewd theater. His scenes are full of dreadful action, circumstantial homeliness, and knowing argot; they are couched in a halting, repetitious, gratingly banal style of conversation that Arthur Miller and Tennessee Williams have taught us is the authentic speech of the people. Gazzo's boss dope peddler is a fastidious sadist who wears dark glasses and giggles (a very fashionable type); his heroine is pregnant; he has written a virtuoso drunk scene for the brother; he stages an almost-seduction that shimmers with incest; he sets down the paroxysms of dope deprivation with clinical detail (and, for all I know, perfect accuracy). Small wonder that the audience emerges from the theater looking as spent as *voyeurs* at a street disaster.

The leads in *A Hatful of Rain* are taken by Shelley Winters and Ben Gazzara. She plays with the admirable directness, the open and strong emotion, that have made her one of Hollywood's really fine actresses. The play will do her no harm at all. But I am less sure that it will not harm Gazzara. It is written too directly to the specifications of his reputation, gives him too much chance to exploit himself—the cold voice, the impotent hysteria, the frenzied athleticism. For Gazzara, *A Hatful of Rain* is an emotional sequel to Tennessee Williams's *Cat on a Hot Tin Roof.* He is an actor of power but little experience, and is in danger of freezing into a type. What he needs is to play a few seasons in a first-rate repertory company. But where would he find one?

Frank Silvera and Anthony Franciosa, as the father and the brother, both create strongly modelled, thoroughly worked out personalities that look capable at any moment of stepping into the thick of the drama that never develops. Frank Corsaro directs the production as though with a whip: he makes every shock hit you between the eyes.

The Lark, by Jean Anouilh (1955)

Winning actress though she is, Julie Harris was not a happy choice for the title role in *The Lark* (Longacre Theatre, Broadway). Jean Anouilh's dramatization of the triumph and execution of Joan of Arc, adapted for the stage here by Lillian Hellman, is at once a clever and a deeply felt work of theater craft. It shows us Joan with pride and love (there is a markedly parental tone in this portrait), and by weaving

128

THE LARK

past, present, and future almost carelessly together in a fabric outside of time, it catches the special pervasiveness of legends.

But there is a hazard in the play, and that is a difference in the level of approach to Joan and to the lords of war, state, and church who surround her. About Warwick and the Bishop of Beauvais, the Dauphin and Captain La Hire, Anouilh is judicious, analytical, seriously concerned with motive and character. He conjures up, thus, an engrossing group of men—not good men or bad, but self-justifying men who are sadly aware that history lies in ambush. These men of power are played by actors of power and fine discrimination: Boris Karloff, Joseph Wiseman, Christopher Plummer, Theodore Bikel, and Paul Roebling most notably. They re-create in immediate focus the terrible dilemma that Joan posed to authority and the hearts of men.

Joan, on the other hand, is treated with indulgent affection, almost playfully, as though an engrossing fable were being spun. We see into her very little, and are asked to satisfy ourselves with the magic of her presence. This could be moving—the lords sitting in council on the lark of promise. But I do not think Anouilh intended the allegory to be carried all the way, as in "a mystic has freed France and a prophet has been burned at the stake." Her presence, however inexplicable, must be tangible.

Julie Harris plays Joan as a sprite. It is not just youth and promise that she expresses, but eternal youth, eternal promise. That can be adorable, but it is also untouchable. Our hearts go out to youth and innocence, but they do not go out to Peter Pan, except when we are young ourselves. There is something complacent about the ever-ever child.

Miss Harris, for all her honest workmanship and sensitive, responsive intelligence, is an audience-actress. She is here in closer rapport with the audience than with her allies and judges; she looks for applause across the footlights, not in the wavering eyes of kinglings. We feel ourselves in cahoots with her against England and the Inquisition; therefore she is not committed to the frame of their reality and their flames do not burn.

The applause for Miss Harris and her great cast is long and genuine and earned. It has been an evening of splendid theater. But it stays in the theater, and we go home in a mood of cheerful sentimentality that is not right for Joan's victory in martyrdom.

REVIEWS

Pipe Dream, by Richard Rodgers & Oscar Hammerstein; *The Most Happy Fella*, by Frank Loesser (1955–56)

The new Rodgers and Hammerstein musical opened at the Schubert Theatre (Broadway) to a more than million-dollar advance sale and cool notices. *Pipe Dream* offers good taste and good humor, a seductive score, lovely sets, and a host of attractive people behaving with an easy self-confidence that is almost unprecedented on the musical stage. It is certainly not as big an achievement as *Oklahoma!* but I like it that the constructors of that gigantic corn opera can work so well in a quieter manner.

The danger for *Pipe Dream* was sentimentality. It derives from John Steinbeck's hobo paradise on Cannery Row, and Steinbeck is a writer compromised by facile tears. The plot, like almost all musical plots, is indeed perilously sweet, but the performers show an edge of ironic self-appraisal that keeps the tone decently dry. Harold Clurman, directing his first musical, is responsible for this astringency. He manages to say that, while it is a nice pastime to pretend that alcoholic bums are brave-hearted lads and café whores their admiring younger sisters, we know—and they know—that it is a pretty lie. You will notice a long-haired madman beating eccentric time to the happy rumpus, an acrid counterpoint to the innocence.

This double tone requires acting at a level not usually attempted in musical comedy, and probably the most remarkable thing about *Pipe Dream* is Mr. Clurman's successful assumption that competent acting is entirely possible on the musical stage. His people do not break character when they sing and dance; no one is permitted to act badly because he does his own specialty well. Mr. Hammerstein's book is sensible and it is sensibly performed, the dialogue being plausible and the mass jollifications being spontaneous outbursts rather than production extravaganzas. The whole show feels spontaneous, a quality that is achieved on the stage only by the most rigorous and purposeful drill.

Judy Tyler, who plays the heroine, is not remarkably pretty and she has a rough, unplaced voice. Her virtue is that she looks like somebody who might hitchhike in dungarees along the California highways and is able to inject an element of individual decision into the inevitable boy-loves-girl story. William Johnson, playing Steinbeck's beloved Doc Ricketts, is a more conventional lyric hero. He sings well, looks fine in a beard, and acts well enough.

130

PIPE DREAM   THE MOST HAPPY FELLA

But the bums from the Palace Flop House are the real heroes of the show. Mr. Clurman keeps them working at a level of unforced buffoonery that spins the show along. They never do anything extraordinary, but they are always up to something that makes amusing sense. There are eight or ten of them, led by G. D. Wallace (straight man), Mike Kellin (tough dope), and Guy Raymond (a lanky man with a witty grace), and they should be final proof that the chorus boy is gone to stay.

Helen Traubel is the only box office name in *Pipe Dream* and the one big problem. She is so obviously a good sport, apparently so free of prima-donna snobbery in the knockabout world of show music, that it seems ungenerous to say that she finds herself on the wrong stage. In fact, she acts the motherly madam with considerable aplomb, but she can't sing the songs for beans. And since singing is her fame, she is given a lot of it to do. Her voice is a formidable instrument; here it sounds as baffled and bored as a diesel pulling a hand truck.

Jo Mielziner's several sets are light and cheerful; they are clever workmanship but unpretentious. Boris Runanin's choreography is not remarkable, but it fits smoothly into the action. Altogether, *Pipe Dream* is a civilized and intelligent amusement, and that advance sale should give time for word to get around.

In the second act of *The Most Happy Fella* (Imperial Theatre, Broadway), a young man stands behind a pretty girl and, putting his arms around her to demonstrate how she is to paste labels on grape crates, repeatedly scrubs the back of his hands across her breasts. The audience is convulsed and loudly applauds these artists when their scene ends. Now what sort of adult laughs at this sorry kind of lechery, and how could the producer guess that hundreds of them would buy admission to this show? How could Frank Loesser, who has written a strong, constantly interesting, often heart-rousing score and adapted Sidney Howard's *They Knew What They Wanted* most sensitively to provide himself with an appropriate and substantial book, permit this episode of cold vulgarity to mar his work?

For that matter, how can he appreciate the great vocal and dramatic skill of Robert Weede in the title role and not hear the cheap dance-band vocalist tricks in the voice of Art Lund, the romantic lead? How can he compose dashing and witty material for his comic trio and ask Mr. Weede to address corny banalities to "mamma up in heaven"? How can a show so secure in conception suffer a succession of queasy details that douse the gaiety so artfully engendered?

REVIEWS

Catering to the public, I think, is what does it. Big musicals are the most commercial ventures in the commercial theater. They cost a fortune, they must take in a fortune for weeks on end, and a pair of tickets to one of them (even at box-office prices) is substantial, conspicuous waste. So onto a good framework the owners hang all manner of crass bait—these entrepreneurs have no respect for the taste of the affluent. *The Most Happy Fella* is a show bursting with talent: Mr. Loesser; Mr. Weede; Jo Sullivan as the sweet-voiced heroine; the trio (Arthur Rubin, Rico Froehlich, John Henson); Shorty Long and Susan Johnson, the antic couple who must perform the sordid business I mentioned earlier; Mona Paulee, who plays an unnecessary part that seems borrowed from Gian Carlo Menotti's *The Saint of Bleecker Street*, but who has a lovely voice. The costumes, scenery, and choreography are always good and occasionally excellent, and the whole show goes at a rousing pace through a story that, thanks to Mr. Howard, has credibility and tenderness. A production so excellent should succeed on its own terms, not require the gloomy bad taste with which it has been embellished.

The Iceman Cometh, by Eugene O'Neill (1956)

As everyone who has sat through it knows, *The Iceman Cometh* (Circle in the Square, Off-Broadway) is an exhausting play. It is long by the clock (four hours and a half) and long for its own content. It repeats, it meanders, it falls into doldrums, it infects the audience with a contagion of impatience. And all of this is quite deliberate.

In the particular corner of hell represented by Harry Hope's saloon, the torment is boredom.

Men without strength to act or courage to think must erase the hours somehow; so they talk—in endlessly spiraling convolutions, treasuring and repeating every inane aphorism and second-hand figure of speech because they have scarcely enough of them to make the time march. The shop talk of alcoholism is the most painful in the world: only numbed brains can tolerate it. Eugene O'Neill's method is not to suggest how it is, but to pour it out undiluted until the audience aches with it. Meanwhile, his plot moves like a heavy snake through the sludge of words.

Each of the derelicts sheltered by Harry Hope—and Harry himself—has a dream. The dream makes each man restless; it nags and worries him and keeps him futilely paddling in the water of ambition.

132

THE ICEMAN COMETH   MEASURE FOR MEASURE   KING JOHN

So Hickey, that mad Freudian priest and drummer of hardware, would purge them and bring them peace. But the bums understand what Hickey is offering, and they fight him with the pathetic astonishing strength of the dying. Oh, the relief when Hickey is destroyed and the dreams recur! Poor bums; we may well give thanks that we are not sustained by bubble-like dreams, that we do not have to live a lie because it is the only life we have. Or at least we may be grateful that we do not have to wrestle with Hickey.

This last is the germ of terror that O'Neill leaves in the mind. It comes as an afterthought—it may come more surely from reading the play than from seeing the production—for the method of *The Iceman Cometh* very nearly frustrates the content. An audience brought to a state of squirming revolt, consciously waiting for the last line and escape into the live street, is in no shape for thought, still less for intro-spection. But O'Neill works with an acid that eats deep. His pessimism is so impersonal and clear of self-pity that you cannot evade it. You must resolve to accept knowledge of it, answering it as best you can with "Yes, but . . ."

José Quintero's production at Circle in the Square seemed to me excellent. Theater-in-the-round (actually this stage has one standing wall) is well-suited to the sprawling structure of the play and it puts us all in the saloon, which is the point. *The Iceman Cometh* makes severe demands on its cast, which must exert sustained and sharply disciplined energy to communicate lethargy and mental squalor. Mr. Quintero's group seems completely saturated in the coma of defeat, and it has the wonderful theater quality of becoming increasingly convincing as the evening wears on. Of course the actors do in fact exhaust themselves, but exhaustion in this case is the essence of style.

Measure for Measure & *King John*, by William Shakespeare (1956)

The second summer at Stratford, Connecticut, will be remembered as the season when the stage designers for the American Shakespeare Festival learned to use its remarkable theater. This is not said to slight the considerable dramatic achievement of John Houseman, the 1956 director; Jack Landau, his associate; or the acting company—and indeed they have taken brilliant advantage of the environment provided for them. But it has been evident from the moment when the

REVIEWS

Stratford blueprints were first published that a stage of such size and opportunity would have to be understood as one of the active elements in any production housed there. You cannot build a production and move it onto such a stage, using the playing volume as neutral space. That was the mistake made in the first season, with the result that the space loomed around the sets, the actors huddled in a world seeming too large for them, and the traffic of dramatic movement was mazed by the seductive license of a stage whose three dimensions are everywhere penetrable.

In the second season, while the level of performance has taken a large step up, the physical spectacle seems to have been solved at one stride. This is not the only way to mount Shakespeare, but it is a noble way and one that uses in full the great resources of the Festival Theatre. Rouben Ter-Arutunian is responsible for the scenery and costumes, Jean Rosenthal for the lighting and stage production. Together they have enlisted the unwonted space and freedom as allies and produced a vision that is not only heart-lifting in itself but urges the importance of whatever takes place within it.

The genius of the setting is that it is entirely simple and completely encompassing. The raked floor of the stage extends at least as far forward of the proscenium as there is depth behind it. There is a broad, easy stair from below stage at the front of the apron and at stage center a trap, also large and of easy access, down which a whole troop can on occasion plunge at full tilt. The three sides of the stage back of the proscenium are framed to immense height and width by horizontal slats of neutral wood hung in a large number of panels and in two or more ranks deep. These panels can be raised or lowered individually in almost numberless combinations to suggest gates, doors, chambers, passageways of whatever importance; segments high in them can be swung up to evoke battlements or the windows of a ribald house (in the present instances; the allusive possibilities are infinite). The introduction of a few vertical bars creates a prison; chandeliers and a green baize table evoke an apartment of state; two stands flanking left and right produce a ceremonial avenue. Light can come from behind the slats, diffused; it can hit against them or glance across them, and the wood offers a warm or forbidding surface as the color and quality of the light determine.

The walls can seem solid barriers or yielding curtains; they can be dappled with shadow as is the world outdoors. Changes of scene take place as it were instantaneously and the swift geometry of the evolutions contributes to the dramatic urgency. Though these slatted walls are tall and frame a huge space, they do not give the eye any units for

134

measurement, and they offer a background against which the actors, when it is useful, can appear in stereoscopic perspective. The result is that the performers are close without being intimate: they stand large and can move with large, carrying gestures. It is a marvelously sensitive setting but so empty that whatever moves onto it is instantly endowed with great moment.

Against this spare framework and with so little furniture that a box becomes a point of focus and a plywood throne an indelible impression, Mr. Ter-Arutunian has designed costumes that bear rich and oversized detail. His colors bite and his haberdashery—civil, military, royal, or bureaucratic—is both bold and a little strange. This also throws attention where it belongs—on the players.

What has been invented at Stratford this summer is not the only solution that will—or should—be made to the challenge of the theater there, but it contains the secret to any successful solution: it takes advantage of size and avoids the traps of scale. Mr. Houseman, meanwhile, has profited from this superb frame to stage *King John* and *Measure for Measure* (*The Taming of the Shrew* will open on August 5th) as strong and driving entertainment.

On paper, these two are not among Shakespeare's most inviting dramas, but in these productions they play their heads off. I have no doubt that more subtle, reflective, even minatory interpretations of the texts can be imagined. Indeed, *Measure for Measure*, as dark a play as a comedy can well be, is here set in nineteenth-century Vienna and played as though to a waltz (with snatches of absurdly appropriate music by Virgil Thomson abetting it). And *King John*, in which honor and virtue are at rare premium, emerges as a conflict among men who are rather headstrong than without scruple. That is all right—no one seeking to demonstrate the deep perspective of Shakespeare's moral landscape, or the lyric passion of his imagination, would try to make a case from these plays. As Mr. Houseman offers them, they seem vital and basic (which they are) and consistently motivated and resolved (which they are not). And as he presents them you cannot fail to see that, whereas King John is not Macbeth and Vincentio is not Prospero, they were shaped by the same hand. As bold, strong-colored constructions for the popular stage, these are wonderful plays and the season thus far at Stratford is a great year for the groundlings Shakespeare knew us to be.

Of the company now performing there, the main point is that it has not yet become a company. There are not, as there were last year, antagonisms of style or individual inadequacies to strike down a play. But one still thinks of the productions in terms of the particular actors

REVIEWS

appearing, says to oneself that certain roles are conceived as they are because that is the way certain actors can perform them. This, as you would expect, is most evident in the leads. The supporting cast is developing a style and a familiarity with Shakespeare's language and conventions that enable a herald, a secondary noble, a townsman, or a bawd to make a sharp and right impression in the second or two that your eye is on one of them. But one feels that Mr. Houseman, for all he is a strong director who shaped the plays according to his advance decision, also to a real extent accommodated himself to the given styles of Nina Foch, John Emery, Kent Smith, Mildred Dunnock, Fritz Weaver, and certain others. They are all good actors and they all offer interesting interpretations. But what one likes or dislikes about their performances, one attributes to them—and that is not what is meant by a company. It is not yet the organization that can undertake the great plays that still lie ahead for the Festival Theatre.

How, in the long run, a company is to be created is not yet evident. The present scheme of inviting a guest director to start afresh each season with guest stars is not likely to produce it. But the Academy at Stratford is in session, the students are carrying spears on the stage, and this branch of the enterprise may in time bear fruit. Meanwhile, one can foresee how such a company would look by observing the present conduct of Morris Carnovsky, Arnold Moss, Hiram Sherman, Earle Hyman, Kendall Clark, Whitford Kane, and some others of as yet smaller experience, who begin to offer a symphonic organism that would permit a director to stage a Shakespeare repertory as great as the capacity within him.

Johnny Johnson, by Paul Green (1956)

Seeing the revival in 1956, I find it almost impossible to recapture the impression *Johnny Johnson* made when the Group Theatre introduced it in 1936. It is not that we are wiser for the twenty years, but we know more, and Paul Green's morality play no longer chastises us or feeds our hope. Mr. Green subscribed to the "they" theory of wickedness, and that was a comfort; "we" were legion and "they'" were few—it needed only a prophet to show us where the strength lay. But that was after one world war: after two such and a cold war, we know that there is no "they," or rather that "we" are "they." Paul Green can no longer invigorate us; it is Samuel Beckett we now attend.

What holds the play's force is Kurt Weill's music. But this score, which I think originally must have italicized and added iron to the

136

staged parable, now seems turned against the audience. It laughs at us because we once believed in ourselves.

Yet I am glad that Stella Adler has revived *Johnny Johnson* (Carnegie Hall Playhouse, Broadway). It is one of the very few revivable products of the polemical theater of the 1930s, a reminder that for a brief but exciting period the American stage became a journal of opinion. We no longer have "living newspapers," satire has almost disappeared from our musical comedies, and the only political voices raised on Broadway today are those of Shakespeare and Shaw.

The production that Miss Adler has staged has the great merit that it grows in power and sureness as it proceeds. Group scenes are its weakness: the director—or it may be the choreographer to whom she entrusted the job—has no eye for a stage in motion. Confusion can be demonstrated in the theater only with purposeful discipline; allowed its own course, it becomes a rumpus, and *Johnny Johnson* ever and again drops into high school jollification

James Broderick in the title role appears to discover the part as he plays it. In the opening scenes he is so pale that the action lacks a center, but once the fable has moved into the trenches he takes command of the text, and in the ultimate scenes in the lunatic asylum he performs with a quiet conviction that is arresting. Gene Saks as the psychotic psychoanalyst offers the greatest *tour de force* on the local stage since Alvin Epstein's epileptic monologue in Samuel Beckett's *Waiting for Godot*. Still, the stature Broderick can recapture for his pure hero is the feat of the production. It is possible to smile at *Johnny Johnson*, but is not possible to laugh at Johnny.

Girls of Summer, by N. Richard Nash, & *The Happiest Millionaire*, by Kyle Crichton (1956)

The critics for the New York press must have access to an ideal theater season that is not available to less-favored playgoers. How otherwise to explain their very grudging reception of N. Richard Nash's *Girls of Summer* (Longacre Theatre, Broadway)? Nash has written a serious and generous play on a theme that most people will recognize as germane to their own experience. He has constructed it with skill, building emotional tension through a series of varied and vivid events, and keeping his solution very ably in doubt. His work has been admirably staged by Jack Garfein, who directs in a bold, unequivocal style that permits the actors to command the stage without strutting. And his principal roles are occupied by Shelley Winters and Pat

REVIEWS

Hingle, who share a gift for accenting a part so that it becomes more brilliantly lucid than life ever is, but without being distorted into an actor's vehicle. All this, I should suppose, is not an everyday achievement on Broadway.

What Nash talks about is the honesty needed to make oneself understood and the resolution needed to cast oneself off into the stream of experience. His heroine, thoroughly frightened by the demands that events have made on her, is hiding behind her own competence, escaping from life by dealing with it forthrightly and at arm's length. His hero is able to rout her out of her wave of fear because he is himself on a holiday from reality and can ask the sort of impertinent questions that come easily to masqueraders. Perhaps disappointment is felt around town because Nash is in Anton Chekhov territory, but certainly no second Chekhov.

Omniscience is Nash's weakness. He works from a psychological blueprint that, however valid it may be, deprives his play of the wonder that is the true life of the theater. He is a superintending playwright, and thus he gets his characters safely through crises where Chekhov found he could be no help at all. He pays the price that characters so carefully attended and manipulated do not assume an independence and stature of their own. So *Girls of Summer* is good workmanship, not great art, but to those who enjoy watching the theater working hard and usefully at its trade, Nash's play is nevertheless recommended.

The Happiest Millionaire (Lyceum Theatre, Broadway), on the other hand, is recommended to those who believe the theater is a place for bubbling nonsense and who can still detect the bubble after one full act of the nonsense. It is adapted by Kyle Crichton from a book, *My Philadelphia Father*, which he and Cordelia Drexel Biddle wrote together, and which is said to recapture the unique personality of the millionaire Anthony J. Drexel Biddle. If Mr. Biddle was unique he had trite ways of showing it—alligators in the conservatory, prize fights in the drawing room, and loud-mouthed, cocksure, warm-hearted bullying all over the lot. Mr. Biddle, as portrayed, is a character wisely cut from Kaufman and Hart's *You Can't Take It with You*, and his wife is the lady Philip Wylie calls mom. (Wylie's 1942 book of essays, *Generation of Vipers*, inspired the term "Momism.")

Walter Pidgeon can literally be seen throwing himself into the title role; he continually demonstrates its risibility instead of playing to the script and letting the laughs fall where they will. This betrays a lack of confidence in the material, for which he cannot be blamed. Ruth Matteson as Mrs. Biddle is so tolerant that I came in the end to feel

138

THE HAPPIEST MILLIONAIRE   THE GOOD WOMAN OF SETZUAN

she was being tolerant of me. The play is best served by Diana van der Vlis as Cordelia Biddle herself, as well as by Don Britton and Dana White as her brothers. They treat the whole affair as an exhausted and hysterical Christmas afternoon, which is astute of them and produces a style suitable to their ages.

The Good Woman of Setzuan, by Bertolt Brecht (1957)

The current revival of interest in Bertolt Brecht suffers a real, though probably not decisive, setback from *The Good Woman of Setzuan* now playing at the Phoenix Theatre (Off-Broadway). The production commits the worst sin of the theater—it is boring.

I think the fault lies with the production, not with the play. Granted that Brecht's "epic" theater is more openly pedantic than the theater of illusion that audiences in the United States are trained to accept, granted also that the political and social teaching of this play is both dated and doctrinaire; still, the text does live and move, the characters are full-standing and varied, there are passion and humor and excitement. But not on this stage.

Eric Bentley translated the play with what sounds to my ear like a warm appreciation of its flavor, but he has displayed it in the theater as though he were dressing a museum. I have attended play readings that engendered considerably more animation. Two things seem to me particularly wrong with the production. In the first place, it has no consistent tone. Brecht set his play in a fictitious China (perhaps because in China also the stage is more a place for ritual than for illusion), and he constructed it as an almost mathematical fable on the impossibility of doing good in an evil world. (This is a somewhat weighted equation, however, since his well-intentioned prostitute is invariably gullible when she is altruistic and invariably shrewd when she switches in self-preservation to her selfish alter ego.) From this base, Mr. Bentley could have pitched his production to a choice of keys. But Uta Hagen is realistic, Gerald Hiken is lyric, Irene Dailey is Grand Guignol, Zero Mostel is burlesque, Albert Salmi is theater-workshop expressive, and Nancy Marchand is musical-comedy sinister. This is all good talent, but it is governed by no one's idea of the effect wanted.

In the second place, the thread of dramatic tension repeatedly breaks from a want of stage deportment. I understand that Brecht wished his actors, when not immediately engaged in the proceedings,

REVIEWS

to go blank. But there is a great difference on the stage between effacing yourself and dropping out of the ensemble, between planned movement and random stir. The actors in *The Good Woman of Setzuan*, when they are not "working," look like a crowd of extras on their lunch hour. You cannot sustain any sort of dramatic dignity or narrative pressure if your actors lounge and have to pull themselves together when the action threatens to come their way. The effect is ludicrously like a class of wool-gathering school children, and Brecht, for all his pedagogical leanings, could not have intended anything so self-defeating.

So a play that could be fleet and lucid wanders and bumbles. The contrasts fail to clash, the wit misses its target, the irony is lost from lack of precision. In short, if the actors seem bored and at sea, how can the spectators be otherwise?

Troilus and Cressida, by William Shakespeare (1957)

The final production of the Old Vic's season here, at the Winter Garden Theatre (Broadway), is a provoking and theatrically exciting *Troilus and Cressida.* Tyrone Guthrie, labeling the play a satiric comedy, directs it for laughs and jangle. He has put it in Edwardian dress and manners, with guards/regiment types out of *Punch* and their light ladies from Mayfair and Leicester Square. Mr. Guthrie invents business with a nervous versatility; he runs his actors up and down the aisles, hangs on them all manner of glittering, rattling accoutrements, and keeps them fretting and jibing like horses too long in their stalls. There was surely never a busier production of the play or one more eager to meet the audience on the easy ground of a broad style. Guthrie competes with Shakespeare for guffaws—the tiny Priam among his giant sons, Helen an aging variety artiste in too-tight shoes, Nestor's shooting stick, Thersites' nasal (and often incomprehensible) Cockney, the elegant Pandarus wolfing after every comely boy on the stage.

This is every bit as good a laugh-riot as George Abbott's *The Pajama Game*, and there are no nagging doubts about the quality of these heroes—they have no quality. Who will wonder about the heart of Cressida, a high-born slut whose very groom knows her too well? Or who will be jealous of the honor of Agamemnon, a blimp grown fatuous punting the years away before the walls of Troy? It is all malice, pose, and larking, and we have no need of Thersites to tell us "Lechery, lechery! Still, wars and lechery: nothing else holds fashion."

140

It would not be true to say that Mr. Guthrie's concept fails to work—you could not sit in the audience and deny that the production is a success. But it may be too small a success. *Troilus and Cressida* is a bitter play, whatever the argument for calling it a tragedy, that strikes out against honor without principle, love without generosity, blood without cause, and Shakespeare did not waste anger on jackdaws. Yet this Hector plays for the varsity, Ulysses is a Noël Coward sophisticate, Cassandra a Bloomsbury eccentric, and Troilus a dear boy caught in a precocious love affair. It is funny and right on the surface.

Then there is Achilles, who can't be made to foxtrot like the others. He is corrupt but powerful; dangerous, passionate, and direct; and he remains fixed in his original context. Mr. Guthrie conceives him as a prizefighter gone to sloth, which is excellent, but his unscrupulous megalomania is much too raw for the surrounding gold braid and tin swords. And what of Pandarus's spitting farewell? The hatred is too sudden after all the easy amorality—the shaft misses.

I recall the acting as a group of splendid individual turns: Paul Rogers as Pandarus, John Neville as Thersites, Rosemary Harris as Cressida, Richard Wordsworth as Ulysses, Charles Gray as Achilles all demonstrate a gift for bold and explicit characterization; but they make their marks as virtuosos and rather apart from the encounters of the play. The rest of the company works with dash, noise, and enthusiasm, without building much dramatic structure either out of their lines or their presence on the stage. Everything gives place to a general impression of feverish brightness. Mr. Guthrie is a showman of almost unmatched energy and ingenuity; what he seems to lack is a good opinion of his material or of his audience.

Purple Dust, by Sean O'Casey (1957)

A good deal of fun can be had at Sean O'Casey's *Purple Dust* (Cherry Lane Theatre, Off-Broadway) if too great demands are not made of the occasion. What you must not demand are substance from the playwright or a high polish from the company. O'Casey's celebrated nationalism takes the form this time of broadest farce, "elevated" at intervals of about twenty minutes by salvoes of pyrotechnic lyricism, just to remind the audience that the old man owns finer tools than the slapstick.

He has set a couple of bally English antiquarians down in a howling, bog-bound wilderness, where the sly but proud natives steal

REVIEWS

them blind, even walking off in the end with their Irish light-o'-loves. I don't quite see the stalwart sons of Eire being content to make honest women of their landlords' doxies, but if O'Casey thought it a good joke, I'm ready to laugh. Certainly he can write funny lines and the play dances—though pretty much on one spot.

Phillip Burton, the director, has failed to convince the cast that farce is funnier when it is played straight. This production is altogether too cluttered with comic attitudes (to say nothing of comic get-ups), and every actor seems to have a relative in the audience. The company displays a dismaying variety of stage Irish accents and, except for Alvin Epstein in the role of a romantic house builder, it has trouble shifting pace from the buffoonery to the poetry. It is, in a word, a less than polished group, but nonetheless ingratiating and enthusiastically occupied in batting out a bit of very skillful nonsense.

The Waltz of the Toreadors, by Jean Anouilh (1957)

The craftsmanship, both of writing and of performing, in Jean Anouilh's *The Waltz of the Toreadors* (Coronet Theatre, Broadway) is a reason for cheers, and the play has been greeted with unanimous published applause. The applause in the theater itself, however, was less generous—at least, the audience around me seemed a little baffled and fretful. It expected either more or less—and this was not an arbitrary expectation, but in the design of the work.

For in the two scenes of the first act Anouilh establishes a farce of wit, at once uproarious and polished, and at the first intermission we were all congratulating one another on assisting at an evening of such capable banter. But in the following acts the colors darken; a rueful good humor turns toward self-pity, exasperation toward hatred, foible toward decay. As a plan, this is excellent—if all goes well, the audience should acknowledge that it has laughed too easily and be the readier to extend compassion when matters are shown in a more telling light.

But all does not go as well as it should, because when the colors darken they do not deepen. The gallant General St. Pé, quixotically in love after seventeen years with the maiden who danced with him once to the "Waltz of the Toreadors," and now dictating his memoirs to a timid seminarian outside the bedroom of his invalid, termagant wife, is a sufficient figure for farce. And the farce detonates with the arrival of the still-chaste but now more-than-a-little-impatient maiden. The two ladies, flinging themselves into gestures of suicide, declare that

THE WALTZ OF THE TOREADORS   A HOLE IN THE HEAD

only embraces will sustain the life flickering in their bosoms, and master and scribe are engaged in lunatic ministrations at the first-act curtain.

The machinery of farce continues to the end. The invalid wife springs to her feet and assumes heroic attitudes in disheveled bed-dress. The priests' boy discovers a Lothario talent in himself. The General's ill-favored daughters catch the suicide contagion. And an inebriated priest arrives with astonishing news that sets relationships in quite new contexts. But the surface dance of gaiety is gone: we see that St. Pé has fallen off into self-pity and feeble lechery with house-maids; his wife's tirade is not only extravagant, it is cruel and ugly; the resolution is apt enough, but mean-hearted. And yet Anouilh has not found enough to say of these people to make their misery signif-icant to anyone but themselves. St. Pé's life is certainly a waste, but it would be hard to show that more than tinsel has been squandered. So an audience that has been abruptly shaken out of its initial high spirits, naturally wonders why it has been sobered. It experiments with a laugh now and then, but without conviction; it tries to respond to the General's misery, but the insights are too meager. In the end it shrugs.

The company under Harold Clurman's direction takes advantage of every hint and clue that Anouilh provides. It is a wonderfully civilized performance, and you will not often see a play so carried by the presence and projective force of its actors. But this has the disad-vantage—most noticeable in the case of Ralph Richardson, but evident too in Mildred Natwick as his frightful wife and Meriel Forbes as his mistress in name only—that the actors not infrequently seem to run out of material. They are alive and strong; their stands and movements on Ben Edwards' splendidly evocative set seem ever poised to launch them into matters of real moment, but then the lines give out and they relapse into gesture and business. The passages of farce they handle with beautiful spirit, like jugglers' bright Indian clubs, and the proper cheers break out; but when the actors come to the heart of the play, it is not there.

A Hole in the Head, by Arnold Schulman (1957)

Television writers have been doing rather well selling their used copy to Hollywood. Now Arnold Schulman has brought to Broadway a yarn he wrote originally as an on-the-air drama. *A Hole in the Head* (Plymouth Theatre, Broadway), which is almost sure to be one of the

143

REVIEWS

spring's most amiable hits, is scarcely adapted to the point where it hides its origin. It is a script (few people, I think, would call it a play) at once full of action and devoid of movement; it contains a series of crises but no conflict; every character is playing on the same team— lovable Sidney's team—and the final curtain means only that the time is up for this evening.

At this level of commercial entertainment, *A Hole in the Head* is a perfect achievement. Schulman writes a combination of sentimentality and caricature that warms an audience like tea. Sidney is a no-good innocent with bigshot illusions, a widower and a sweet, exasperated father to his twelve-year-old quiz-kid son. He runs a bankrupt Florida motel (a busy, confectionery set by Boris Aronson, which revolves in an arc of thirty degrees for no particular reason) on the strength of a gaudy wardrobe and the grudging support of a successful New York brother. In this episode, brother and sister-in-law have come down to adopt the boy in exchange for a new loan.

Other possibilities are suggested: a widow with a modest competence is materialized for Sidney (but there is also a toothsome divorcee upstairs), and something is said about a nice little five-and-dime just waiting for a sensible couple in a small New England city. The widow can cook and the divorcee takes herself off to Cuba, but we viewers know that nothing real is going to happen to threaten the sure-fire storyline of Sidney and his kid running that Florida holiday flophouse.

The dialogue is a distillation of the conversation heard from the next booth in any Sixth Avenue delicatessen—extravagant, ironic, glittering with incongruity, always skirting rage or tears. The lines fairly bounce with vitality—and it is by the lines that you must judge the success of dialogue comedy.

Absolutely successful also is the production. A cast headed by Paul Douglas, with David Burns and Kay Medford as his relatives and Tommy White almost eerily on the right note as his son, moves under Garson Kanin's direction with the confidence and homogeneity of a strong repertory company. They are not playing Chekhov or O'Casey or Shakespeare—they are playing Schulman at so many yaks per minute—but on the score of matching style to content, they are the equal of any fabulous theatrical enterprise you care to name.

A Hole in the Head earns your respect, and in large measure your affection, by understanding itself so thoroughly. Professionalism at a high enough level becomes its own subject matter. There is no creative life in it; in fact its perfection is a mortal danger to creation, which is never perfect. *A Hole in the Head* is so good that it is a direct threat to the future of tragedy, comedy, melodrama, and even the bedroom

144

EXILES   ORPHEUS DESCENDING

farce. Professionalism, not vulgarity, is the gun that television holds at our head—by which I mean the head of the theater.

Exiles, by James Joyce (1957)

The Renata Theatre on Bleecker Street, newest of the Off-Broadway houses, has begun its career with a handsome staging of James Joyce's *Exiles*. John Boyt has designed the best-looking production I have seen downtown. His two sets and his costumes have a coherent style and an unobtrusive wit. There is no suggestion here of warehouse hand-me-downs—on the contrary, Mr. Boyt manages to imply a lavish budget that I don't for a moment suppose he enjoyed.

Against this look of success Walt Witcover has mounted a vivid interpretation of Joyce's play. You can scarcely fail to be caught up in it or to withstand the very considerable charm of its powerful egos. It is played with assurance and a warm individuality by a handsome and competent cast.

But, it must be said that, for all its strength and color, *Exiles* is a curiously evasive play. It suffers from the fact that the characters are all so preoccupied with stating ultimate truths about themselves that they have little time to heed one another. Communication flags and they are indeed all exiles. Joyce wrote the play at a time when he greatly admired Ibsen, and it comes perilously close to being a parody of Ibsen. Everyone is both attracted and repelled by everyone else, and everyone is motivated by the noblest and/or basest impulses. Four egomaniacs on one stage are surely a parody of something.

I rather sided with the wife (Jutta Wolf) for the old-fashioned reason that she was a damned fine-looking woman and I didn't care at all for her husband's fishy smile. As a matter of fact, a director of *Exiles* has to make up his mind whether we are for or against this husband. Mark Lenard played him with equal measure of pale suffering and slippery fishiness, and this contributed to the atmosphere of limbo.

Orpheus Descending, by Tennessee Williams (1957)

One critic of *Orpheus Descending* (Martin Beck Theatre, Broadway) is struck by its extreme bitterness; another finds that this revision by Tennessee Williams of an early work is noticeably less baleful than the

145

REVIEWS

plays he has been writing in recent years. It is a matter, I suppose, of whether the observer is more oppressed by exterior brutality or interior cruelty.

Orpheus Descending is social protest, almost a tract; it is as ugly as bigotry and as vicious as power in mean hands. It is also relentless. Williams loathes the vacuous bully-bosses of his rural South, and fears them. In his story the impulses toward life and generosity of spirit are overwhelmed; the law of ignorance is enforced by flaming gasoline and half-starved hound packs. Nevertheless, compared with such a work as *Cat on a Hot Tin Roof*, this play has almost a sunny disposition.

Orpheus, a vagrant folk singer, finds himself stranded in a town that is itself stranded. He becomes the sustaining son to an old woman who paints visions, the corrective brother to a girl who employs debauchery as protest, the lover of a wife married to hatred and death. He is not a remarkable boy and he does not assume these roles deliberately, or even willingly; but he is alive and what still lives in the desert immediately responds to his presence. No one who lives survives; still, they have recognized one another and they are a promise.

It is easy to say, and it is being widely said, that *Orpheus Descending* is discursive, indecisive, awkward as to its machinery. I could quote lines so ringing with philosophy that they were obviously written by a much younger Tennessee Williams. But it is a great thing at a play to be able to take sides; to know that a war has been waged; that virtue spoke even though it did not prevail. Anger and sorrow are valid experiences in the theater. The later Williams of *Cat on a Hot Tin Roof* uses shock to induce audience reaction in a situation too extreme for allegiance.

It is hard to separate the vigor of *Orpheus Descending* from the vitality of Maureen Stapleton in the central role of a live woman among the cruel dead. She is so bold in her broad characterization, so precise in the enlightening details of manner, she shifts mood with such accurate pose and inflection, that you laugh aloud from the pleasure of such creative skill. Mr. Williams wrote a rich part in this Italian wench so improbably and unhappily cut off from decent joy, and Miss Stapleton embodies her magnificently.

Harold Clurman has built the production around her, which was the obvious thing to do. Less obvious was the construction of a supporting cast that would give her a wall to beat upon. The hateful and pathetic gargoyles of Southern lust, suspicion, and vulgar gentility he establishes with quick, sharp statements from extremely apt performers. The difficult title role he keeps exceedingly quiet and

146

uncomplicated. Cliff Robertson, who plays it, is a graceful young actor with what seem instinctive good taste and good ideas. He has as yet no great power, but he does have a stubborn presence that admirably supports Miss Stapleton's virtuosity. Boris Aronson has designed an intricate set that nevertheless looks open and untricky, and on which the sweeping action can move without stumbling.

The play is ragged in spots, sententious in spots, but it is *about* something and cares about it—which makes it as welcome as spring in this winter of sterile theater amusements.

A Moon for the Misbegotten, by Eugene O'Neill, & *New Girl in Town*, by George Abbott (1957)

When Eugene O'Neill escaped from the family suicide implicit in *Long Day's Journey into Night*, he deserted his older brother, James; in later years he paid for this with an irrational sense of guilt. In *A Moon for the Misbegotten* (Bijou Theatre, Broadway) he dramatizes an episode from the family history that suggests that James found at least a moment of companionship, understanding, and love before he died. By attributing a measure of fulfillment to his brother, O'Neill could accept a measure of peace for himself.

Or so we are tempted to speculate. We are assuming these days an identity between the various Tyrones of the plays and the members of the O'Neill family who obviously inspired them. I suspect that in time we shall find we have been too literal about it. But in the case of *A Moon for the Misbegotten*, it is hard to avoid the notion—and the notion is what gives the play its poignancy—that O'Neill was trying to lay to rest the ghost of his brother.

It seems a *rationalized* play, skillful as to plot but uneasy, even specious, in its motivations. Unless you assume that it is factual, you may have trouble believing that it is plausible. Since Jean Genet's *The Maids* I have not seen a play in which the truth was so evasive. Toward the end of his life Jim Tyrone inherited a worn-out Connecticut farm that was being worked in a desultory way by a drunken Irish tenant and his almost ludicrously Rabelaisian daughter. Jim liked to drink with Mike Hogan and he soon came under the spell of the sluttish Josie. When he threatened to sell the place, however, Hogan and his daughter cooked up a badger game, and late one moonlit night the scapegrace landlord walked into the trap.

Up to that point the play sounds a likely sequel to the sour miseries of *Long Day's Journey into Night*, but then, the focus changes. Jim

REVIEWS

was only kidding about the sale and Hogan, knowing it, was only trying to promote a romance that he thought would bring joy to the lonely pair. For Josie is really an idealistic maiden, yearning with mother love, and Jim is a tired little boy who wants to weep and sleep on the bosom of an understanding nurse. In the dawn light everyone is transformed: the crafty Hogan is a kindly old cupid, the foul-mouthed Josie is a monument of self-denying love, and Jim has found the grail of understanding and forgiveness.

It is an affecting scene and would make you glad about the ways of men and women if you could accept it. But the Hogans ring false as ministering angels and the theory that true confession is good for the soul seems an easy solution to the terrible experience of being a Tyrone. It is unlike O'Neill to force a play into reconciliation, and I cannot escape the feeling that in this, his last work, he wrote not what he understood, but what he wanted to believe. The trick behind the trick, says Hogan, is the spice of life. It is also a device by which a dramatist's heart may deny what his mind knows.

Cyril Cusack, a veteran of the Irish theater, plays the crafty farmer. He uses all the tricks—the falsetto voice, the jabs, winks, leers, pate-scratching, and dead-pan sallies—of Abbey Theatre knockabout farce and he makes great fun with the material O'Neill supplies.

Wendy Hiller and Franchot Tone have a harder time. Miss Hiller appears to be unfamiliar with farm-wench behavior and displays a rough, immodest awkwardness that seems almost spastic. She is presumably haunted also by the knowledge that in the closing scenes she will have to assume a wise and suffering nobility for which she can find little forewarning in the earlier pages of the script. And Mr. Tone is in the thankless position of author's pawn. He overacts heartiness, he overacts contrition, he even hams pouring a drink or lighting a cigarette, and he is convincing only in the rather long stretch at the end when he is asleep in Josie's arms. I see nothing in the text to justify this hollow behavior—Tyrone was supposed to feel at home around the Hogan farm—and I attribute it to an experienced actor's feeling that his part does not hold together.

All this, I fear, is also a reflection on Carmen Capalbo's direction. He wisely gave Mr. Cusack his head, but he seems not to have found any solution to the problems of his other two principals.

This being the year of O'Neill, it was almost predictable that one of his plays would come to town as a song-and-dance show. I would have bet on *The Emperor Jones* with Harry Belafonte, but *Anna Christie* with Gwen Verdon is not a surprise. George Abbott has taken as much from O'Neill as he can use in a musical—he has borrowed

148

SUMMER OF THE 17TH DOLL   THE MUSIC MAN

the basic situation and the central characters and then gone off on his own to cut the expected comedy capers. The resemblance of *New Girl in Town* (46th Street Theatre, Broadway) to *Anna Christie* is apparent but not striking. The smart trick was to build the role of Marthy Owen up to co-starring stature and then give it to Thelma Ritter. Miss Verdon is an *ingénue* with scarlet petticoats; Miss Ritter is a ribald, apple-cheeked gnome who appears to move on concealed springs. Each in her way is a superb showman, and neither is inclined to step aside for the other. The result is an invigorating neck-and-neck race for the applause of the final curtain.

The two ladies work their heads off against a conventional but pleasant background of music by Bob Merrill (there is at least one tune you can whistle), sets by Rouben Ter-Arutunian, and dances (including the now-obligatory dream ballet) by Bob Fosse. The male leads are George Wallace as Anna's lover and Cameron Prud'homme as Chris Christopherson, Anna's father and Marthy's old man. Sensible actors with good, strong singing voices, they are quick enough on their feet to keep out of the way of the main contest.

Broadway is as rich in technical know-how as General Motors, and *New Girl in Town* is the product of that applied skill. I applaud it: I think *New Girl* is a great show, just as I think my Chevrolet is a great car. Both cost more than I like, but it is impossible to resist the absurdly efficient machinery.

Summer of the 17th Doll, by Ray Lawler, & *The Music Man,* by Meredith Wilson (1958)

The critics of the daily press, almost without exception, have declared that *Summer of the 17th Doll* (Coronet Theatre, Broadway) is not blended for the American taste. Its Australian accent, they say, is so exotic as to be virtually unintelligible. Still worse, the play is about some dim people whose circumstances are too remote from ours for the spark of sympathy to jump the gap. The New York theater being the shopping center it is, this judgment will probably be fatal to Ray Lawler's play—unless the Theatre Guild membership is sufficient to keep it going until word of mouth comes to its rescue, as I believe it then would.

For *Summer of the 17th Doll* is a good play, a strong play that deals in fresh terms with a theme of almost universal application. And it is performed by a company whose wit and eloquence are not often surpassed in the Broadway neighborhood. I cannot account for the

REVIEWS

fretful bafflement with which it has been greeted. The Australians speak a kind of simplified Cockney that no doubt sounds vulgar to ears trained on Michael Redgrave or Dame Sybil Thorndyke, but which is no more difficult to understand than the voice of Mississippi, one of our more popular stage lingoes.

The only thing exotic about the circumstances of the play is that the men in it are sugar-cane cutters who labor for seven months in Australia's tropical north, and then come down to Melbourne for a five-month vacation, known, not very obscurely, as "the lay-off." There seems nothing in this to trouble the least flexible of playgoers, and surely the reviewers are not thrown into confusion because Australians celebrate Christmas with fireworks in the summer.

I suspect that what really strikes them as passing strange is the normality of the people Mr. Lawler has caught in his tragedy. It is a long time since we saw on the stage a working man who was not frightened by his own strange appetites, or an old crone who was not hiding a bloody axe in her bureau. We have been sensationalized by our playwright-moralists and are puzzled by the suggestion that psychopathology is not the only road to human understanding.

The theme of Mr. Lawler's play is the wages of illusion—the more perfect the illusion and the longer it endures, the more shattering the price it finally extracts. He chooses to work with the lives of very simple people who express themselves with an openness that is almost embarrassing in this era of oblique comment (clinical shoptalk is a form of emotional evasion). But the theme itself, Lord knows, is one we all recognize.

Two sugar-cutters have been coming south for sixteen years to spend the off-season with a pair of barmaids in a house owned by the mother of one of them. For both couples these reunions have been perfect, unchanging, inviolable recurrences of happiness—five months of heaven every year, as one of the girls describes it, saying that she would not exchange what she has known for any marriage in the world. But this is the seventeenth summer.

Without quite realizing what they were doing, the men and their girls have stylized and ritualized their relationship. (One of the men has brought his sweetheart a kewpie doll each year, if you were wondering about the odd title.) They have always exchanged the same jokes, eaten the same meals, drunk in the same bars, gone on the same excursions, and parted with the same promises of love and renewal. Thus they have worked a miracle—they have made time stand still.

This year, though, the tableau has been broken. One of the girls has married, one of the men has lost his gang leadership to a younger field

150

SUMMER OF THE 17TH DOLL   THE MUSIC MAN

hand; and, though another girl has been found and all the proper forms have been observed, the well-loved ceremony will no longer work the magic. With the magic lost, they are lost entirely. As in any fairy tale, their youth falls from them in rags—there is no transition—and they are old. They try to embrace, to comfort one another, but who can embrace, or speak even, over a gulf of seventeen years? They do what charmed lovers must always do when the charm breaks: weep, smile, and turn apart.

I think this is a tragedy of substance and pertinence—at least I have no trouble translating it into settings closer than Australia and into contexts other than romance. Lawler has worked it out with admirable compassion and an expert understanding of the dynamics of the stage. He has no bizarre secrets to disclose; he is not dealing with extreme experiences; his people are strong and will no doubt survive somehow. In these respects he may be unfashionable, but in deeper respects he is important, and it seems too bad to dismiss him as a stranger from that odd country where people walk around upside-down.

There is not much point in giving you the names of the actors (Lawler himself plays one of the men), for they are all Australians appearing here for the first time. They have been acting in this play for a long while—both at home and in England—and they now work together with a harmony and individuality that are magnetic.

The dietary equivalent of *The Music Man* (Majestic Theatre, Broadway) is a tunafish sandwich washed down with a with a frosted chocolate. I eat this sort of thing when I am on the run, but I don't take the theater on the run.

Meredith Wilson's musical machine is bland, prettily tuneless, competently banal, and entirely unnecessary. I don't understand why it attracted any audience at all, and yet its success is so great that just to have seen it is a mark of sophistication—and success. Having exercised the ingenuity and paid the price necessary to get into the theater, the audience will applaud its own taste and good fortune, and let it be known around town that it has seen pure beauty, embellished by Robert Preston (who is not at all bad). So the myth prospers and tunafish becomes a feast for the aristocracy of the expense accounts. Nothing succeeds like snobbery reinforced by indifference.

REVIEWS

Endgame, by Samuel Beckett (1958)

Use your head, can't you, use your head, you're on earth, there's no cure for that!

There is no bottom to the nihilism of Samuel Beckett, but each time, as he is going down forever, he finds a flicker of wit and kicks on for another few strokes. For a poet, total renunciation is probably impossible—he is forced to believe in his own poetry and from that he can rebuild a universe.

So *Endgame* (Cherry Lane Theatre, Off-Broadway) is not really the end; it merely approaches the end as the parallel lines approach infinity. However, it is much further along than *Waiting for Godot*: it looks as though we might be extinguished at any minute, not with a bang and not with a whimper, but stuttering importantly like a rundown clock. The past ("accursed progenitor") is refuse. Ancient father and mother, they stand in ash cans on the stumps of their legs, having lost their shanks "in the Ardennes" . . . "on the road to Sedan"—which may suggest where and when Beckett thinks the end officially began. The lord of the present is blind and paralyzed, enthroned in his filth, sardonic and mawkish with the worn-out poses of an eternity of posing. The slave is truculent and spavined, but still slaving—out of habit, and perhaps because it is the only activity left on earth. It is something to be able to get around, however painfully.

There has been a disaster (at least we are now deep in a "shelter"), or perhaps it is just cosmic fatigue; the tides no longer flow, nothing moves, nothing grows, there is no sunlight "out there." Or *was* that a child, flashing just past the edge of the window? Impossible, absurd, ha ha! And yet if it were so, we could give up this silly game, this wordplay, this humiliating crawl to infinity. We could die without committing the treason of extermination. Beckett will not quite give up the hope he does not have:

Hamm: The bastard! [God, that is.] He doesn't exist!
Clov: Not yet.

"This is not much fun," says Hamm the master, and compared to *Waiting for Godot* it really isn't. The mad dialogue still rings like china, and shocks of wicked laughter still spill out of the surrounding gibberish:

ENDGAME THE VISIT & THE FIRST BORN

Clov: Do you believe in the life to come?
Hamm: Mine has always been that.

But when two of your four characters are stuck in ashcans (with the tops on a good part of the time) and a third is confined to a throne on castors, you must rely for action on the comings and goings of the one remaining on his feet (just barely on his feet). This degenerates fairly soon into a sorry pendulum of business, even when so resourceful a mime as Alvin Epstein is engaged In it. *Endgame* is in one act and runs for about ninety minutes, but it seems a long evening.

The new parable lacks the playfulness, the lovable naughtiness of its predecessor. That was not all Bert Lahr's doing: Beckett kicked up his own heels. Now it is so much later in the day that defiance and gaiety are almost used up—the effect is powerful enough, but there is less theater to it. And more poetry, perhaps. The characteristic staccato lines clash against one another like cymbals, the voices within voices are like the supporting and echoing choirs in an orchestra. It is the song of final dissolution by a minstrel-prophet with the logic of death in his mind and the conviction of life forever in his blood. The great drama of Beckett is always his inability to subdue himself.

Lester Rawlins, as the blind Hamm, controls the center of the stage with hypnotic black glasses and a warlock's repertory of vocal changes. P. J. Kelly and Nydia Westman, our elders in the ashcans, tremble between slapstick and horror with a dexterity won from long experience in more mobile comedy.

The Visit, by Friedrich Dürrenmatt, & *The Firstborn*, by Christopher Fry (1958)

Leaving the Lunt-Fontanne Theatre (formerly the Globe, Broadway) after the third evening performance of *The Visit*, I heard someone at the rear of the orchestra crying "boo" with self-righteous vigor, and I was glad to hear it. I don't agree that the play or performance deserved this comment, but it shows much more clearly than applause—a standardized rite in our theater—that the play arouses ponderable reactions.

The Lunts have often been reprimanded for putting their talents to frivolous ends, and it is a pleasure to report that, for better or worse, they are currently engaged in a work that has more character than their own charm. *The Visit*, by a Swiss dramatist named Friedrich Dürrenmatt, could be rather easily dissected by any bright student of

153

REVIEWS

theater form. The central conflict has been staged and decided by the end of the first act. Moreover—and stemming really from this circumstance—a good deal of the later detail seems motivated as much by the needs of the playwright as by the imperatives of his characters, and an inconvenient proportion of the impact has no deeper source than carefully staged visual effects. It may be that Peter Brook, the director, has over-embellished the play—a transparent vehicle for this almost legendary couple—but he did have the problem of keeping the audience occupied for a long time after the trap was sprung.

Despite such reservations as I have, the play is arresting and memorably odd. The plot is as simple as an aphorism. The richest widow in the world returns after many years to the place of her birth, a town in an unspecified but Germanic section of Europe. The town is almost dead, and it develops that she has impoverished it by secretly buying and suspending all the small industry on which it had depended. But the natives do not know this and anticipate great assistance from a lady whose philanthropy is world-acclaimed. She does make a stunning offer—she will give the town a billion marks (wild rejoicing), but on the one condition that the town will kill the well-loved Anton Schill, local grocer (the two protagonists are of course played by Miss Fontanne and Mr. Lunt). It is recalled that, when a youth, this man denied being the father of her child, produced witnesses (now shown to be perjured) to name her a trollop, and caused her to seek her fortune as a whore. She subsequently married Levantine oil. The shocked town cheers Herr Schill to the echo, but Madame Zachanassian remarks that she is quite prepared to wait, and that concludes the first act.

The rest of the play works at details: how the townspeople begin to buy on credit in a mood of optimism whose source they will not acknowledge; how their would-be benefactor gets married but sends her husband back to South America so that she can resolve in death her love-hate for Schill; how the town rationalizes what it will do in the operation of high, though delayed, justice. The nice irony, what holds you, is that Schill really does deserve punishment and that his neighbors are his proper judges. The billion marks corrupt them even as the money wakes them to their duty.

The tone of all this is curious, but nevertheless insinuating. If one were being rigorous, it might not hold together, partly because of the author's eclectic restlessness, partly because of the surface gaiety the Lunts like to stamp on everything they do. Madame Zachanassian travels with an entourage consisting of the judge who presided at her trial, now called Bobby and acting as an entranced major-domo; the

THE VISIT & THE FIRST BORN

two false witnesses, blinded and presumably emasculated and now serving as attendant musicians; a pair of American thugs who double as torturers and bearers of their lady's sedan chair; and a black panther (her nickname for Schill had been "black panther"). It is a little difficult to maintain serious attention in the presence of so much *outré* luggage from Beckett, Sartre, Kafka, and the sideshow. American audiences can scarcely fail to drop occasionally into the mood of comic-strip frightfulness.

Then, too, the behavior described is concentration-camp desperation, but the town of Güllen does not appear to have been pushed to the simplicity of the concentration camp. The citizens talk of desperation, but no one looks desperate—only rather down at the heels. I suspect that the Lunts do not like real pain to appear on their stage: a genteel shabbiness is as far as they are prepared to go. Therefore, if you wish really to be attacked by *The Visit*, you must make yourself unusually vulnerable. Otherwise, it is very obviously a play.

As for the production, Miss Fontanne and her husband provide two bright pools of competence around which some excellent acting is done. With the Lunts, of course, competence has become an art in itself—only I felt that they were acting according to their unsurpassed stage knowledge, not according to what these parts impelled from them. The work is perhaps too easy for them—what they do works so well that they are rarely forced to *be*. The supporting cast is large and I cannot itemize it. There are no false or ill-proportioned performances—Mr. Brook's professional good taste has touched everyone, and I call particular attention to the conduct of Eric Porter as the burgomaster and to Peter Woodthorpe as the school master. Each, when the occasion comes, steps forward as a firm center of human personality. As much as anything, their work is what makes this production disturbing and more than a somewhat novel shadow box for the high pantomime of the Lunts.

Because it is written in blank verse and deals for the most part with "great matters," Christopher Fry's language evokes in all of us an echo of the Elizabethans. It is, however, a disheartening echo. The Elizabethans beat out a new language, a bright weapon, whose richness and drive supported the energy of their passions. Fry is a devotee of words; language is for him a romp—all the bright adjectives, the agile verbs, the charming plays of juxtaposition and surprise. As the tension of his plays rises, so does Fry's loquacity. He drowns passion in speech, makes actors of his characters, and has

REVIEWS

never considered the heart too full for words. He is not interested in the battles of the drawing room, and lacks the assassination of wit needed for such encounters, but he makes an ingenious plaything out of a heroic style.

In *The Firstborn* (Coronet Theatre, Broadway), the manner is peculiarly depressing. The book of Exodus will not lend itself to brocade; it is a terrible story, a parable of stone, and it cannot by verbal embellishment be made palatable to humanists. Fry has supposed that the tyrants of Egypt and the children of Israel were people not unlike ourselves, except that they conversed rather more eloquently. His Moses is an idealist, a social reformer; his Pharaoh, a manager of Empire who comes from his siestas in a mood that could be induced by reading in Voltaire. Faced with the punishments of an implacable Jahveh—the plagues of locusts, of frogs; the Nile water turned to blood—he says in effect that people are forever blaming the weather on the administration. And Pharaoh's sister, she who found Moses and gave him his life, appears in her years of late maturity as a maiden lady whose cultivated intelligence and strong feelings have been turned toward wry melancholy by lack of commitment. Her contemporaries live in Jane Austen.

The theory that human nature is pretty much the same anywhere and any time is one of the superficialities of world-mindedness and liberal brotherhood. It makes our dealings with the Chinese, the Arabs, and the Russians even more difficult than they need to be; in the cause of psychological identification, it extracts the armatures from the great legends of our heritage. If you think of Moses and Pharaoh as two pig-headed men, one of whom possessed the secret weapon of God's wrath; if you must sympathize with Moses because, although his team wins, victory costs him the life of his old playmate, Ramses—you have lost a great deal and gained, I think, very little. Exodus is not social history, however much it may be based on events; it is a concept of man's relationship to God through which the human race has passed. Traces of that concept color our spirits, but that is not to say that God spoke from a storm cloud to men and women aware of themselves as post-Renaissance individuals. This is anachronism, not imagination.

In this production, *The Firstborn* plays better than it is. Katharine Cornell, Anthony Quayle, and Torin Thatcher give it considerable visual and oratorical dignity. They move well and they speak impressively; being actors of some virtuosity, they obviously enjoy the exercise of Fry's ornate language, though inevitably it makes mouthpieces of them. The result, nevertheless, is turgid and non-

156

communicative; the action stalls and the cataclysms turn perversely funny in this rational atmosphere.

A Touch of the Poet, by Eugene O'Neill (1958)

Seven or perhaps eleven plays to encompass all things American from the Revolution to The Way We Live Now; after a number of false starts, the solemn burning of aborted fragments in a hotel room in Boston with only one completed play surviving, *A Touch of the Poet*, set in 1828. What could sound more unpromising? Especially in the wake of that stunning, mawkish bore *Long Day's Journey into Night*, whose production and reception on Broadway resembled nothing so much as a state funeral, with black plumes waving and sonorous eulogies of the dead master from those who gave so little aid and comfort to the living master for his *The Iceman Cometh* in 1946.

I went to the theater expecting the worst. Even before the curtain went up, irritable phrases formed In my mind (how often, I wonder, does this happen to professional reviewers?). "Rhetoric is the attempt of the will to do the work of the imagination": W. B. Yeats. . . . I would definitely use that one, for if there was ever a rhetorician, it was the late master. Then I recalled my old resentment against his misuse of the *Oresteia* when, having crudely borrowed the relationships, the melodrama, the portentousness of Aeschylus, he blithely left out the whole idea of justice, which was, to say the least, the point of that tragedy. And, finally, the maddening urge of American primitives to include everything—to write cycles, tetralogies, epics, the whole hee-haw of the Thomas Wolfes as they list the rivers of America in alphabetical order, their minds innocent of civilization, their self-love filling the empty plains of a new continent that ought to have a tragedy, though just what it is no one has yet discovered.

The curtain rose. Two minor characters started talking. One's heart sank as they explained at length necessary secrets. By then I had worked through Henry James: "It takes a very great deal of history to make a very small bit of literature," when suddenly the stage was bathed in light: Helen Hayes and Kim Stanley were on; the drama had begun, and O'Neill blazed.

A Touch of the Poet is a beautiful play, beautifully presented (at the Little Theatre, Broadway). The presentation has but one fault, to which I shall come last; its virtues more than compensate. The play is *rose*, not *noire*, and it has a deliberate artifice, which I prefer to the shapeless black melodramas O'Neill usually preferred. Then, too,

REVIEWS

1828 is just right. Andrew Jackson; the rise of the democrats, the fall of John Quincy Adams and with him that oligarchical, gentlemanly society that began the nation. All this is symbolically right, and pleasing. It is time we used our bit of history, especially since the New York audience has practically no sense of the United States before the First World War. Lincoln, of course, is recalled, glumly. It is known that there was some sort of Revolution at the beginning, and that's it—almost as if the critic-historian Van Wyck Brooks had never lived.

O'Neill reminds us of our past. He indicates the rise of the Yankee merchants, busy, practical, contemptuous of the old aristocratic principle. With precision and—for him—economy, he sets the scene for his moral action, which is the crushing of a man's false pride, his absorption into the main, his final realization that he has lived a bogus life, presuming to a position both worldly and moral to which he has no right but the one—and this is significant—of wanting.

Cornelius Melody (Eric Portman) was born of Irish peasants, served bravely in the Peninsular campaign, became a British officer, got pregnant a peasant girl, married her, came to America, opened a tavern, and failed. He torments his wife (Helen Hayes) and his daughter (Kim Stanley); he quotes Byron to himself in a mirror. He assumes the manner of a king in exile. He is laughed at by the Yankees but adored by his wife, who understands him perhaps more profoundly in O'Neill than she would in life: she sees how lonely he is in his vanity (very much like George Meredith, this), and she loves him. He is alternately mocked and served by his daughter, a finely realized character: part dreamer, part materialist, veering this way and that, ambivalent and strange.

The story is simple. The daughter loves a Yankee of the new merchant class. He has escaped his family to write poetry but eventually he will go into business—happily. The girl must marry him to escape the world of unpaid bills and false pride. She also loves the Yankee and wants to cheat neither of them. His family deplores the match. They try to buy her off. Melody, drunk, goes to challenge the boy's father to a duel and is beaten up (dressed as a major of the British army) by the police; he returns, pride gone, and in an incredible *volte-face* chooses reality to prideful illusion: he is only a Mick and a failure who loves his wife. The girl gets her Yankee, and all ends well.

What makes the play work thematically is the examination of Melody's dream world. It may well be that this is the most significant American theme, at least in the twentieth century. Reality does not please Melody; he chooses to invent his past; he tells lies; he believes

158

A TOUCH OF THE POET

the lies and for various reasons is abetted in them by those about him. O'Neill has often dealt with this theme (in *The Iceman Cometh*, for example) and so have many of our best writers, most notably Tennessee Williams in *A Streetcar Named Desire*.

Which brings me to an interesting question: What is it in modern American life (1828 is as good a date as any to start the "modern") that forces so many to prefer fantasy to reality? One observes them, at any cocktail party: charming people, boring people, intelligent, dull—people of all sorts, telling lies, which no one much minds. It is all a game. Who shall I be? Who am I? And the person who drops the brick of truth is the only villain. It is to this that the audience of *A Touch of the Poet* most responds. There is an element of Melody in all of us, and one watches with horrified fascination as he is brought at last to the truth about himself.

As for the production, it is splendid. Harold Clurman has taken the three most mannered actresses in our theater and imposed the play's manner on them with complete success. Miss Hayes is strong and direct and very moving; her cute pony-prancing has been severely curbed. Betty Field, whose old voice I always liked, has quite a new one that works admirably in her single scene. But the production's glory is Kim Stanley's performance. The old tricks are there but they glitter, and she gets the character's ambivalence with such fairness that one is reminded of a character in Dostoevsky: light and shadow mysteriously fluctuating; the "yes" and the simultaneous "no." It is fine work.

The production's flaw is the performance of Eric Portman. He is a fine technical actor whose attack here is unfortunately wrong. He belongs, at least when he plays bravuras, to what I think of as the "voice-music" school of English acting, whose honorary president is Sir Ralph Richardson. The voice-musicians hear some strange melody in the wings to which in counterpoint they sing their lines. Their songs are often fascinating but almost always irrelevant to the play's meaning. Mr. Portman is far better in the small, neat plays of Terence Rattigan, because in the superficially realistic idiom one can gobble and honk and sigh and mumble and the meaning is always clear. Major Melody needs grandeur and thought, neither of which Mr. Portman provides. As I watched him strut about the stage on his spindly legs, his swollen body held tightly erect, like a pineapple on two sticks, I was haunted by *déjà vu*; not until the final scene did I recall who it was he reminded me of: a maleficent Mr. Micawber, from Dickens' *David Copperfield*—and the moment one plays Melody like Micawber, O'Neill is brought down.

159

REVIEWS

Happily, there are so many good things in this production—including the play—that the thing works, and one is pleased that Eugene O'Neill's last play should be at once so human and so gently wise.

Epitaph for George Dillon, by John Osborne (1958)

If the point of your play is to be that your hero is a hollow sham, prudence suggests that you contrive to conceal it until quite far along in the proceedings. In *Epitaph for George Dillon* (John Golden Theatre, Broadway), John Osborne and Anthony Creighton make Dillon's emptiness clear before he has ever set foot upon the stage and devote the rest of the evening to showing the various ways in which a vacuum is without content.

The play has a certain virtuoso appeal, for not only is Dillon without any qualities that could move you to response, but everyone around him shares in the negation, and it is surprising that a stage can be kept looking lively and varied while the actors work out permutations on the concept of zero. Perhaps the fact that the cast, led by Robert Stephens, Eileen Herlie, and Alison Leggatt, is composed of resourceful actors adept at making their presence strongly felt (Stephens is a regular windmill of self-generated emotion) has something to do with it; but it is also true that Mr. Osborne showed early a brilliant understanding of stage situation.

That is a mechanical affair, though, and not to be confused with dramatic situation. Dramatically, the play defeats itself by telling you that these are negligible people, incapable of growth or change, and then proving it by permitting nothing to grow or change. The stage does not offer either enlightenment or entertainment when all that is to be discovered about the characters is evident in the immediate impression each one makes.

George Dillon, self-styled artistic failure, is patently a parasite living on the general credulity that does not look under the bushel when a petulant loafer says his light is hidden there. The Elliott family on which he feeds is patently meant to be fed on and will be no better and no worse for the experience. (The Elliotts are representatives of the middle class, which the *nouveau* literates in England feel compelled to denounce in filial horror.) The notion of a thin-skinned man doomed to live among people who say "this occasion calls for a drink" does not rouse pity if he has made no slightest attempt to escape. The

160

maudlin deflation of Dillon in the closing scene looked, thus, like a good actor's trick of shrinking in his clothes.

A playwright cannot trot a lot of people on stage and simply say, "Did you ever see such a bunch of fools and phonies?" The answer is that we have seen a good many fools and phonies, that we think we are pretty good at spotting them, and that it is the playwright's job to show us either that our acumen is less sharp than we had supposed or that there are curious reasons behind the distressing waste. Anyone who really believes that there is nothing to be said beyond that flat angry question has a right to his opinion, but the theater is not his *métier*. He belongs in some work where people are counted, not discussed. And I am not talking about the artist's supposed obligation to society—only about his obligation tb show us what he has discovered when he calls us to his booth. *Epitaph for George Dillon* is not a discovery, it is a tautology.

Gypsy, by Arthur Laurents (1959)

When a show fails, you can usually filter out from the debacle a whole series of contributing errors. But when a show succeeds, the triumph is apt to look so inevitable that you can only wonder why success occurs so seldom. *Gypsy*, for example: this new show at the Broadway Theatre (New York) looks as easy as swinging in a hammock. True, it has intelligence, imagination, talent, and taste, but are these virtues so rare in America's thriving commercial theater? A good question, if rhetorical.

Anyhow, *Gypsy* is a soaring delight: funny, moving, brilliant, satiric, beautiful, bitter, perceptive, rowdy—in short, great. It is based on a valid story and put together by experienced theater people who knew exactly what they wanted to achieve and who made no mistakes at all. This results in a steady progress, a consistent tone, and a general relevance that can best be summed up in the generalization "style." It would be boring if I were to list the whole roster of credits, inserting a rapturous phrase after each name.

Nonetheless, for the record, here are the principal heroes of the occasion: *Gypsy* is produced by David Merrick and Leland Hayward; the book is by Arthur Laurents (from the memoirs of Gypsy Rose Lee, a.k.a. Rose Louise Hovick), the music by Jule Styne, the lyrics by Stephen Sondheim; Jerome Robbins directed; the sets are by Jo Mielziner, the costumes by Raoul Pène du Bois; the three leading performers are Ethel Merman, Sandra Church, and Jack Klugman.

REVIEWS

That summary, however, by no means exhausts the talent—if I could, I would list every name in the program, right down to house physician Benjamin A. Gilbert, who I am prepared to believe is the best all-around medical man practicing between Times Square and Columbus Circle.

What gives *Gypsy* depth and substance is the tension between its surface pleasures and the underlying bitterness of its story. It is, for a wonder, a musical based on an ugly state of affairs. June Havoc and her sister Louise were the child slaves of a mother driven by the fury of frustrated ambition. From babyhood, they toured the third-rate vaudeville houses of the United States in a dreadful song-and-dance act of their mother's concoction. June was the star; Louise, in boy's clothes, was her untalented support; there was a chorus of dejected moppets.

This "child act" continued long after its performers had ceased to be children; in fact, the ordeal went on until June eloped with the troupe's male dancer. Mother, her ego courageously surviving this betrayal, rebuilt the act around the faithful Louise. Then one fateful and starving week, they were booked into a burlesque house. They had been hired as a sop to the police, but on their last night one of the theater's regular *artistes* failed to return from the saloon and the hangdog Louise was pushed out through the curtains as that new and sensational stripper, Gypsy Rose Lee.

What sort of woman the mother really was I do not know. For the purposes of Ethel Merman, she is drawn as a creature of powerful, earthy charm: witty, resourceful, courageous, infectiously optimistic—in sum, a monster of unrealized talents. This gives Miss Merman scope to display her thoroughly realized talents. Even so, it must have cost her some anxiety to take on the part. Successful entertainers do not act; they project themselves. Unlike actors, therefore, they will usually refuse hostile parts as damaging to their carefully constructed image. The last exception I can recall was Bing Crosby in the movie of Clifford Odets's *The Country Girl*; Miss Merman's part is not that cruel, but it falls short of being endearing.

It is also not customary for the star of a big show to work like a stevedore for just short of two hours and then to turn the climax of the evening over to a relatively unknown actress. The last twenty minutes of *Gypsy* belong to Sandra Church. Miss Merman, It is true, has the last scene, but what you carry home with you is the memory of Miss Church prowling the stage in that strange, ritualistic stripper's lope. Every stripper needs a gimmick, the show says in one of its most uproarious scenes. Gypsy Rose Lee's gimmick was refinement, and

162

Miss Church, who suddenly emerges out of misery into heart-pounding loveliness, shows precisely how the gimmick worked. It is beautiful mimicry, and it is beautiful sex.

I should have placed in the honor roll above Karen Moore and Jacqueline Mayro, who play Louise and June when they were genuine children. They are the horrible essence of juvenile talent, and their performances are one of the feats of Mr. Robbins' almost miraculous direction. I will just add that Jack Klugman, playing Mother Rose's lover and the act's booking agent—an intelligent and sensitive man who sweats with weakness—gives a performance more eloquent than you will often see on the dramatic stage; that Mr. Styne's music is crisp and witty; that Mr. Mielziner and Mr. du Bois have put together a set of beautiful stage pictures that are also full of funny and nostalgic comment; and that the show boasts the most elegant two-man dancing cow in recent stage history.

Now I will stop—I sound to myself like a water spaniel wagging his tail over a piece of steak. Still, how often does the musical theater serve steak?

The Tempest & *Henry V*, by William Shakespeare (1960)

Over the past several summers, the American Shakespeare Festival at Stratford, Connecticut, has developed a distinct style for presenting the great repertory. Taste is so creamy at Stratford as to be almost edible; it is a designer's theater.

This emphasis on a confectionary vision stems no doubt from the current scholarly position that the Elizabethan stage, far from being bare space cloaked only in passionate imagination, was a sumptuous tabernacle hung with rare stuffs, peopled with fabulous throngs, and capable of marvels. Even so, I think it an error today to set Shakespeare's plays as though they were jewels. Ours is a rich and materialistic culture, but true flamboyance does not come naturally to us. If Shakespeare flung gold and ermine over his players, doubtless his players had exuberance enough to carry the elegance; ours simply do not. When in *The Tempest* Alonso's followers appear in suits and trappings out of a conquistador fairy tale, they may delight the eye, but they are also reduced to manikins. Every extra, every halberd-bearer, would have to glow with Hotspur's panache to prevent a scene so dressed from becoming a waxworks. We don't have the resources for such riotous expenditure of energy, and it is a question whether

REVIEWS

we would profit from the effect if we could stage it. Wealth and busyness do not uplift us—we have too much of both.

Furthermore, the spectacles that Stratford has encouraged its designers to stage are less elegant than showy. They would appeal most powerfully, perhaps, to an audience that had dined at Longchamps and driven to the theater in a Thunderbird. Surely there is something wrong with a scheme for *Twelfth Night* that urges the critics to refer coyly to *H.M.S. Pinafore*. And surely it is a sad waste, in *The Tempest*, to have Prospero conjure up a three-part, stage-crowding tableau for the delight of the betrothed lovers, only to produce a conversation piece that could be duplicated from the gimcrack shelves of any Mexican import shop. I know the idea is to be amusing, but the effect is to be cute; I suspect that the designers have been encouraged to look on Shakespeare as an excuse for their fertile whimsicality.

Against such background, the plays themselves seem smooth but uncommitted. Insofar as one remembers them, it is in terms of individual performance rather than organized productions. Katharine Hepburn's Viola in *Twelfth Night*, for one, is surprisingly convincing. Miss Hepburn's innate gawkiness serves her well in the masquerade, and this year she has considerably curbed the suburban whinny that gives her stage voice its weird individuality and can turn Shakespeare's purest music into slapstick. For his part, Morris Carnovsky is an elegant, often penetrating Feste; he gives a substance I haven't seen conveyed before in impersonations of this most agile of clowns. Loring Smith and O. Z. Whitehead as Toby Belch and Andrew Aguecheek, on the other hand, are at once hectic and pedestrian. They suffer the most from the transposition of the play to what appears to be a pre-Victorian Cowes regatta. As for Richard Waring's Malvolio, he is lackluster, and that is the role that keys the play. The theory that Shakespeare, being immortal, can speak against any background, breaks down soonest with his eccentrics and his bawdry. What shows as wit and high spirits in a Renaissance context becomes vulgarity and debauchery in the straitened atmosphere of Jane Austen's England. *Twelfth Night* is not a work of surpassing poetry; if it does not jig and sparkle, it is mere foolishness.

In *The Tempest*, Clayton Corzatte offers an Ariel that is seldom embarrassing—no faint praise, considering the Ariels that customarily skip about our stages. And Earle Hyman's Caliban is first-rate—he conveys the brute's poignant glimmerings of the soul that eludes it; that, rather than virtuoso beastliness, is what counts in the part. But Joyce Ebert is a dim Miranda, John Ragin a sheepish Ferdinand; and, surprisingly, Mr. Carnovsky falls completely short of Prospero. He

164

THE TEMPEST & HENRY V

works his miracles with a stiff caution, like a vaudeville magician who is not sure his offstage accomplices will catch the cues. He chops the air with the basic manual of stage gestures, and he recites at the audience as though lecturing it on the special meaning of *The Tempest* in the Shakespeare legend. All the tricks show and none of the magic takes wing.

Certainly, *The Tempest* is difficult, but if it is to be played at all, it must be done with confidence. If Shakespeare was running through his illusionist's repertory for one last time—offering, as it were, a farewell evening of star turns—then director and cast must believe that he knew how to bring it off. Timidity is disastrous and a lavish timidity, as though to help the old man through a dubious enterprise, is fatal. Productions like this of *The Tempest* are what give the impression that Stratford adores Shakespeare as a monument but does not really believe in him as a playwright.

Belief in Shakespeare is not just a critic's banality. You can see how well it works in Central Park these evenings, where the New York Shakespeare Festival is again offering its free productions (a largesse so bountiful as to sweeten the summer temper of the whole city). The Festival's style was established in previous years by Stuart Vaughan. Its method is to present the plays with maximum clarity of line and movement, to let them run fleetly and unembellished, and to assume that the audience will be caught up in the excitement of momentous deeds and bold personalities. The Central Park productions are staged as though they had been written for this company by a master craftsman who knew precisely the interests and appetites of his audience. It is a simple theory, which is not at all to say that it is easy.

Joseph Papp, the Festival's producer, also directed the first play, *King Henry V*; *Measure for Measure* and *The Taming of the Shrew* will follow at approximately three-week intervals. For the initial production, the minimal platform stage beneath the Belvedere served admirably as Shakespeare's "wooden O," and Leonard Cimino, as the Chorus, swept the bannered hosts of England and France across the scene with bravura zest. Mr. Papp's *Henry V* was a tapestry of proud enterprise pricked out with spirited personality. James Ray, as Henry, was perhaps better able to convey the young king's coltish charm than his ambitious mettle—it is a fault common to our present-day Hals; we seem unable to rear actors who can express command within a context of youth. And I thought that Arthur Malet's Charles VI was more waspishly funny than the text justifies. It played well enough this way, but the King of France is not meant to steal laughs from the clowns.

REVIEWS

But the other leading figures, as from time to time they swung into focus on the merry-go-round of the action, were a varied delight. Louis Zorich, Roberts Blossom, and Albert Quinton, as Bardolph, Nym, and Pistol, were rogues right off the streets; John Call, as the Welsh captain, Fluellen, touched the dignity beneath the bantam; Kathleen Widdoes made a delicious Katherine, and she and Jacqueline Chambord played the famous English lesson with infectious pleasure in their own foolery; Thomas Aldredge's Dauphin compelled respect as a dangerous fop. The large company of princes and men at arms was handsome and moved with a hard masculinity that gave the largely implied clash of armies an impact you felt in your own spine. Moreover, the love and intelligence that went into this production became evident from such small matters as the protective tenderness that Henry and his brothers feel for that decent old man, Sir Thomas Erpingham. The scene is exceedingly brief, but Karl Williams played Sir Thomas with an antique valor that etched itself sharply into the effect of the evening.

I can guess the reasons, but nevertheless I regret two of Mr. Papp's cuts. The omission of the opening scene between those calculating prelates, Canterbury and Ely, blurred Shakespeare's bitter understanding of the causes of war; and the failure to record the death of Falstaff robbed the friends of that mighty barrel warrior and catch-as-catch-can philosopher of the chance to mourn his passing. Otherwise, I scarcely see how a better scheme could have been devised for bringing Agincourt to the attention of the people at large—which is what both Shakespeare and Joseph Papp understood to be the job at hand.

Krapp's Last Tape, by Samuel Beckett (1960)

Sleep is lovely, death is better still,
Not to have been born is of course the miracle.

I quote these lines from Heinrich Heine, as recently translated by Robert Lowell, because I'm tired of people pinching their mouths at Samuel Beckett for celebrating the nausea of existence. Most men feel it, certainly all poets do—Heine's lines are a paraphrase of Sophocles—and it has nothing to do with despair, which is the related charge leveled against Beckett. He states his case—the most recent of many similar statements—in a one-character, one-act play, *Krapp's Last Tape*, which opened last January at the Provincetown Playhouse (Off-Broadway) in New York's Greenwich Village. As I expect to

166

KRAPP'S LAST TAPE

make clear shortly, the hero of *Krapp's Last Tape* has been trapped in a cage for thirty years, but I doubt that the least sensitive member of the audience would care to put his arm through those bars. Krapp has the stare of a badger; despair has not tamed it.

It is curious about Beckett that, though he deals in the most dire experience, his fables do not depress. There is a salty virility to his people, an assumption of equality with juggernaut, that gives off the exciting smell of human pride. "Use your head," says Hamm in Beckett's play *Endgame*, "use your head, can't you, you're on earth, there's no cure for that!" No more is there, but it does not occur to a Beckett character to take that grim fact lying down. Figuratively speaking, that is. His heroes are not infrequently lying down when we first meet them.

Prone or supine—Beckett's people give a good deal of thought to the relative advantages of the two positions. Supine, one enjoys a breadth of vision, but prone, one can get over the ground more readily, gripping with the knees and digging forward with the fingernails. Proceeding that way, you may advance a good twenty yards in a day, and who's to say that a man should reasonably aspire to more? The hub of Beckett's insight—the recurring vision of his recent novels *Molloy, Malone Dies, The Unnamable*—is that experience is subjective, inviolable, and immeasurable. Molloy, finding himself on the beach, gathers a little trove of sixteen stones, admirable for sucking, and works out a procedure for enjoying them in orderly rotation. Is this an achievement of less stature than Isaac Newton's formulation of the laws of motion? Well, that would depend on whether you put your question to Newton or to Malloy. Or do you say that society will judge such matters? I refrain from telling you what Malloy would say if you came at him with a word like "society."

Or consider Malone, also representing the human race. He is almost dead when we first encounter him, and at the end, there is just the difference that he is quite dead. He lies on a bed, he knows not where; brought to this pass, he knows not how; fed by anonymous hands that come no more. He has possessions—one yellow shoe, a hat with the brim gone, a photograph of a donkey with downcast eyes, a needle embedded in two corks, a scrap of newspaper, a stone—and these he can reach and stir with a long stick, for he enjoys the use of his arms. In bed with him are two pencils, one of which he can no longer find, and a notebook. That is important, for in the time left to him Malone will tell stories—write them, rather, because the "others do not endure, but vanish, into thin air." Then he will make an inventory of his possessions, and then he will die.

REVIEWS

I cannot possibly say whether we are with him for twenty minutes, or two months, or ten years. What I can be sure of is that the acquaintance is amusing and enriching. That virtual corpse, abandoned in a bed of casters, is an adventurer and commander to shadow Alexander. I am not trafficking in paradoxes; Malone is man stripped to artist.

We are the only animal that sings its own saga, and which is more important, the singing or the doing? It is immaterial in Malone's case, for he *does* in order to sing. He grasps life because it gives him a story to tell, and when it is done, he is done. Malone, infinitely vulnerable and infinitely tough: "This club is mine. . . . It is stained with blood, but insufficiently, insufficiently. I have defended myself, ill, but I have defended myself."

With Krapp, though, the adventure is different. The others—Molloy, Malone, Hamm, etc.—as good as dead to begin with, live off the transfusions of their art. Krapp, on the contrary, suffers art to cut him down in his prime and then lives on to see himself as a mirror of snapshots receding through the years. If science has its martyrs, so does art—men withered by the invisible, burning rays. Krapp, I believe, is one of these.

Krapp's Last Tape is the outrageous title of an outrageous play. Imagine! A feeble, nearly blind and deaf, solitary and half-drunk old man, crouching in a squalid room, subsisting on bananas and playing to himself (commenting the while) old tape recordings of his own voice—recordings, moreover, that consist in no small part of comments on still earlier tapes. Is this theater? Well, yes, it is, outrageous, of course, but very much theater. Being outrageous in the theater is nothing new for Beckett. There was that matter of Godot who never showed up, and of the animated *Endgame*, three of whose four characters were immobilized, and two of those in ash cans. Another play, among Beckett's many, is *Act Without Words I*. It takes place in a featureless desert and involves the pantomime of man beset by objects—a tree, a pair of scissors, a carafe of water, a knotted rope, etc., all lowered from the flies—and by a commanding whistle that emanates from various points offstage. It reads as though it would play like man's fate, caught beneath a burning glass.

These capers of Beckett's are a function of his virtuosity. He plays in the theater as a hawk plays in the air currents—with the exuberance of being at home. Beckett carries a stage within his head. When he writes a scene, he knows how it will materialize, how long it will take, where its center of gravity will lie, what impact it will make. This is something outside, in addition to, the dialogue—it is the kinetic sense

KRAPP'S LAST TAPE

of the theater. (O'Neill, I would guess, was like that.) When Donald Davis, who created the role of Krapp in New York, and Alan Schneider, who directed him (and directed also, in earlier seasons, *Waiting for Godot* and *Endgame*), began to move the old man around the stage, they found that Beckett already had the whole piece moving in the script. Every pause, every repetition, every agonized progress from A to B had been timed with that enigmatic metronome that sets a play's pace.

I mean this sort of thing:

> *fumbles in his pockets, encounters the banana, takes it out, peers at it, puts it back, fumbles, brings out the envelope, fumbles, puts back envelope, looks at his watch, gets up and goes backstage into darkness. Ten seconds. Sound of bottle against glass, then brief siphon. Ten seconds. Bottle against glass alone. Ten seconds. He comes back a little unsteadily . . .*

When Messrs. Schneider and Davis stuck to the letter of such instructions, the play marched. When they experimented with sequence, or invented or subtracted, the action stalled. They added an overhead light and, in correspondence with Beckett, worked out some business to italicize a phrase they feared the American audiences would ride over. Otherwise they worked as did Arturo Toscanini with a score— they materialized what was given.

Acting in a one-part play is an odd experience. Mr. Davis, who talks of *Krapp's Last Tape* with loving possessiveness—it has been, after all, *his* play, in a way not often given to an actor—says that the problem is to keep the acting alive, performance after performance. In the theater, he says, you expect to feel minute differences, from evening to evening, in the thrust and parry of your colleagues, and adjusting to these keeps the blood running in your own performance. With *Krapp's Last Tape* there is only the recording machine for foil, and it makes the problem the more difficult, for it never varies by a hair or a decibel. (Most spectators, by the way, assume that the machine onstage is a dummy and that the sound is controlled by a hand offstage. Beckett, who had never seen a tape recorder, thought it could be worked that way, but Messrs. Davis and Schneider found that, what with the repeats and jumps called for in the script, the hazards of synchronization were too great. During the long rehearsals, Mr. Davis acquired Krapp's own cranky mastery of the gadget, slapping it around as he would a wife who had lost her charm and putting it scornfully through its paces.)

REVIEWS

The resilient give-and-take that Mr. Davis needed in the months of his performance (he left the play late in the spring to join the American Shakespeare Festival at Stratford, Connecticut) was supplied in large part by Mr. Schneider, who, whatever his other projects, made it a practice of dropping in on the show every few days. Once, when Mr. Schneider was out of town for a time, Mr. Davis felt his performance slipping and could not put his finger on the trouble. Mr. Schneider spotted it his first evening back in town. Mr. Davis is a vigorous man of thirty-two: Krapp, a phenomenon of decrepitude ("The sour cud and the iron stool"), is sixty-nine. The strain of maintaining this gap of years is considerable, and Mr. Davis, with no one to react against, had been the lopping the years off.

There is no curtain at *Krapp's Last Tape*. When you take your seat, a dark, fusty room confronts you. There is a table at stage center, with a recorder and some cardboard boxes on it, a light overhead, a shabby chair alongside. That is all you can see, and you can imagine what you care to imagine beyond vision. After a time the lights go down. When they come up again, Krapp sits in the chair (in a coma?), the recorder cover in his lap. It is his birthday, the one day each year when he records a new tape. He sits there a moment, staring blindly, and then begins one of those great vaudeville pantomimes that are Beckett's hallmark: the fumble through the pockets, the watch held painfully to the eye, the aimless shifting of papers, the bunch of keys to the eye, the right key in the fingers, the shuffle around the table (good God, the painful shuffle!) to the first drawer.

Unlock the drawer, open it, peer in, pull out a tape, hold it up to the light, put it back, close the drawer, lock it; keys to the eye again, select another, open the second drawer, peer in, feel around with the paw, out comes a banana (laughter—you always laugh at your own risk at a Beckett play), hold up the banana (Beckett says in a letter to Mr. Schneider that Krapp displays objects with the overweening candor of a stage magician showing his innocent props), close drawer, lock it, keys back in the pocket, straighten up and face audience, stroke the banana, peel it, drop skin to floor, stick banana into mouth and stare vacantly into space (you may be wishing now that you could have your laugh back), suddenly chomp down on it and gobble it with soft eagerness (no teeth), pacing the while. Stumble on the banana peel (of course), kick it into the pit, finish the fruit, hobble back to chair, full stop.

Then a sigh, then out with the keys and up to the eye, and we're off again. Not quite the same, though, for this time Krapp resists the banana even after it is in his mouth (a tape of thirty years ago, which

170

KRAPP'S LAST TAPE

he eventually will play, says, "Have just eaten I regret to say three bananas and only with difficulty refrained from a fourth. Fatal things for a man with my condition. . . . Cut 'em out!"). He stows the banana in a vest pocket. (This became an increasing trial to Mr. Davis, and on some evenings he omitted the rediscovery of the banana.) Krapp shuffles off with lunatic briskness into the darkness, and a cork pops—the first of several such pops from the dark. He emerges with an old ledger, puts it on the table, wipes his mouth with his hand, his hand on his coat, and rubs the hands briskly together. Life, it appears, is about to begin.

What life? Why, the only life that matters to this diseased, dirty, drunken old hermit—the recording of Krapp's story. But Krapp has no story. What he has is the iteration of a spot on a tape where experience got stuck thirty years ago. Krapp, as I have said, is a martyr to art, one who was burned. It is dangerous work—we've known that from as long ago as the caves—but we choose to overlook the hazards, for we need the product. Has Krapp himself been an artist? Quite probably—at least he was a man overwhelmed by language: the sound of words, their power to make experience real, their power, in the end, to supplant experience. In fact, Krapp was too vulnerable to words; he should never have taken up the trade.

There are all sorts of signs. Looking up the tape he wants in the ledger, Krapp reads out (they are his first words): "Ah! Box . . . three . . . spool . . . five." Abruptly his head goes up, he listens, and then, "Spool! Spooool!" The sound spirals out and up like a lovely curl of light—the sensuality of words. After much more business with boxes, keys, and drawers, he locates the tape and flings it on the recorder like a practiced but drunken engineer. When it has been running a while, with pauses for Krapp to savor the old presence of himself, this passage occurs: ". . . there is of course the house on the canal where mother lay a-dying, in the late autumn, after her long viduity . . ." Krapp starts up, switches off, reels back again: ". . . after her long viduity." He switches off, stares, tries the word on his lips, gets up (no joke for him), stumbles off, and comes back with a dictionary—an unabridged—lays it on the table, and fumbles through the pages: "State—or condition—of being—or remaining—a widow—or widower. (*Looks up. Puzzled.*) Being—or remaining? . . . Also of an animal, especially a bird. . . the vidua or weaver-bird . . . Black plumage of male. . . . (*He looks up. With relish.*) The vidua-bird!" The audience laughs over "spooool" and "viduity" as over the banana. Quite right; it is very funny business—but there is also a chill to it.

Krapp speaks well—that is the link between the youth, the man,

171

REVIEWS

and the old wreck. Words are his tools: a nursemaid (she had threatened to call the police when he had spoken to her) has eyes "like a crysolite"; a ball he is throwing for a dog is a "small, old, black, hard, solid rubber ball"; the shade on his mother's death-room window is "one of those dirty brown roller affairs." Words, it seems, are taking over; "crysolite" is more important than the policeman, the characteristics of the shade weigh more than the death.

See, or hear, what happens. The tape of thirty years spins on:

> . . . at the end of the jetty, in the howling wind, never to be forgotten, when suddenly I saw the whole thing. The vision at last. This I fancy is what I have chiefly to record this evening, against the day when my work will be done and perhaps no place left in my memory, warm or cold, for the miracle that . . . (*hesitates*) . . . for the fire that set it alight. What I suddenly saw then was this, that the belief I had been going on all my life, namely—

But Krapp will not listen: angrily he switches off and reels ahead, picking up: " . . . clear to me at last that the dark I have always struggled to keep under is in reality my most—" Krapp curses and reels on: " . . . unshatterable association until my dissolution of storm and night with the light of the understanding and the fire—" This is awful; he can't get away from it.

Cursing and reeling ahead, he comes at last on a passage he will play again and again. It deals with yet another occasion. I won't quote much of it; there is the danger, when you start quoting Beckett, of going on to the end. He makes a kind of poetry. But the Krapp of those days was in a punt with a girl:

> I noticed a scratch on her thigh and asked her how she came by it. Picking gooseberries, she said. I said again I thought it was hopeless and no good going on, and she agreed, without opening her eyes. (*Pause.*) I asked her to look at me and after a few moments—(*pause*)—after a few moments she did, but the eyes just slits, because of the glare. I bent over her to get them in the shadow and they opened. (*Pause. Low.*) Let me in. (*Pause.*) We drifted in among the flags and stuck. The way they went down, sighing, before the stem!

And so on. It is beautifully stated, and it is the end of Krapp. Aged thirty-nine. What he had discovered that night on the jetty he can no longer bear to remember. Lies, probably the death of life. Whatever it

KRAPP'S LAST TAPE

was, it led him soon thereafter to that "suicide" in the punt. Men live their lives; artists must both live and celebrate; those who are destroyed by art celebrate instead of living. For Krapp the reality became not the punt and the girl and the sun and the flags—but the tape that records all those things.

Now, thirty years later, when he takes up the microphone to record: "Nothing to say, not a squeak. What's a year now? . . . (*Pause.*) Revelled in the word spool. (*With relish.*) Spooool! Happiest moment of the past half million." Then he puts on the old tape again, and the last we see of him he is lying with his head on the machine as the voice memorializes that afternoon and ends: "Perhaps my best years are gone. When there was a chance of happiness. But I wouldn't want them back. Not with the fire in me now. No, I wouldn't want them back."

Krapp's Last Tape is a sad play for anyone; for artists it could be an object of terror. What it means to Beckett, I shall not presume to say, but I could guess that it represents a nightmare escaped. People are always comparing Beckett with James Joyce: they are both Irish, and Beckett is said to have served as Joyce's secretary. In fact, his debt to Joyce is no greater than that of half the writers in his generation, and as for working for him, Beckett says he used sometimes to write letters for him or run literary errands—as did a good many in the English and American colony in Paris of those days. There are, for example, only two references to Beckett in Joyce's letters. One related that Beckett had devised an acrostic on Joyce's name; Beckett now says that he cannot even remember how it went.

What is forgotten is that Beckett's second book was a study of Marcel Proust, written in 1931, before any of his novels or plays. After that he wrote for twenty years with almost no recognition. As for Krapp, shifting around the table, he dislodges a little pile of books. He picks one up: "Seventeen copies sold, of which eleven at trade price to free circulating libraries beyond the seas. Getting known." This remembrance of all things past also brings a laugh.

When you realize that Beckett was forty-six before *Godot* threw him a bridge to the world, you may guess why the unappetizing Krapp, with his bananas and his "spooools," his "viduity," his "crysolite," his visions on the jetty and renunciations in the punt, crawls with such terrifying authority through his litter of impoverishment: "Sometimes wondered in the night if a last effort mightn't—(*Pause.*) Ah finish your booze now and get to your bed. Go on with this drivel in the morning. Or leave it at that. (*Pause.*) Leave it at that."

An artist may go on for quite a time, seeing himself as Molloy or Malone or whichever of those clowns and desperate pilgrims crying

173

REVIEWS

out their stories in a lunar landscape. But when he sees himself as Krapp in his den, cursing and drinking and searching out the right word, fighting terror—"Last fancies. (*Vehemently.*) Keep 'em under!"—and recording new reflections of old reports of sterile years; when that is the way he sees himself, he is going down for the third time. No wonder the play fascinates—we are always asking one another what it must feel like to die.

The Hostage, by Brendan Behan (1961)

This period of our early manhood, perhaps the most impressionistic years of one's life, was an age of revolution. . . . We felt ourselves to be the second generation in this exciting movement of men and ideas. . . . After the 1914 war, and still more after Hitler's war, the young who are not conservatives, fascists, or communists are almost certainly defeatist; they have grown up under the shadow of defeat in the past and the menace of defeat in the future. It is natural, inevitable that they should suffer from the sterility of being angry young men.

Thus Leonard Woolf, in *Sowing*, the first volume of his memoirs, contrasts Lytton Strachey, Clive Bell, John Maynard Keynes, and the other elegant intellectuals of Cambridge just at the turn of the century with the young, influential spirits he sees around him today.

Thus also, from some distance in time and climate, I approach the roaring presence of Brendan Behan. I doubt that Behan would have found himself suitably employed passing tea and advanced sentiments in a Trinity College study, and I feel certain that Woolf's circle would have found little to commend in Behan's *The Hostage*, which blasted Broadway (Cort Theatre) back into life last September. And yet of all the writers who have come up since World War II, Behan has the best right, I think, to identify himself with Woolf's words.

Behan is in rebellion against establishment and propriety; his heroes are tough and disreputable; his speech is rude, and his ability to seize and shake the imagination of his time is prodigious. It is convenient, then, almost to the point of being inevitable, that he should be thought of in company with such marauding talents as Samuel Beckett, Jean Genet, and John Osborne. But the association is more evident than it is comfortable. These others, whatever their differences of manner and attainment, have in common a vision of society in decay: their scenes smell of bad teeth and septic flesh, and the condition they diagnose

174

THE HOSTAGE

does not seem to be reversible. Furthermore, diagnosis is the function they perform. They do not rebel from within a community; they have removed themselves in order to draw up a report, a forecast, if necessary an epitaph. The loneliness such men endure in their work is in itself a heroic renunciation.

There is none of that in Behan. He insults you with his arm around your shoulder and invites you to join in a song dedicated to your own asininity. He himself is always felt to be in the thick of his plays, and he throws abuse and ridicule on authority and respectability as though blasphemy were his native tongue. In a real sense it is: unlike the others, Behan was born and raised in revolution. Rebellion is not associated in his mind with lonely withdrawal and frustrated rage; it is the way you join your pals and get the job done. It is easy today to laugh at the Irish Nationalists—and Behan, who is no professional Irishman for all his blarney, is a leader in the laughter; but it should be remembered that they carried out the only successful war of independence that the West has known in the twentieth century.

Behan recently remarked to a New York reporter, "The first duty of a writer is to let his country down. He knows his own people the best. He has a special responsibility to let them down." Behan doesn't say this sort of thing just to be outrageous; it is an expression of his real patriotism. He is loyal to the subversive principle in human affairs and has gone to jail in its behalf. The difference between Behan and his contemporaries may be a matter of subversiveness, but it is not a matter of excellence. Certainly, on the basis of what he has done so far, I would not give him place as an artist over the others. I cannot help feeling that his cocksnookery is more valid than the clammy, irresolute whining that pervades Osborne's work; yet Beckett's man alone among the lunar stones, and the grinning obscenities of Genet's paradoxes, may be our truer, more prophetic monuments.

But views of the future are not only prophetic; they are aspects of our present temper and can have an effect on our course. In the midst of death we are still alive, and Behan's subversion explains why his pull on the audience is close to irresistible. Irreverence has almost disappeared from our common speech, and we miss the salt of it. When the curtain of *The Hostage* went up last fall on a spectacle of whores, odd boys, and assorted ruffians dancing a jig with the innocent pleasure of children let out of school, a rush of blood seemed to sweep through the stagnant arteries of Broadway. We were back again at the old business of being vulgar, raucous, incorrigible children of God.

REVIEWS

The story, as must be known by now, concerns a young English soldier, seized as hostage for an Irish lad who has had the bad judgment to shoot a policeman and is about to hang for it. The Cockney boy is brought to an old Irish Republican Army (I.R.A.) hideout, now converted from lack of patriotic funds to a bawdy house, and there takes part in the general larking about while awaiting final word on the fate of his opposite number. The English hostage dies in a bitterly pointless accident. But the plot is only a trampoline from which Behan can launch gymnastic sallies against crowned heads and commissars, churchmen, patrioteers, and dreamers. The play is staged by Joan Littlewood, director of the Theatre Workshop in London, in a style of danced reality, a choreography of personality at full tilt, that makes much of our local work look solemn and lumpy.

It could be that Behan is too much aware that his mission is to liven things up a bit. He reminds you at times of the guest who takes to throwing the cold cuts about on the misapplied theory that a touch of wit, or wildness, will save the party. Pretty much anything goes at *The Hostage*, and what rescues it is the speed with which the author recovers from his lapses. Perhaps there is a theory here—that Behan is a phenomenon of nature and not to be distilled through art. If so, that phenomenon is arrogance: a peculiar virus for a man of Behan's comic sense to pick up.

The play recalls a good many sources: it is part music-hall turn, part gaslight melodrama; it inherits an attitude from Sean O'Casey and derives incidents from Behan's own life as well as the morning papers (lines change a bit as the weeks pass). It is as slapdash as a club amateur night, with the action stopping any time someone wants to belt out a song, the characters making broad-winked asides to the audience, and the dead hero hopping up at the end so that everyone can go home happy. Behan is quite willing to coax a laugh out of someone's inability to get to the toilet, and he doesn't hesitate to milk the sentiment of two homeless orphans falling sweetly into love (and, since it is Behan writing, also into bed). He sees nothing odd about putting a bawdy song into the mouth of a convent girl from the countryside. *The Hostage* does not subscribe to the laws of classic unity.

And yet the point and drive of the thing belie its squatter carpentry. Behan doesn't set his stage in a brothel to catch onto a stylish cliché, nor does he have a mad Anglo-Irishman skirling bagpipes through the proceedings from wistful memories of Kaufman and Hart's *You Can't Take It with You*. He doesn't break into his action with implausible arias, or otherwise shatter the stage illusion, by inadvertence. He does these things because the remnants of the I.R.A. are the sons of heroes

176

THE HOSTAGE

sunk into seediness, crazy with the wail of old glories, and falling out of the frame of reality like fragments from a cracked mirror. And by implication that is the status of fanatic nationalism everywhere—it is a passion that has outrun its time.

Pat, the caretaker of the rooming house and former comrade-in-arms of Monsewer, the daft piper, is closest to being Behan's own voice in the play. Meg, his old girl, says to him: "You're always singing about them ould times, and the five glorious years, and still you sneer and jeer at the boys nowadays. What's the difference?" And he answers:

> The H-Bomb. I'm nervous of it. It's such a big bomb it's after making me scared of little bombs. The I.R.A. is out of date and so is the R.A.F. [Royal Air Force]. So is the Swiss Guard and the Foreign Legion, the Red Army, the United States Marines, and the Free State Army.

Behan throws in rousing ballads about Michael Collins and Easter Week; but he also sings "Don't muck about with the moon" and "There's no place on earth like this world," and those are the songs you remember. Behan the boy terrorist, captured in Liverpool at the age of sixteen with a suitcase full of dynamite, has changed the focus of his outlawry. He is being subversive on the side of sweet reason and a little more tolerance, please, before we blow ourselves off the map. The particular quality of Behan's tolerance is the most attractive thing about him and the mortar that holds his jackstraw constructions together. It has nothing to do with innocence or indifference; he possesses an encyclopedic knowledge of mischief and depravity and, though unconcerned by copybook morality, is implacable in the face of real wickedness. The tolerance that sustains his writing and gives it a health uncommon in our day stems from a rueful confidence in man's ability to be decent in a modest sort of way. I attribute it to the teaching of his early prison years.

As Behan points out in his autobiographical *Borstal Boy*, England can maintain its boast of having no prisons for political prisoners by the expedient of throwing such politicals as it wishes to punish into the common pool of felons. Thus, when he was put away over the matter of the suitcase, Behan was sent to a Borstal institution, where he found himself in the company of a desperate sample of Britain's youth. Thieves predominated, but there was also a substantial representation of armed robbers, pimps, murderers, and rapists. Behan was no lamb among the wolves—he had been reared in the streets of

REVIEWS

Dublin and the ranks of an illegal army—but he was a clean and honest boy who went to Confession regularly (until the English put a stop to that). However, he was also obsessively gregarious—if pimps and murderers were the only society available, then pimps and murderers must be his friends. He moved in with his fists and his songs and found that where he assumed good faith, he usually found it.

Behan was probably lucky to be thrown in with criminal society at this youngest level; ten years later he might not have found his way so easily behind the masks. But having once seen men in terms of what can be expected of them if you don't ask too much, he has never lost his bias of modest optimism. Years later in *The Quare Fellow*, that cold-eyed attack on capital punishment, Behan constructs horror and pity out of small vignettes of courtesy, tact, humor, slyness, and above all tolerance. And so in *The Hostage* he mixes wit and foolishness, pomposity and humor, selfishness and compassion, until you can't tell the saints from the sinners and are reduced to blessing them all.

Behan, who never misses a chance to catch the Catholic Church under the ribs, calls himself a Christian. It is this faith in the not excessive decency of unremarkable men that he means.

Period of Adjustment, by Tennessee Williams, & *A Taste of Honey,* by Shelagh Delaney (1961)

A disconcerting experience at the theater is the sensation of inadequate response. To be present when matters of urgency are examined, and to know oneself uninvolved, produces a spiritual scruffiness akin to the guilt induced by moral evasion. In our day there are dramatists of high resolution and impressive power—Tennessee Williams is the most notable one in the United States, as John Osborne is in England—who send me home in the late evening dispirited and estranged from whatever is creative in my own make- up.

Although Williams and Osborne are above all else plausible writers, and each has a bird dog's instinct for the presently relevant theme, what they lack is the love for individual personality that is the fever of true storytellers. In its stead they display a preoccupation with general symptoms that is the bias of therapists. They automate fashionable predicaments, but they do it so cleverly—and I will believe honorably—that one's senses cannot tell the human surrogates from God's creatures. But a kind of animal instinct rejects what schooled eyes and ears may be willing to accept; therefore one slopes along home in a

178

PERIOD OF ADJUSTMENT & A TASTE OF HONEY

yellow mood, depressed because such excellent simulacra did not pass the tests by which every species recognizes its own.

The dramatist's problem of securing an adequate response was brought into focus for me by seeing recently, on successive evenings, performances of Tennessee Williams's *Period of Adjustment* (Helen Hayes Theatre, Broadway) and Shelagh Delaney's *A Taste of Honey* (Lyceum Theatre, Broadway). Both plays are skillfully written in the vernacular of present-day concerns; both are admirably produced and performed. Mr. Williams calls his work a " serious comedy"; Miss Delaney offers no label, but hers could fairly be called a witty tragedy. It comes to much the same thing; but *Period of Adjustment* dulls the spirit, and *A Taste of Honey* puts new shine on the human race.

Subject matter is not at issue. Mr. Williams, to be sure, has changed his mask without making any notable shift in his fixed gaze: he is concerned, as in his succession of violent tragedies, with the guilt of impotence, the horror of castration, and the danger of the devouring female. But these are valid concerns—symbolically, they certainly are —and in any case Miss Delaney's material is scarcely more gladsome. She offers a chronicle of life in a Lancashire slum wherein a girl is deserted by her trampish mother, made pregnant by a Negro sailor on leave, befriended by a homosexual art student, and last seen crouched alone in her tenement flat, crooning to herself a nursery rhyme and enduring the first spasms of labor. It sounds stubbornly sordid when you omit the humanity of these people, but that is precisely what Miss Delaney does not omit. Indeed, it is her reason for writing.

Tennessee Williams's reason for writing is not so quickly stated and in the end must be more inferred than proved. One thing seems certain, though; he is driven from within, not attracted from without. At the time when he was working on *Period of Adjustment* he had this to say: "My back is to the wall and has been to the wall for so long that the pressure of my back on the wall has started to crumble the plaster that covers the bricks and mortar." A man who senses himself to be in that extreme situation must necessarily be intent on extricating himself; and, in fact, a little later in the same article, written for the *New York Times*, Mr. Williams confesses: "At the age of fourteen I discovered writing as an escape from a world of reality in which I felt acutely uncomfortable."

Speculation on that statement would lead me into the area of art as therapy, where debate is savage and endless, and I want to stay with *Period of Adjustment*. It concerns two couples who, at the beginning of the play, find themselves mentally and physically estranged and who, at the final curtain, are tumbling into their respective beds with

179

REVIEWS

the happiest anticipations. Bravo! And good for them. But we, unhappily, have been obliged to stand by for two hours while they made their trek through the psychological rain forest, and a melancholy session I, at least, found it to be.

Conformity is depressing, and these Williams characters are worse than conformist—they are composites. They are so, probably not by design, but as the inevitable result of Mr. Williams's method. Standing there with his back crumbling the plaster, he knows himself beset by harpies; and it seems to him that the way to make these evil birds significant is to show that he is no special victim, that in fact they will devour the most unremarkable flesh. That bespeaks a kind of modesty and a decent concern for others; it may even be true. But I am persuaded that it leads Mr. Williams to work with clay so commonplace that the breath will never enter. He seems to derive his people as Mr. Gallup derives his opinions—by averages that approach homogeneity.

The characters in *Period of Adjustment* are real not by intuition but by definition: they are compiled from all the television commercials, suburban sociologies, Norman Rockwell magazine covers, and master-of-ceremonies jokes that have ever passed before Mr. Williams's suffering eyes and ears. The results are not genuine people; they are genuine statistics—and statistics burdened with a characteristic Williams tic. The tic is something we are expected to recognize and sympathize with; but neuroses do not look plausible in manikins, and sympathy wavers and turns rancid when its object is a generalization. So one retreats from this "serious comedy," baffled and dismayed by the insipidity of suffering humanity. Relief comes when you see that though the suffering may be genuine, the humanity in this instance is only an advertising dummy.

Miss Delaney was just nineteen when she wrote *A Taste of Honey*, and she naturally went about the job in a much simpler way. She has said that she was prodded to write by a dissatisfaction with the way people of her world were portrayed in plays she saw while working as a theater usher: "The North Country people usually are not shown as they are, for in actual fact they are very alive and cynical. I write as people talk." That is as quiet—and as bold—a boast as a writer can well make, and Miss Delaney quietly lives up to it.

Jo Smith, the girl, is a vulnerable little bitch with a sharp tongue and a ready heart, both engendered by loneliness. Helen, her mother, is an overblown peony, with a mind as errant as a kite let loose and appetites as sharp as a fox's. Geoffrey, a sort of Dutch aunt to Jo, saves his dignity from the traps of pettiness and a tendency to flounce by

PERIOD OF ADJUSTMENT & A TASTE OF HONEY

a real generosity of concern. One falls quickly, almost eagerly, into intimacy with these people because they possess that most engaging virtue of understanding themselves.

Helen, in brief, lapses from avid sensuality, grimacing sourly at the comedy of her aging susceptibility; Jo is rarely quite free of a self-mockery induced by admitting that the very real misery of being a waif is considerably softened in her case by the virtuosity with which she rings changes on the role. And Geoffrey's too fragile outburst of masculine aggression not only defines for us his essential femininity, as no amount of attenuated extravagance could do it, but confirms himself to himself. He becomes a denser, a more substantial, figure after one flaccid embrace has shown him pitilessly what way he will never go.

When these three defiant egos cross one another, wit flashes, the sensibilities bleed, allegiances are sprained. It is a battle for communication, a struggle for security, a search for purpose; and it is not resolved—except for the resolution that it will go on. When the curtain falls on *A Taste of Honey*, Jo and Helen and Geoffrey are licking their paws and planning their next sorties on life; when it falls on *Period of Adjustment*, the characters are stacked in the wings, ready for the next demonstration.

A final note: it is being said that Joan Plowright makes a personal triumph of *A Taste of Honey*. So she does, in the sense that she turns Jo into a miracle of meager vitality. Her gestures are half woman, half don't-give-a-damn; she can crow like a young rooster, and she has a way of smirking when hurt that I doubt I shall ever forget. But it is not a triumph in the sour sense that she outclasses her company. Angela Lansbury's earth mother turned barmaid and weekend wife is brilliantly discriminating where she could be just blowzily smothering; and Andrew Ray has probably made American theater history with his unabashed, unsentimental portrayal of Geoffrey; his gentle, waspish boy is the first stage homosexual I have seen who was not an invitation to guffaws or pious horror.

The New York production was directed by Tony Richardson and George Devine after the pattern established in London by Joan Littlewood. A jazz quartet in the background underscores the syncopated realism of Miss Delaney's tribute to the people she knows. And that I now know, as well.

181

REVIEWS

Roots, by Arnold Wesker (1961)

Roots, the middle play of Arnold Wesker's social trilogy (which includes *Chicken Soup with Barley* and *I'm Talking about Jerusalem*), is at the Mayfair, an Off-Broadway house that, lodged in a sub-cellar of the Paramount Hotel, is buried in the heart of Broadway.

It turns out that Wesker's play is very difficult to import, not because conditions are so different in England, but because in certain basic aspects they are the same. An American is lured by familiarity into thinking he is at home with the problem, and then the details sound off key. In our terms there are no such people as the Bryant family of rural workers against which the "awakened" daughter, Beatie, is so stridently rebelling. We are rootless in the sense that we are moving without direction, consuming without need, prevailing without understanding. Wesker's people are rootless in the sense that they have been cut off where they stand, their traditions atrophied beneath them and their likes rotting. He is in effect calling on the British masses to rouse themselves from a sleep that is sliding toward death; our rootlessness induces intoxication rather than somnolence.

If the production were more British it would be easier to understand, but this is an American project in cast and direction. It feels like O'Neill with assistance from Odets, assuming that both had abruptly lost contact with their sources. Because of this ambivalence of milieu, the audience falls back on the theater itself as the only place where the events occur. The play becomes "realism" rather than real; that is always embarrassing, the more so here because *Roots* is frankly hortatory. Yet Wesker, though he is a socialist, puts little faith in programs, manifestos, or leaders. Individuals' helping individuals to safe footing is what he envisions as the way ahead. He believes in missionaries, which in the American context is not unlike believing in fairies. You must feel helpless to accept the helping hand, and helplessness we are not prepared to admit in our fuel-injection society.

Given this indecisiveness of attack, Mary Doyle had an impossible task as the impatient daughter. Beatie has come home from London, filled with half-heard theories about Art, Life, Love, and other capitalized generalities that she has caught from her half-baked rebel of a boyfriend. We can sense so little about where she "fits in" that we take her at face value and blink at her feckless banality. Wesker, I would suppose, means us to see in Beatie—and thus in her section of a generation—the struggle of a girl who senses a truth but lacks the background, training, and time to bring it to pass. But there is no sense

182

of struggle in Miss Doyle's Beatie; she is more like a Bennington girl working off energy.

Wesker is a dramatist of formidable technical skill, which today is not so very rare. But he is using it in an effort to split a way into the monolithic inferiority of his times, and that today is so rare in the theater as to evoke wonder and gratitude. The present production, however, is one that can only be filed pending further information.

The Death of Bessie Smith & *The American Dream*, by Edward Albee (1961)

Western drama was created to celebrate legends and perpetuate mysteries, and plays were housed in the porches of cathedrals before they had homes of their own. I hope I will not spoil anyone's fun, therefore, if I point out that, more than other literary forms, the theater has reached its peaks in an atmosphere of moral vehemence. Novelists and poets have often written out of a sense of outrage and a passion for improvement, but few of them have dared to wag a finger with the open assurance of Ibsen, Strindberg, Shaw, or Brecht. Molière cloaked homily in wit; Shakespeare ticked off the major vices with the zeal of a catechist. Tennessee Williams has lectured almost exclusively on moral dyspepsia, illustrating his talks with charts as lurid as any displayed by the Anti-Saloon League. A playwright's great advantage over other writers is that he speaks to congregations. Only the preacher enjoys the same power, and beneath the different trappings of place and circumstance the message is the same: "Go, and sin no more." Implicit in a sermon is the belief that people can be awakened to take action against their moral decay.

The shock we have experienced recently in the theater comes, I think, in considerable part from the fact that several of the most forceful writers have foregone their hortatory role and become dispassionate chroniclers of humanity's swift and irreversible decline. In such plays as *The Chairs*, *The Balcony*, and *Endgame* the playwrights Eugène Ionesco, Jean Genet, and Samuel Beckett, with varying degrees of directness and in contexts of humor, disgust, or pity related to their own personalities, have been telling their audiences that social decay has passed considerably beyond the point where exhortation would be relevant. A preacher could derive no more devastating act than to take a bowl of water with him into the pulpit and there wash his hands of the congregation. It might also be the most therapeutic act he could devise (and some such motive may lie behind the exploits of the

REVIEWS

aforementioned writers), but it would be abnormal, desperate, and spoiled by repetition.

For this reason it had seemed to me odd that these writers—I would add John Osborne because his work, though styled in what looks like the theater of protest, is in fact a counsel of revulsion—were engaged in so violent a dislocation of the theater's natural course that a return to the tradition of moral suasion was predictable. Some of the most interesting work of the past, not very interesting season suggests that this is happening.

What started me thinking along these lines were two one-act plays by Edward Albee: *The Death of Bessie Smith* and *The American Dream*. For Albee, whose moral fervor is as urgent as a war cry, writes in the vernacular of the Theater of the Absurd, another name for the disengagement of Ionesco-Genet-Beckett. The heroine of *Bessie Smith* is less a woman than a hieratic monster, akin to the three-nosed bride of Ionesco's *Jack, or The Submission*. The people of *The American Dream*, like Beckett's stumblers and gropers, are grotesquely deprived of their faculties, live in a setting of dreamlike anonymity, and agitate the audience into almost constant laughter by the irrelevance, incongruity, and ironic juxtapositions of their conversation. As with Beckett, our horror at the statement of an Albee play comes as an aftertaste; but, unlike Beckett, it also comes as an admonition.

Bessie Smith, one of the great black blues singers, died in 1937 after an automobile accident near Memphis, Tennessee. She died in the street because the first white hospital to which she was taken would not admit her, and she did not survive to reach the second. It would be convenient, especially in the North, to suppose that Albee's play is about race prejudice, but the theme is not that easy (in the sense that most of us now have available an automatic and almost guiltless sense of indignation in the presence of discrimination).

Bessie Smith herself never appears in the play that bears her name, nor is her death its subject. The subject is mutilation as a substitute for love. The hospital nurse who dominates the action, growing rankly and unfruitfully in a sterile community, can reach out to the two men in her orbit only to blight them. The intern is white, the orderly black, but she amputates their pride and promise with cold impartiality. Her savagery is hysterical, a kind of perverse rape, and the men accept it because if they did not feel her knife, they would feel nothing at all. When Bessie's gentleman friend storms into the hospital office, he does not affront the staff because he is black; he frightens them because he is in honest agony. And when the orderly and intern return from the car outside, their hands are covered with more blood than you would

184

THE DEATH OF BESSIE SMITH & THE AMERICAN DREAM

think possible—unless, desperately and hopelessly, they had been washing in the ebbing life of Bessie Smith.

The critic Kenneth Tynan has expressed some scorn for *The Death of Bessie Smith* as a drama opposing discrimination, because of the degenerative effect such work may have upon whites. I think he misunderstands. Albee is alarmed by a general failure of the channels of awareness, an inability of the public body to regenerate itself. He had also treated the subject of violence as it beats vainly on the beast of insensibility in the earlier *Zoo Story*, which first brought him to public notice when it was presented on a double bill last year with Beckett's *Krapp's Last Tape*. Now, in *The American Dream*, produced in tandem with *Bessie Smith*, he has shifted his preoccupation into a world of more evident fantasy and symbol, couching the play in a chilling humor that suggests an evening of high spirits in the morgue.

The American Dream combines elements of science fiction (in that several of the characters seem to have had their brains replaced by servomechanisms) with elements of Grand Guignol (in that a baby, adopted some years earlier by the couple of the play, had been reproved for his infant indiscretions by the surgical loss of each offending limb and organ). Not surprisingly, that baby dies, and the adoption agent has finally shown up to replace it—with its (by now) teenaged identical twin. This young man is The American Dream: seeming on the outside as succulent as an apple, but as crippled psychically as his brother had been surgically.

Allegories do not fare well in paraphrase, and I shall not do further damage to this one by completing the summary. The play's wild humor is occasioned by the fact that whereas the automatized characters respond with ludicrous precision to one another's clichés, any odd remark fails to stimulate the receiving mechanism (and there are many odd remarks because the instruments are not equipped with censors). The machine folk are also egged on a bit by an old party named Grandma, who is both senile and crafty, and who enjoys the flexibility (let us call it), even in her dotage, of being human. I got a bad scare at the end of this play by hearing, from the row behind me, some comments about *The American Dream* so insensitive, so brutal, that they differed in no essential quality from what had been coming earlier from the stage. As Grandma says when, stepping out of character, she freezes the action just before the final curtain, "This is a comedy and we had better stop it right here."

Albee is young, and his "promise" has become a catchword of the contemporary theater. He knows how to engender stage excitement,

REVIEWS

he can borrow without imitating, and he is beset by ideas. In his zeal to get a message across, however, he seems to put himself too evidently on the stage; and for a man otherwise so much at home in the theater, he has a surprisingly hard time with his endings. He tends to lurch in the home stretch, like a boy who has learned everything about riding a bike except how to get off.

In Arnold Wesker's *Roots*, the urge to preach becomes so insistent that the main character, Beatie Bryant, periodically hops up onto a table or chair, the better to harangue her associates and, of course, the audience. The trilogy consisting of *Chicken Soup with Barley, Roots,* and *I'm Talking about Jerusalem* has pushed Wesker in three years to the front rank of England's younger generation. The pivotal figure of the three plays is Ronnie Kahn, a restaurant worker with a large collection of long-playing records and a deep contempt for the passivity of the masses. He thus immediately fits the Angry Young Man category invented by Osborne, John Wain, John Braine, *et alia*. But Ronnie is also related to the placard-waving, *agitprop* heroes of the American thirties, when Clifford Odets was urging us to awake and picket. One reason why Wesker is an exciting playwright is that he has had the nerve to make Ronnie a man who is both fed up and a crusader. In *Jerusalem*, Ronnie's brother-in-law, a utopian socialist, gets caught in a petty theft. We have suffered recently from the conventionalized views of the young Jeremiahs; Wesker's people, like the brother-in-law and Ronnie, jump out of pigeonholes in an irritating way that is strikingly lifelike.

The trilogy spans the history of a lower-middle-class London Jewish family from 1936 to the present, and swings in political conviction from a communism espoused in the spirit of middle-European socialism to a restoration of the principles of William Morris, including garden crops and a distaste for machinery. Wesker himself, when he is not writing plays, exhorts the British trade unions to recognize that a regard for the economic welfare of their members is not enough. He declares that the great mass of the people is entirely outside the culture of its age (that, indeed, is why it is a mass), and he implores the unions to open theaters, support orchestras, underwrite publishing houses, sponsor exhibitions. Slogans and programs, he holds, are useless because they only enforce the monolithic conformity of the public. Individual awakening, a jump of the spark from man to man (perhaps through art), is the only answer.

Roots is the most explicit statement of Wesker's position; the other plays deal more with dreams that failed. Ronnie does not appear in this middle play; he is represented instead by his girl, Beatie, who is

186

THE DEATH OF BESSIE SMITH & THE AMERICAN DREAM

visiting her farmworker family and who, in anticipation of Ronnie's arrival, is stridently sounding the call to truth and beauty. Every third speech by Beatie is a quotation from Ronnie, often delivered from a perch. It is evident that she doesn't understand a fraction of what she is saying and just as evident that Ronnie, himself a spruced-up social illiterate, has been feeding her second-hand generalizations. Wesker is an unusual missionary in that he clearly expects no quick road to salvation. But the point of the play is that after Ronnie has welshed on his engagement, after the family has said its "I told you so's" and has (quite humanly) scored its points off their arrogant city sister, Beatie is still talking—and suddenly talking in her own voice.

The play is vivid and poignant. The country people are far from clods, and though the author has fetched Beatie a terrible blow, he has measured it to her powers of recuperation. From about the time of Jean-Paul Sartre's *No Exit*, in the mid-1940s, playwrights have been closing all doors on their characters. Wesker, for whom the stage is again a pulpit, not a killing ground, leaves a way out.

The whole trilogy should be brought to the United States. *Roots* itself distorts Wesker's ideas by making them seem more naïve than they are. Without the other plays, moreover, Ronnie looks to be a villain, and that compromises the author's purpose. Ronnie is a latter-day everyman, flawed, confused, driven by the genius of self-dissatisfaction. He is a considerable creation: in his own Jewish way, the sort of man the Irish put on their stage.

Roots was not very well produced in New York; it is a difficult play to stage with American personnel. The kind of country worker Wesker describes does not exist here, and though our culture may be debased, it is not stagnant. Cut off from our roots, we racket all over the place; Wesker's people are withering, like marrows with their roots severed beneath them. The cast seemed to be visiting the play, not living in it; and the production, lacking a security of location and tone, fell off into staginess. Further, the young actress who played Beatie displayed the wrong kind of vitality. She suggested a sociology major on a rampage, and since much of what she mouthed was platitudinous, she sounded more stupid than ignorant. Wesker does not waste pity on stupidity: he is the champion of the uninformed.

But despite a fallible production, and although I have reservations about the Wesker gospel, *Roots* goes on ringing in my ears as few plays have recently. Causes make theater, but you needn't join up to enjoy their power. Bernard Shaw did well for the stage, but anyone who swore allegiance to his banner would have lost his mind before half the plays were staged.

187

REVIEWS

All the plays here mentioned were produced Off-Broadway (*Roots* at the Mayfair Theatre; *The American Dream* and *The Death of Bessie Smith* at the York Playhouse). A couple of years ago, the future of Off-Broadway theater seemed more than dubious because it was not finding playwrights; everyone agreed that it could not live indefinitely on the established repertory. But new plays are now popping up like toadstools (by Americans in addition to Albee, as well as by Europeans); the mortality, as with toadstools, is high, but the theater is a wasteful—and difficult—medium.

Purlie Victorious, by Ossie Davis (1961)

A few years ago, a great search was on in the united States for social satire, and no examples were to be found. Dwight D. Eisenhower's conduct of the Presidency defied caricature, and his immunity to acid wit seemed to cast a haze of solemn conformity over a nation previously celebrated for irreverence. Sincerity prevailed. I would not credit John F. Kennedy with having deliberately invited cock-snookery; nevertheless, moving day at the White House did seem to coincide with a new spirit of mischief in the land. This tendency may be seen in an early arrival to the Broadway season.

I'm speaking of *Purlie Victorious* (Cort Theatre, Broadway), a farce by Ossie Davis, a young black playwright and actor who applies laughter to the classic Southern race melodrama. The ingredients of his play are as hallowed as Harriet Beecher Stowe's *Uncle Tom's Cabin*: the field hands are exploited; the white master carries a whip; the virtue of a black maiden is toyed with at the great mansion on the hill; the young hero pits his defenseless body against the horrors of sadistic sheriffs, slavering bloodhounds, and the entrenched might of white despotism. Only in this case, the white overlord is too doddering to administer an effective beating and clearly represents no threat to a girl's honor; his sheepish son is, at least in spirit, a member of the NAACP; the sheriffs are a pair of butterfingers; the bloodhounds do not materialize; and our hero's headlong attack is diverted into an exploit of prudent and virtuous larceny. The exploitation of the field hands remains and becomes the focus of the sly and preposterous plot.

Debunked heroics of this sort can be very funny. Mr. Davis has written his play in a style of hallucinated grandiloquence and himself plays the title role with a self-intoxicated extravagance that lends a fantastic levity to his perfectly sober social point. He is beautifully abetted by Ruby Dee in the role of a bumpkin beauty; by Godfrey M.

188

PURLIE VICTORIOUS   THE BLACKS

Cambridge (late of the related but infinitely more savage *The Blacks*, by Jean Genet) as a sardonic "last of the Uncle Toms"; and by Sorrell Booke (who last season was the virtuoso star of three Chekhov comedies Off-Broadway) as a spavined survivor from the glorious old Confederacy. Mr. Davis plays reasonably fair with his subjects—he kids the blacks while he derides the whites; and he manages to smile wryly at Purlie, his alter ego, even at the moment of final victory.

Morally, *Purlie Victorious* is a considerable achievement, and as entertainment it is more often than not a success. But I think it has been overpraised, as men will rhapsodize over good well water after a long march in the dust. It is a fine effort, but it is not a great play, and the disposition to thrust greatness upon it may dull its real edge. For one thing, the play talks too much and does not do enough. For another, the characters are not certain whether or not they are supposed to know that they are funny. (This may be in part a matter of direction, but the ambiguity is also in the lines.) For a third, Mr. Davis is better able to set up his climaxes than he is to bring them off. For all of its gusto, therefore, the play has a disconcerting way of losing power as it rides into its crises. The second act chugs.

I don't mean this as a veto (the "hit-or-bust" phobia has become so virulent among present-day audiences that a critic must hesitate over the mildest "however"). Mr. Davis has exercised his fertile good humor in the cause of a new freedom for the theater as well as for blacks. His play should be seen, enjoyed, and applauded—if he gets those deserts, he may go on to write a still better play the next time.

The Blacks, by Jean Genet (1961)

At a time of sit-ins and freedom rides and Africa's astonishing birth of nations, it is almost inevitable that we should expect a play performed by blacks, obsessed by ritual killings, and clanging with cries of hate and defiance, to offer some relevant comment on the race issue. Writing *The Blacks* in this era, Jean Genet has counted on our so reasoning.

The play is now being excellently performed in a production staged by Gene Frankel at St. Mark's Playhouse, Off-Off-Broadway. But if you go to it in expectation of constructive discussion, ready to assist in proclaiming the long-deferred brotherhood of man, you may feel yourself cruelly rebuffed. People say glibly that Genet lives outside society, but they do not really consider what that implies. They continue to regard him as a rebel (i.e., a kind of violent reformer) and

189

REVIEWS

assume that, since he has undertaken a social theme, he must be moved by some impulse of good will, some wish to instruct or improve. But there is not a trace of good will in Genet, and the question of whether society is to be integrated or segregated is to him a matter of perfect indifference. It would still be society, and he would still be outside it.

It is in fact absurd, whatever the emphasis of the times, to expect this terrifying Frenchman to devote himself to civil rights, national aspirations, or in any way to produce a play of constructive social significance. What intimation has he ever given of such virtuous behavior? In his own life he has been a thief and a bawd (thrown out of five countries, tossed into thirteen jails before the age of thirty-five); in his plays he is an illusionist. As a youth he pursued a visionary absolute of degradation; the largely autobiographical *Our Lady of the Flowers* and *A Thief's Journal*, both written in jail, read for pages on end like the hallucinated ecstasies of an anti-saint. Both books, by the way, are scheduled for publication in America, an event that may finally break the back of our official censorship. The obscenity and scatology of these fictive memoirs are so perverse as to be numbing; the books are no more exciting—in the police sense of the word—than the fumes of ammonia are intoxicating.

It would be hazardous to guess what influences and experiences shaped this exuberant gymnast of evil. Criminals do not leave clear records, and Genet, naturally enough, is a liar. In *A Thief's Journal* he refers to himself as a foundling, and it may well be so, but I think he must have passed some of his earliest years outside public institutions. In *Our Lady of the Flowers*—also autobiographical, though more ambiguously so—there is a little boy who lives with his widowed mother, a woman of fierce French respectability. He lives better than his fellows ("in the only house in the village, except for the church, that had a slate roof") and probably a good deal more gloomily—set apart and surrounded by Gothic dreams; apparently he chews the leaves of aconite for the visions. A man corrupts this small child, and for this child corruption becomes a vision of the absolute. Similarly, the young Genet consecrated himself to wickedness with the fervor of a seminarian giving his life into the hands of the Almighty. But, alas for his vows, he was also an artist, and, in the end, he turned from the religion of vice to the aesthetics of subterfuge. "Metamorphosis lies in wait for us," he once wrote; also, "I am mad for fancy dress."

And metamorphosis in fancy dress is what he has been giving us ever since. "Disturbing" is, I believe, the adjective most commonly applied to Genet's plays. But he does not disturb so much by what he puts forward—in the manner, say, of Henrik Ibsen or August

190

THE BLACKS

Strindberg—as by the dislocation of expectation. His is the malaise of the missing stair tread, the question unanswered, the image that can be caught only as the eye blinks. Whatever is looked at straight-on in a Genet play disappears on the instant, or is transformed into something else.

But why be concerned with such a perverse fellow? The idea under the shell, the hall of mirrors, are diversions for yokels ; we are responsible men with a regard for logic and a respect for our own dignity. Woe on us, we are therefore the very ones who were ever Genet's prey. In his youth lie he picked our pockets and trafficked in our lecheries; now in maturity he shatters the authority of our senses and poisons our faith in our rectitude. We can pretend he isn't there, but that is a lie and makes us his timid henchmen. It is possible to get the better of Genet's trickery: you have only to be perfectly sane and entirely candid. But this coincidence of health and virtue is not so common as to have restricted him much in either of his lives.

If we were talking only of the prose (based on *Our Lady of the Flowers* and *A Thief's Journal,* which are the two I have been able to get my hands on), we might perhaps decide to sweep past Genet. These books are works of prismatic brilliance, containing scene after scene of bizarre or sordid incident caught as in amber by the preservatives of symbol and metaphor. Their motivation, however, seems fatally miscalculated: when perfect evil is the goal, the issue is no longer art but sanity. Genet is sane, and as dramatist has turned from the abyss of pure negation. His plays are calculated attempts to dislodge society from its underpinnings. A man alone against society does not perhaps strike one as a patently reasonable encounter. But the enemies of society almost invariably strike from within; Genet is outside, and it remains to be seen whether or not he has a lever long enough for his job.

The Maids was his first play, and it first brought his name into general currency in America when it was produced in Greenwich Village in 1955. It deals with a ritual. Indeed, almost everything Genet writes for the stage is couched in rites and ceremonies (from outside, apparently, these look to be our exposed flank). In this case, two maids are discovered rehearsing the murder of their dear mistress. Claire is playing Madame, and Solange, her sister, is playing Claire. (Genet wished the parts to be taken by boys, thus raising the pretense by one more power; but we are not Elizabethans, and this has never been tried.) By the transposition of roles Claire can both revile and caress herself, in the person of Solange; and Solange, hating and fawning upon Madame (whom the sisters also love), can at the same time

191

REVIEWS

loathe and fondle Claire, her alter ego. The servant is the image of himself reflected from the master.

Jean-Paul Sartre, who has written a long introduction to this play, traces the whirligigs of pretense in a circular alternation of truth with falsehood (real boys, playing false maids, who are real women enacting a false hate that is inexorably confused with self-love). The metamorphoses can be proliferated almost at will, for the essence, the wicked heart, of this play is that Genet deftly avoids the single fixed datum that would give it an anchor and arrest the nauseating spin. The maids have never accomplished the murder because Madame has always come home before they had completed their elaborate incantations and were ready for her. But this time Claire, as Madame, drinks the poisoned tea, thus committing in real suicide a symbolic murder and assuming in death the identity of the person who gave her substance. The attack of the play, exceedingly disconcerting, is on the observer's sense of objective identity, his conviction that he can tell a hawk from a handsaw.

The forces of conflict in Genet's theater are not confined to the stage; they are directed into the audience. The characters seem engaged in a conspiracy against the spectators, and hostility flows strongly from stage to auditorium. *The Balcony* (which, at Off-Broadway's Circle in the Square, has become one of New York's impressively long runs) was Genet's first full-length play and a more elaborate tapestry of ritual and impersonation than *The Maids*. The place of the title is a bordello that caters to fantasists. Here come ordinary persons, clerks and plumbers and the like, to be dressed in the trappings of power— as a bishop, a judge, and a general, which to Genet are the personifications of society—and to use the girls who attend them, not as women, but as the objects of their authority. The eroticism of fancy dress is a scarlet thread through this play.

The action takes place in a time of revolution, and while the patrons of *The Balcony* are acting out their dreams of power, the real custodians of power are liquidated. Except, that is, for the chief of police, who acts as a bridge between the house of illusions and the world outside. He continues to function in a desperate attempt to hold the state together because his life is unfulfilled: no one has ever come to *The Balcony* and asked to be decked out as the chief of police. Until someone does—and at the end it happens—the chief cannot rise to the hierarchy of symbolism, where power no longer expresses itself in action but in mere being.

Genet concocts in *The Balcony* an image of society in which real authority has been absorbed by the apotheosis of authority. Out in the

THE BLACKS

streets the princes of church and state lie slain but within the bordello, priest, judge, soldier, and finally chief of police attain omnipotence by sacrificing their ephemeral potency for a place in the permanent wardrobe of illusion. (The patron who asks for the role of chief of police castrates himself in a climax of ecstasy.) The play breaks down the distinctions among the individual, his functions, and the symbolic efficacy of his office. Function annuls person, and symbol obviates function, until at the end the brothel and its denizens become surrogates for the world and its people. The audience is defied to keep its eye on the individual—the pea beneath the shell—in this game of devil's sophistry.

In *The Blacks* Genet has written the only play I can recall where the purpose is to insult and confuse the audience. I doubt that what happens on the stage can ever be made entirely clear down to its fine detail (though in a moment I shall have a stab at the broad construction); but there is no doubt about what happens to the audience—it is humiliated.

This is a work written for an all-black cast, to be played for a white audience. Genet instructs in a foreword to the printed text: "If, which is unlikely, it is ever performed before a black audience, then a white person, male or female, should be invited every evening.... A spotlight should be focused on this symbolic white throughout the performance." Thus, at the very start, hostility is established—not because Genet prefers black society to white society, but because, for the time being, white society is the group in power.

I would like the reader to visualize the scene, at least as it is presented at the St. Mark's Playhouse, which seems to me splendidly designed for the purpose. This theater is a cockpit, a miniature arena for gladiators, with the seats raked steeply in a semicircle. Opposite the audience and beyond the playing area, which is quite bare, spiral gangways circle up from either side to a high platform that is occupied for most of the evening by several blacks, whose faces are partially covered by white masks that represent a queen, a missionary, a governor, a judge, and a poet-lackey. (Genet here enlarges his symbols of society, but the context is unchanged.) Thus the white audience faces the patently false embodiments of its institutions across a stage peopled by blacks.

The Blacks is constructed of two simultaneous plays-within-the-play, one performed on stage, the other out in the wings. When the lights come up, several couples are discovered turning to a minuet. They break off on becoming aware of the audience and are introduced by their spokesman, one Archibald Wellington, who explains with icy

193

REVIEWS

politeness that, in deference to the audience present, his friends will enact a drama of black behavior as whites envision it to be. (Roscoe Lee Browne's disdainful but not quite natural elegance in this role is subtle and brilliantly controlled acting.)

Thereupon, with many false starts and outbreaks of their own personalities and concerns, the company unfolds a pageant in which a white woman (played by one of the men, who dons a sweet-grand-mother rig for the purpose) is raped and murdered. Thus the blacks earn the punishment that their white masters (those ranged on high, in their masks) have decided in advance to mete out to them. To heighten the effect, this play-within-a-play is performed around a catafalque that, we are assured with much circumstantial detail, contains the body of the murdered white woman, transported hence in a Cadillac for the occasion.

Now it is clear that our black hosts cannot take this charade seriously, however hard they may try out of deference to our known prejudices. There is no body, there is no murder, and when the "whites" descend from their safe premises to administer justice in the "steaming jungle," it is they who expire, apparently by prearrangement: one of them has been heard, early in the evening, rehearsing his death speech. I take this detail to be a comment on the whites' understanding of the benevolent demise of colonialism.

At the same time, it is also clear that this inept drama—the performers who are vivid "out of character" become wooden as "actors"—is introduced not only to entertain us but to divert us from what is taking place elsewhere. And that is the offstage play-within-a-play. A messenger named Edgar Alas Newport News (the names in the play are all wicked parodies of the white man's concept of black nomenclature—Felicity Trollop Pardon, Adelaide Bobo, etc.) keeps running in with word of a trial. A traitor has been caught, there are cryptic asides about the black man's learning to take responsibility for his own justice, eyes are rolled at the audience, and there is a good deal of shushing. Then, as the onstage play is approaching its climax in the jungle, word comes that justice has been carried out. All crowd around the messenger, who affirms that it is so and adds that "another" has been appointed in "his" place and is "on his way." The masks are forgotten, and various people start to wander off, remarking that they have jobs to do. But then they bethink themselves of the audience sitting there all agog and decide that the flummery had better be carried out to the end: "as we could not allow the whites to be present at a deliberation . . . that does not concern them, and as, in order to cover up, we have had to fabricate the only one that does concern them."

194

THE BLACKS

It is at this point that Genet's trap is set to snap. When someone throws up a screen, we believe instinctively that it is designed to hide something. And when we penetrate a subterfuge, we believe instinctively that what we have come upon is real. It is not easy to remember that Genet is a liar. But our hosts have told us several times that they are performing not what they are but what we believe them to be. How then do they describe this offstage "other" who is "going off to organize and continue the fight"? "Just as you would imagine him," says Newport News, smiling. "Exactly as he must be in order to spread panic by force and cunning." What about his voice, someone asks. "It's deep. Somewhat caressing. He'll first have to fascinate and then convince. Yes, he's also a charmer."

And he's also a figment of generalizations and clichés—just as the audience would imagine him. The trick behind the trick is obvious enough, set down so; but by the time *The Blacks* gets to these lines, the audience is feeling as white as bone. It has been made to feel excluded by its color (a rare sensation for whites); it suspects that baubles have been danced before its eyes to obscure the real affairs of life. So now it hears in those empty words of Newport News a charming menace, and its hair stirs along the spine. Being very much on edge, made acutely conscious that "we" are not "they," it is not quick to notice that one of the girls asks, "But . . . at least he's black?" At that everyone laughs. You bet he's black—indeed, that's all he is, a blackness in the white man's blood.

Of course, we would recover ourselves in a moment, but before we can, the minuet resumes and we are smilingly dismissed. Thus Genet puts to the test the vaunted tolerance and humane flexibility of contemporary society. "All men are brothers" is our fervent carol, but how well does it stand up to a little insolence, a little exclusion, some enigmatic mumbo jumbo? It is humiliating to find one's façade of good will so thin.

At the end or the play one has a most curious sensation while going through the conventional courtesies: the bows of the performers seem insulting; the applause of the audience sounds defensive, as there is no cordiality about it—we were told we could be had, and we were had. Because, as it turns out, we too can have our color used against us.

Genet is now quite the lion of the Paris salons, and I'm told that hostesses are wont to put a piece of silver, or some charming *bric-à-brac*, temptingly within his reach: there is always the chance of enjoying the glory of being robbed by so distinguished a guest. Such a man must have a particular understanding of what it means to let bygones be bygones. For he, too, is one of the blacks—one of those on

REVIEWS

whom we others have sat in judgment. It is remarkable how clean of heart one must be to come safely within the spell of this black and unrepentant sinner.

A Man for All Seasons, by Robert Bolt, & *The Caretaker*, by Harold Pinter (1962)

Our generation, at least in the non-Communist world, is in difficulties about its heroes. Heroism, understood as courage in action, we can still recognize and applaud; but the individual hero, defined as the personification of what the age intends to be, has become a wraith. Heroes will not thrive in every moral climate; today they do not seem to thrive even in England—after Greece their natural habitat. But English writers are still out hero-hunting, a proposition that can be demonstrated by three plays from London that have endowed the current Broadway season with such distinction as it has had. The quarry that they have brought home is another matter.

Robert Bolt, author of *A Man for All Seasons*, went seeking one hero and came up with another. His subject is Sir Thomas More, and he celebrates this noble, wise, and beautiful man in a play of such elegance as we now rarely see. Its speech (which is not infrequently the speech of More himself) flows with the smooth strength of fine cloth; its machinery is ingenious to the point of wit; it is concerned with lofty and universal issues. And it is performed by the large Anglo-American company—especially by Paul Scofield in the title role—in a style of crystal sharpness and sparkle (ANTA Theatre, Broadway). This company makes of acting not only an art but the most enticing of sports. I cannot imagine a more appetizing theatrical occasion.

The playwright believes that the magnetism of an absolute principle is what gives life meaning and flavor, and is at pains to demonstrate the accessible humanity of his subject. More, who moves in Scofield's conception with the bent shoulders of a scholar and the reaching stride of a Crusader, is a wit and a gourmet, a man readily amused by folly, delighting in the duel of intelligence, immersed in love—for his wife and daughter, for his sporting friend the Duke of Norfolk, for his king, and for his valet. And immersed most deeply of all in love for his God.

At the moment when he is a pivot to the conscience of the Christian world, More is a man at ease. He is probably the most reasonable man of his age, but it is an age when reason and faith can be synonymous. More understands the ways of men and states; more pertinently, he

196

A MAN FOR ALL SEASONS & THE CARETAKER

understands young Henry VIII. He knows that Queen Catherine will be put aside and Anne Boleyn will achieve the throne; he appreciates the reasons of state and of passion that will make this inevitable, as well as the scholastic argument that will make it palatable. But the Pope has set his hand against the deed, and the Pope speaks with the voice of God. To flout that voice is heresy, and heresy is folly. More cannot be moved from his stand because he cannot be made to take leave of his own reason. He is thus a man at ease.

To our eyes he is also a man in a frame: he could have been painted by Hans Memling. Bolt conceives him as perfection made animate. There is not much room for movement in that concept, and movement is the genius of the theater. Furthermore, movement is the substance of our society. We are defined, not by our creeds, but by our orbits; our science is a system of relative truths, our souls are the sums of warring impulses. So to say of a character that he is perfectly good is as estranging as if one were to say that he is completely mad. We cannot relate to such men. I find in retrospect that the More of this play has turned as still as a tapestry; another figure beckons to me as hero.

This one is carried on the program as the Common Man. As played by George Rose, he is the evident crony of Shakespeare's citizens of the town; he would have torn Cinna apart for his verses and urged the crown on Richard III. He is variously employed in the play as More's valet, a boatman, a spy, a tapster, a jailer, and ultimately as More's headsman. He is also the interlocutor, reading out bits of history, explaining where we now find ourselves, whisking properties and bits of costume about to change scenes. Bolt uses this character with marvelous dexterity to lend crispness and speed to his pageantry, as well as to season his solemn deliberations with shrewd digs in the ribs. Bolt, an aristocrat, adorns his palace of the mind with a gargoyle, but invites us to remember who we are and disown the fellow.

Alas, we cannot. For Bolt's gargoyle is a surviving sort of man, and that is what we are—a surviving sort of men. The lyric grace of *A Man for All Seasons*, the banners and bugles of its testimony to God's truth, are beauties that fade with poignant speed. What remains strong and warm in the mind is the ape at Sir Thomas's elbow, the antic opportunist who claims no more for himself than that his humanity is a persistent germ on the earth. It is a bitter kernel within the rich fruit of humane and elegant poetry, and not the point intended. But adoration does not make heroes; recognition is what counts.

That being the case, we should find a hero in the wounded, neurotic, self-besotted man known variously as Ross, Shaw, and

197

REVIEWS

Lawrence of Arabia. If More was the hero as perfection, Lawrence was the hero as enigma; that should be more in our style. But Terence Rattigan, whose *Ross* (Hudson Theatre, Broadway) is a dramatization of the desert warrior's glory and eclipse, is not the writer to reveal him. Rattigan deals in another kind of perfection—perfect theater. For him, reality, morality, and beauty are whatever plays. I do not mean that rudely, as an accusation of dishonesty. We all perceive selectively, and the more expert a man becomes at his trade, the greater danger he runs that his trade will filter his perceptions. It is almost certain to happen to artists who offer the world their crafts and withhold themselves. Rattigan knows a human life in acts and curtain lines.

Ross is a consistently absorbing and seriously motivated play; it contains all of Lawrence that the playwright could discern, and that is quite a lot. But the character lacks the overtones that might suggest where his life extended beyond the frame of this particular stage. Rattigan's Lawrence is as overt as a marionette and, once the curtain is down, he stores as conveniently.

That is true generally of Rattigan's characters, and in part it is what makes them so vivid. He can construct a sergeant major with a heart of gold, or a scholar-warrior like General Edmund Allenby, who is as complete and satisfying as an egg. Such characters are realer than life because they have no unprojectable, private dimension to blur them. That may do very well for the supernumeraries, but if your purpose is to bring a complex man like Lawrence into communion with your audience, it will not prove sufficient. A Lawrence complete on stage is no more meaningful than a Hamlet complete on stage. And a play that does not allow for intuition cannot be tragedy, can scarcely be a drama. It may be—and in this case certainly is—engrossing entertainment.

Glen Byam Shaw, who directed *Ross*, and John Mills, who plays the title role, are in such rapport with Rattigan that they underscore his limitations. Mills's characterization is a series of tableaux in which, one by one, he mimes the facets of this notoriously many-faceted man. He enters in turn as the boyish romantic, the fanatic ascetic, the cocky nonconformist, the grieving father of his troops, the tortured animal, the humble penitent, the genius hiding behind an R.A.F. serial number. Each "impression" of Lawrence is instantly recognizable and theatrically interesting; no one, presumably, is supposed to ask whether he was a man or a string of beads. I enjoyed this bravura work, but Lawrence's candidacy for the hero's laurel will have to wait for a more encompassing, less Procrustean advocate. Bolt and Rattigan, in their very different ways, approach the hero by way of legend.

198

THE CARETAKER

The approach of Harold Pinter in *The Caretaker* (Lyceum Theatre, Broadway) is by way of allegory. The instant Donald Pleasence, as Mac Davies, alias Bernard Jenkins—stubble-cheeked, mean-eyed, and swaddled in rags—steps into view, one recognizes a popular spokesman of our day: the anti-hero. A hero may be a creature of history or of fiction, but in either case he can be real. An anti-hero, however, is by nature a thing of myth, a philosophical concept arrived at by reversing all the signs of heroism and drawing a graph of the result. The "real" opposite of a hero is a villain; an anti-hero is a construct, a conception peculiarly appropriate to an age that discovered the neutrino, a particle of matter that has no mass and carries no electrical charge and is therefore undetectable, but must exist because it permits certain calculations to balance. We have our own kind of faith, and the anti-hero has his own kind of reality.

On a factual level *The Caretaker* recites a brief and melancholy episode in the life of a bum who knows his rights. Davies bas been fired from his job as dishwasher in a cheap café, as the result of kicking up a row, and has been brought to a derelict house somewhere in West London by Aston, who looks out for the place for Mick, the owner and his younger brother. Aston gives the old man a bed, some shoes, a few shillings—for which he gets small thanks and no gratitude. They talk in each other's presence; but since neither is attentive, they cannot be said to converse. This exasperates Davies, who wants charity but still more wants to be noticed. Aston is as dispassionate as a board. (His brain, it turns out, has been hobbled by electro-shock therapy.)

Mick, who pops in and out unpredictably, gives Davies no charity but a great deal of attention. He threatens him, flatters him, schemes with him, calls him friend. The job of caretaker seems to be in the offing. The old man is alternately terrified and tickled pink. But what with the impassivity of his benefactor and the instability of his friend, what with his immunity to kindness and defenselessness against daydreaming, Davies is edged into a tighter and tighter corner of the rubbish-laden room. Until suddenly the brothers revile him for a stinking nuisance and throw him the hell out of the place. Curtain.

This is performed with a brilliance I should be quite at a loss to recapture on paper. The effectiveness of Pinter's prose is not only in its spare precision, but in its aching pauses and jumbled profusion of secondhand ideas and inapplicable observations. It is the language of men caught in the plumbing of society, scraps in the sink trap. And the three actors sustain the suspended action with a pretense to reason and purpose that is, quite literally, hideously funny. Pleasence's accent is an insult to sound, his face a social blight. He gestures with an

REVIEWS

expansive vacuity that catches exactly the blind feelers of the stupid conniver. It is beautiful work. Aston (Robert Shaw) is large, pale, and saltless. He is that modern remittance man, the fellow who lives somehow on welfare. He has a screwdriver and a tin of small parts, and he "fixes" things. He is turned off. His brother (Alan Bates) is a more active modern type: the kind who has it made—some day. Uneducated, undisciplined, deceived by the egalitarianism of the times into thinking himself as good as anyone else, he has no skill but lingo. (Mick can talk décor like a Mayfair interior decorator.) He wears a leather jacket and tight trousers.

There is electricity, certainly, in the unsparing accuracy with which Pinter catches these three casualties of our abundant age. (I wish, though, that I understood why he inflicts brain surgery on Aston: it seems to make him an accident rather than a casualty.) But the reporting is not the limit of the excitement. *The Caretaker* is allegory, as it would have to be with an anti-hero at its axis. I don't approve of translating allegory; it is like explaining jokes. But in a sketchy way, the older brother behaves rather like destiny, existence, what we used to call God—doling out impassively the things a man needs to go on breathing. He is never exactly present, but he is around. The younger brother—popping in and out, always ready with a smile or a kick in the teeth, handsome and flashy—could be taken to represent luck, what a man cozies up to at his desperate peril. And the old man— appointed caretaker (at an unspecified fee and with undefined duties) of a cluttered and decaying room surrounded by a planetary system of empty, unfinished, forbidden rooms; kicking at fate, flirting with luck, and flung at last into oblivion by the two of them—this Mac Davies of the itching garments and blindly working mouth bears a grisly resemblance to the whole pack of us.

Pinter is no optimist, and the hero he offers us is a joke in questionable taste. But he is, after all, a playwright and not a magician (though his skill has touches of magic) . A hero is the image of itself that the age projects, what it intends to be. According to Pinter, we project Mac Davies; Samuel Beckett calls him Molloy or Krapp, Edward Albee calls him the American Dream, Eugène Ionesco calls him a rhinoceros. Can all these playwrights be talking about us? It grows chilly.

The Merchant of Venice, by William Shakespeare (1962)

The New York Shakespeare Festival, having survived extreme financial hazards and petty bureaucratic jealousy, resides today in a permanent amphitheater that must be one of the most beautiful outside of Greece, and is certainly one of the most efficient for the outdoor performance of drama.

This exemplary Shakespeare repertory, performed free of charge six nights a week (weather permitting) during the summer months, withstood its recurring crises in part because its director, Joseph Papp, is an idealist with an excellent sense of politics and the uses of publicity, and in part because the citizens of New York, for once in their lives, recognized that something good was being done for them and raised a powerful howl when it was threatened. Made bold by this success, the people of the city went on to snatch Washington Square away from the traffic engineers and real-estate promoters—perhaps they will eventually free themselves of the lethal fumes now pouring into their streets from private cars and public buses.

The permanent theater in Central Park, built with a combination of private and public money, is a platform stage from which rises a steep-raked horseshoe of bleachers that seats 2,300 spectators within a reasonable distance of the stage. Loudspeakers are unfortunately necessary for most of the seating area: I doubt that they can ever be avoided in a city with as strong a ground noise as New York (to say nothing of airplanes), and where there is no natural back-wall to confine the sound. The axis of the structure is just south of east; the audience looks through the skeletal set across a lagoon and a wooded hill to the distant lights of Fifth Avenue. On the right, a feudal castle (the old weather observatory) stands on its rocky crag and flies a banner from its turret; from the left, until night falls, can be heard faint shouts of baseball and soccer players spread out on the fields to the north. Seated there, waiting for the flourish of trumpets, one understands the pride of belonging to a great city—this is how the Athenians and the Elizabethans must have felt. It is not the least of Mr. Papp's accomplishments that he has given back to his fellow New Yorkers at least a trace of the civic dignity that one feared was drowned forever in the humiliations of megalopolitan life.

The 1962 season opened with *The Merchant of Venice*, to be followed (July 16th) by *The Tempest* and (August 13th) by *King Lear*. As always happens when *The Merchant of Venice* is produced, there

REVIEWS

have been protests from official Jewish quarters, made the more uneasy this time because one of the performances was shown on television. I cannot argue with Jews who deplore the play—they have suffered much in the name of Shylock—but the fact is, and Mr. Papp's production makes it perfectly clear, that *The Merchant of Venice* is an anti-Semitic play only to those who are already anti-Semites.

As performed here by George C. Scott, Shylock is a proud, powerful man, deeply committed to his traditions and driven to the point of insanity by the hostility and (worse) contempt of the proper Venetians. He demands the forfeit of Antonio's pound of flesh, and certainly it is a piece of wicked vengeance to act so. But the Christians, making much of their superior charity, demand of Shylock the forfeit of his God (he must turn Christian); and they lack the excuse for their cruelty of years of persecution.

The Merchant of Venice is one of Shakespeare's dark comedies, and its lyricism, its buffoonery, bawdry, and high spirits, do not hide the ugliness of its main narrative. It is possible to neutralize the gall by making of Shylock a monster or a clown, but when he is played with straightforward clarity, when as here the whole motivation of the play is lucid, one feels that somehow the Antonio-Portia-Bassanio crowd has gotten away with it again. The fact that Portia lives in the suburbs does nothing to allay this social itch. The play is really about the momentum of the organization, with some of the most darling lovers in all Shakespeare thrown in to make it a (sometimes troubling) treat for a summer's night.

Nan Martin plays Portia with fine spirit and wit, and she is very lovely. But her voice sounded a little harsh at times; perhaps she was not trusting the microphones at the start of the run. Lee Richardson is a properly dashing (and feckless) Bassanio, Bette Henritze a most winning Nerissa. James Earl Jones is spectacularly funny as the Prince of Morocco without falling into the trap of caricaturing his own race (he keeps it personal). John Call stops the show as Launcelot Gobbo, but I have seen Mr. Call in several such roles, and I begin to suspect that he has invented an all-purpose Shakespearean clown. Gobbo, after all, is not Fluellen and Fluellen is not Dogberry; but in Central Park they are all becoming John Call.

Ming Cho Lee has designed a set of cantilevered grace and strength that is bodied out with light and on occasion with two beautiful screens that fill the central opening; Theoni Aldredge designed vivid and flattering costumes on a budget that must have far exceeded the pin money formerly spent on festival dress.

Mr. Papp, finally, staged *The Merchant of Venice* with the direct-

202

A MAN'S A MAN, OH DAD, POOR DAD & WHO'S AFRAID OF VIRGINIA

ness, the clarity of speech and movement, and (with one or two lapses) the confidence in Shakespeare's stage sense that is the hallmark of the Central Park seasons.

A Man's a Man, by Bertolt Brecht; *Oh Dad, Poor Dad, Mamma's Hung You in the Closet and I'm Feelin' So Sad*, by Arthur Kopit; & *Who's Afraid of Virginia Woolf?*, by Edward Albee (1963)

During the past ten to fifteen years it has become increasingly hazardous to laugh in the theater. An entire generation of audiences has come of age since the stage last rocked to the innocent, unmotivated, and inconsequential merrymaking of George Abbott's *Three Men on a Horse* and Kaufman and Hart's *You Can't Take It with You*. For the contemporary playwright, humor is a tool—in fact, it has become one of his weapons. Nowadays we implicate ourselves by our laughter; more often than not, we are the victims of the jest and, as it were, hoist on our own guffaws.

The tactical use of humor is not new to the stage; one has only to recall the porter in *Macbeth* or the gravediggers in *Hamlet*. Such comic scenes and figures worked as catalysts for the tragedy to come; laughter relaxed the audience, opened its senses, and the blade struck home with the greater force. But Shakespeare did not contrive ludicrous deaths (there was, I admit, the malmsey-butt in *Richard III*, but it stood offstage and presumably Clarence was dead before ever he went into it); he did not mix absurdity with terror or hilarity with disgust. Early in the present era Jean-Paul Sartre announced in *No Exit* that hell is other people; to that has been added more recently the observation that the ultimate cry of agony is laughter.

The new chimeras of the stage range from tragic farce (Eugene Ionesco's *Rhinoceros*) to slapstick horror (Samuel Beckett's *Endgame*), to lethal fantasy (Jean Genet's *The Balcony*). They were written in the knowledge of antic scarecrows frozen to the electric fence; in anticipation of a war that, not content with corpses in quantities beyond precedent, will produce good sports—funny-looking people. Happy laughter presupposes a considerable confidence in the stability of custom (such that it won't be toppled by one unguarded shout) and a structure of values that is generally understood if not scrupulously observed. Gilbert and Sullivan were forever inveighing against the smugness of their society, but in fact only a society secure

REVIEWS

enough to be smug could have given them relevance (their operettas are not relevant today, only nostalgic). The speed with which we have been deteriorating as a society can perhaps be gauged by recalling the joyful caricature that animated George Gershwin's *Of Thee I Sing*. The Eisenhower administration was easily as laughable as Hoover's, but by then we had so lost a sense of destiny that attempts to lampoon Ike and his entourage turned rancid. Humor, in fact, has become a tough business.

Bertolt Brecht was one of the earliest of the modern dramatists to bully his public with laughter. He took fullest possible advantage of the fact that anything presented in a state of unaccustomed nakedness—from a plucked chicken to an unfrocked priest—is ludicrous, and that the humor it generates is amoral. The subject Brecht chose again and again to display in its birthday suit was villainy; his plays are crowded with greed, lust, larceny, hypocrisy, stupidity, all parading around the stage in bland nudity, as though they were babies pink from their baths. The effect has been admirably demonstrated this winter in Eric Bentley's adaptation of *A Man's a Man* (Masque Theatre, Off-Broadway). Galy Gay, a laborer who is goodhearted almost to the point of simple-mindedness, is converted during eleven scenes of vaudeville into a compulsive military killer. What makes the play funny, in its grim, dangerous way, is that the British soldiers (the play is set in a place called India) who reconstruct Galy are easily his peers in transparent fecklessness. We laugh to see their boyish tricks and are left with our mouths hanging open when the blood begins to run. Brecht has a ferocious way of making funny faces at us and then, when we laugh, telling us sharply that we have a peculiar sense of humor. He seeks to unmask, thus, still another kind of villainy—that of irresponsibility.

Brecht was certainly a moralist; nevertheless, the fault I have to find with this excellently ribald and circus-like production is that it so insistently wags the moral at us. Bentley is a diligent student of Brecht and has, I am certain, good grounds for the tone he develops. But the director, John Hancock, might have ruled that the dose of admonishment prescribed by Brecht for a pre-World War II audience could be so large as to stupefy a generation sensitized to propaganda. We expect irony and don't require a "Now, students" tone to recognize when we are being exposed to it. It would have been better, perhaps, to play *A Man's a Man* "straight," trusting the grisly comedy to make its point. Nevertheless, this production is brutally funny—the dead and the damned, off on a carefree binge.

A much more advanced (I don't say better) use of laughter is on

204

OH DAD, POOR DAD   WHO'S AFRAID OF VIRGINA WOOLF

view in Arthur Kopit's *Oh Dad, Poor Dad, Mamma's Hung You in the Closet and I'm Feelin' So Sad* (Phoenix Theatre, Off-Broadway). The humor here is characterized by the title—there is nothing inherently funny about it; one laughs because it is so inappropriate that one doesn't quite know what else to do. This is another kind of bullying—the tactic of putting your opponent off balance by behaving in a way he has no possible reason to expect. The effect usually is to induce a nervous and debilitating giggle. It is good mental jujitsu, but in this case I am not persuaded that Kopit has a valid reason for tripping us up. I suspect that he enjoys watching people sprawl, and that is unamiable of him.

The way to deal with such a title as his is to cut it, as everyone does, to *Oh Dad* . . . And the way to deal with his very clever and totally disconcerting play is to define it as a homosexual version of Little Lord Fauntleroy. Because, although its significance may be baffling, its imagery is tiresomely clear; the giant Venus flytraps that snap at unwary males with fleshy, teeth-rimmed lips; mother's suitor, who is paralyzed by her sustained and suffocating kiss; the pet fish who eats kittens alive (curiously, the play contains no instance of cannibalism); the huge, homemade telescope with which the son confuses his girl caller; the enormous and chaotic collections of stamps, coins, books; and of course the corpse of Dad, which falls out of the closet and becomes entangled with sonny, who is timorously trying to lose his virginity with a possessive hussy on mamma's bed. The result of this sort of thing is that the in-group laughs gleefully at how killingly the author has worked private signals into his public script; and the out-group laughs hollowly in the realization that it has come to the wrong party. I admire Kopit's stagecraft, and I don t doubt the reality of his nightmare; but I hope that another time he will sublimate what's biting him enough to implicate a larger segment of his audience.

If you laugh at Edward Albee's *Who's Afraid of Virginia Woolf?* (Billy Rose Theatre, Broadway)—and everyone does—you may come to accuse yourself of heartlessness. It devotes itself to a very long night in the living room of a university couple who torment each other with wit, or at least witticisms. Ostensibly, the source of their mutual viciousness lies in her contempt for a man less successful than her father and his revulsion against the means by which such success is attained. Another, much younger faculty couple is also present during the night-long bout of drink and vivisection (a good deal of the laughter is engendered by their bewilderment at being under the knives of their hosts), and the husband of this pair is shown to represent the kind of cold-blooded calculation that does lead to departmental chair-

REVIEWS

manships. Nevertheless, I came to believe that the assassinating impulses of the main couple were compulsive, remote from real clashes of principle or character; they fought because they had been warped to fight. This does not invalidate the play, but it places a clinical limitation on its tragedy.

Albee is the most talented of the young American playwrights who have won wide attention in the past ten years. No one since Tennessee Williams has taken such sure and ruthless command of the stage. It troubles me that in his most ambitious play to date, and his first to be offered on Broadway, he is so severely a spectator of his own creation. To use an old-fashioned term, *Who's Afraid of Virginia Woolf?* lacks catharsis: at the end, it merely turns disconcertingly and inconclusively soft. And that, I think, is because the playwright is working from data rather than conviction. It seems that he cannot resolve what he did not instigate—which is common enough in life but not sufficient for art. In retrospect the heartlessness of the audience's laughter may be laid at the door of the playwright's neutrality. Asked to describe the play, one is forced to say: "It is about this man and this woman who. . . ." That is much too particular to justify the intensity of the evening's pain and horror (we do not go to the theater to see accidents). It is not the way one would describe *A Doll's House*; for that matter, it is not the way one describes Albee's *The Death of Bessie Smith*. Only farce can limit itself successfully to the singular.

Albee is a playwright who has come to Broadway after a considerable apprenticeship in the outlying houses. Herb Gardner, author of *A Thousand Clowns*, on the other hand, writes as though Broadway had invented him. This is his first play, but already he is master of that most saleable gambit, the pulled punch. He tells us of an individualist who rebels against the conforming, conniving, humiliating mores of American business life. How, then, can American businessmen and their wives, who make up almost the whole of Gardner's audience, laugh at his jibes with quite unguarded pleasure and march out of the theater with their faces creased by smiles? Because the rebel is pictured in terms of such immature and irrelevant naughtiness that rebellion is plainly seen as kid stuff; and because his business-obsessed brother, who candidly admits that he cheats a little and cringes a little, is applauded (I mean, everybody claps) for doing the best he can. Phooey! Gardner pretends that rebellion is a stroll up Park Avenue on a Sunday morning, to shout taunts at the blank windows; at the same time he defines real grown-up life as providing the right toys for the wife and kiddies and never mind if you cut a few corners and lick a few boots—who doesn't? He must know better (he's smart enough to

206

write a very negotiable play), but he gives his audience a painless laugh at themselves and a warm feeling in the belly. I predict a most successful career.

From here on we can move a little faster. Jean Kerr's *Mary, Mary* (Helen Hayes Theatre, Broadway) and *Take Her, She's Mine* (Biltmore Theatre, Broadway), by Phoebe and Henry Ephron, are routine laugh machines of the sort that are always around and never remembered. They are not imitations of life; they are imitations of other plays. The former concerns a divorced couple who discover that they really love each other best of all; the latter is about a father who must learn that his daughter is a big girl now. The audience laughs because, well-educated in such fare, it knows that certain words ("virgin," for example) and certain situations (a man trying to maintain his pugnacity while under the influence of sleeping pills) have been tested and found risible by the most astute box-office practitioners. There is nothing wrong with plays of this sort—the theater is a store as well as an art, and there are never enough artists around to keep all the shelves filled. You could maintain, in fact, that workmen like Mrs. Kerr and the Ephrons hold the franchise for the much slower and less reliable real playwrights. I found *Mary, Mary* amusing and *Take Her, She's Mine* embarrassing, but that is accidental and the next time around the situation might be reversed.

Finally, and in contrast to the general situation described at the beginning of this piece, the four-man British revue *Beyond the Fringe* (John Golden Theatre, Broadway) offers a wit that is sharp, contemporary, and satiric, but which can be laughed at with relative impunity. That is so especially for an American audience. The kaleidoscope of accents is a wonder to hear, but it scarcely sorts out into anything we can identify as "ours" or "theirs"; and though we may be able to sense the other nuances of class, they are not details that arouse any personal response. We may suspect that C. P. Snow does not enjoy being named the exemplar of the innocuous Briton, but it is not a point on which we would rise to cheer or to stalk from the theater.

The four recent university graduates who wrote and who perform these skits (none considers himself a stage professional and all have other careers to pursue) are gloriously acute observers of absurdity, pomposity, and sham, and hilariously accurate mimics of their victims. England still retains a high degree of tolerance for eccentricity, and the satire in *Beyond the Fringe* focuses less on the venalities of society than on the crotchets of individualistic extremes—from Prime Minister Macmillan to a coal miner with aspirations to abstract thought. Low

REVIEWS

Church obfuscators, elderly and inarticulate clubmen, dotty university philosophers, civil-defense enthusiasts, are the targets. An American audience laughs because these cartoons are inherently funny (and because Messrs. Alan Bennett, Peter Cook, Jonathan Miller, and Dudley Moore are astute and resourceful clowns); an English public would be more apt to feel that its own observations were being brilliantly materialized. But I doubt that even in London many spectators found themselves caught in the line of fire. This limits the bite of the satire, but it also endows the revue with a combination of wit and good nature that is rare to the point of being phenomenal on our stage.

It is hard not to envy the British for being able to turn out such a work as *Beyond the Fringe*, impossible not to wonder whether there are any recent Harvard or Yale graduates who could handle the Bible and Shakespeare with such witty familiarity, could observe their elders and their times with as much irony and as little hostility. England today has its corrosive comedians (Osborne, say, or Pinter), and France nourishes the almost lethal jesting of Genet. But the older societies also support a sophisticated geniality of the sort represented by *Beyond the Fringe* or Giraudoux. Here in America we seem to swing between a grin that is all teeth and a guffaw that is decerebrated. We have always been a very funny people, full of pranks and hyperbole, but wit has largely evaded us. And now that we find ourselves the rather youthful custodians of man's fate, it is a real question whether we shall ever learn to smile.

The Dumb Waiter, by Harold Pinter; *Desire Under the Elms*, by Eugene O'Neill; & *The Milk Train Doesn't Stop Here Anymore*, by Tennessee Williams (1963)

Grammarians of the theater distinguish four principal dramatic modes: tragedy, comedy, melodrama, and farce. Another way to handle this structural pedantry is to borrow a word from antique physiology and define these terms as the humors of the theater. For just as the learned doctors could scarcely expect to find a man who was totally choleric or utterly phlegmatic, so it is almost impossible to cite a play that is, say, tragedy pure and simple.

An exception may be that nerve-shattering machine of careening ice floes, blazing orphanages, screaming buzz saws and virgins outscreaming them that, from about 1850 to World War I, set the tone

THE DUMB WAITER, DESIRE UNDER THE ELMS, & THE MILK TRAIN

and made the money in the commercial theater. This was melodrama, 200 proof. But it was so because it was a synthetic concoction, made by abstracting from drama an element that had existed there long before the word melodrama was coined. It is as though a culinary sensationalist, knowing that garlic is the most arresting ingredient in a salad, were to present his diners with a garlic salad. Such a dish would predictably dominate the meal, as indeed melodrama for a while dominated the theater. But it would likely give garlic a bad name, as those plays have turned melodrama into a term of abuse. We pretend to be offended by the taste of it, whereas in fact our theater would be pale and insipid without it.

Just what is it that we are talking about? Unfortunately it is easier to assume that everyone understands what melodrama is than to define the term. Stark Young, coping with the problem in that superb breviary known as *The Theater*, says:

> One of the traits of farce and melodrama . . . is exaggeration. . . . Their flight is reckless, they are the playwright's trip to the moon. . . . Melodrama is free to avoid the tragic finality, to evade its conclusion. . . . Both farce and melodrama take the cash and let the credit go; they eat their cake and have it, too.

That says something about how melodrama functions; it certainly suggests why melodrama invigorates the stage and the audience.

Eric Bentley, writing a few years ago in the *New Republic*, may have come closer to a definition with the following: "If art imitates life, it should be added that while naturalistic art imitates the surfaces, 'melodramatic' art imitates what is beneath the surface. It is a matter, then, of finding external representation—symbol—for what cannot be photographed or described." And that ties in with a remark by M. Wilson Disher (in his book *Melodrama*) that "insensibility to the absurd" is always a hallmark of melodrama. What goes on beneath the surface, the Freudian motion, is indeed absurd; and it is no coincidence, I think, that the reek of melodrama is particularly strong in the playhouses during this era of the Theater of the Absurd. Melodrama does not prevail merely because it keeps us on the edge of our seats; by its use the fires that rage in our bosoms, the rats that gnaw at our brains, are brought on stage to be faced and, just possibly, faced down. Which foregoing will have to serve as a definition.

In view of all this, it may be entertaining to trace the vein of melodrama in the current season. And that may serve the purpose of stopping people from crying out, as though they had discovered a toad

REVIEWS

in their bath, every time someone on stage does something or says something that the observer would not attempt in his wildest moments (however often he may have cherished the thought of it in his secret reveries).

Calculated Risk by Joseph Hayes (Ambassador Theatre, Broadway), whose *The Desperate Hours* was an almost inexhaustible success as novel, play, and movie, is a good point of departure because it is a melodrama in the old gaslight sense, and we no longer see many of them. It lacks any of those climaxes of fire or flood that punctuated the most ambitious of the earlier thrillers (an airplane does not roar in through a fearful fog, but the runway is offstage). However, the villain is a creature so besotted by greed and hate that he trembles and jerks and suffers a repertory of disfiguring tics.

The plot is a variation on the widow's foreclosed mortgage. In this case a splendid old New England woolen mill, an enterprise dignified by the highest craftsmanship and the warmest paternalism, is threatened with worse than death by a raid on its common stock. The day is saved by the profligate elder son (played by Joseph Cotten), who in the hour of crisis is able to meet the scornful eyes of his dead father (a bust is provided for the purpose) and who shows an unsuspected, but apparently inherited, capacity for board-room trickery in a righteous cause.

Calculated Risk balances on the situation made immortal generations ago in the line, "There is a traitor in our midst," and all in all I spent an excellent evening. I suspect, however, that nostalgia gripped me as powerfully as the proceedings on stage. Thirty years ago, Grey's Drug Store, that lodestone for stage-struck youths, could supply cut-rate seats for a show like this almost any night in the week.

At the other end of the scale is Harold Pinter's *The Dumb Waiter*, which has been offered this season in a double bill with his *The Collection* (Cherry Lane Theatre, Off-Broadway). This is anti-drama, Theater of the Absurd, or whatever term you apply to a play whose main theme, whose central character, you might say, is unspoken implication. The situation in *The Dumb Waiter* is certainly melodramatic: two gunmen, Ben and Gus, are waiting in a basement room for someone unknown to them who will presently come through the door and whom they will kill according to orders. They are great men for orders, these two; and the play turns to farce when the dumb-waiter in a building they had thought untenanted springs into action and sends down a succession of peremptory chits for dishes so numerous and varied that one must envision a bustling restaurant on the floor above. The two make hysterical, hopeless efforts to comply with an

THE DUMB WAITER & DESIRE UNDER THE ELMS

authority that is manifestly irrational—authority is their religion, and reason is not at issue.

The play bristles with melodramatic detail—the tense waiting, the quick glares of rage, the shocking eruption of the dumb-waiter (I was reminded of secret passages and bodies in closets), the book of matches slipped quietly under the door, and the empty corridor when th door is snatched open. Gus and Ben are two more men in thrall to Godot; like all true believers, what they expect for their devotion is justice ("Why did he send us matches if he knew there was no gas?"). The horror for them is that theirs turns out to be a personal Godot.

I won't stop over Pinter's *The Collection*. It is a drawing-room comedy, with the difference that of the three men in the cast (there is also a woman), two are homosexual and one is ambiguous. This makes room for lively permutations, and the proceedings are witty at the expense of our skin-deep conventions; but the extravagance of the conflicts and alliances here is more ironic than melodramatic.

José Quintero has revived Eugene O'Neill's *Desire Under the Elms* at Circle in the Square (Off-Broadway). It is a play animated by melodrama as the Greeks knew it: a father and son mortally opposed, a mother destroying her child in a mad attempt to end the struggle. Whenever *Desire Under the Elms* is revived in New York (and it happens frequently), it is like a gale sweeping the contemporary stage clean of trivialities and the fine shavings of sentiment. Therefore, I think it is a case where melodrama may be used as a term of criticism.

O'Neill rouses pity and terror with his melodrama, but he cannot sublimate them in his tragedy, for it lacks the stature that would allow an audience to find its own significance in a universal design. Tragedy is no longer held to be the exclusive realm of gods and kings, but to quote Stark Young again, in a paraphrase of the standard definitions: the tragic in drama is "the struggle of the individual will against eternal law, the struggle of the good with the good." Old Ephraim Cabot seems to be generating his own law; it is not the inescapable one that tempers us all. And Eben, his son, and Abbie, the wife of one and step-mother of the other, lack the virtue that might give their fate the permanence and breadth of legend. A tragedy that does not rise to inevitability subsides into morbidity.

This latest production was built upon the extraordinary energy and projective powers of George C. Scott, Colleen Dewhurst, and Rip Torn. It was a muscular and compelling presentation, but I felt it did not congeal into a unified work. The solo resourcefulness of the actors may have been too pressing for Quintero to harness in the time available. More likely, theater-in-the-almost-round works to the serious

REVIEWS

disadvantage of a play set on three nearly equal and mutually antagonistic points. A centrifugal motion is almost unavoidable, with the actors hurling themselves at the audience instead of at one another.

What everyone noted about Peter Feibleman's *Tiger, Tiger, Burning Bright* (Booth Theatre, Broadway) is that at last we are shown a play about blacks that is not about the black problem. But I don't think anyone has made the related point that it is not about the black question only because, with one inconsequential exception, there are no white people in the play. It is not yet possible to mix races on stage (or that matter in fiction) without race's becoming an element in the plot. This is a reflection, surely, but it is a reflection on society, not on the theater.

Color still makes a point that is additional to whatever point the playwright is concerned about, and as long as that is true black actors, however accomplished, we will find the great majority of central roles closed to them. That it will not always be true can be predicted from the increasing frequency with which blacks appear on stage (and in the movies) in situations where color is irrelevant. I don't mean the traditional parts of domestics and raffish hangers-on; there is now a wide area of supporting roles in which the color of an actor's skin sets off no response. An interracial *Romeo and Juliet* or *A Doll's House* may someday be a matter of no special moment, but in this area the theater will follow the mores, not create them.

Meanwhile one can judge from the production of *Tiger, Tiger, Burning Bright* how much the barrier of racial awareness is costing us in stage talent. Few productions display such a consistently high level of individual craft or so unified an embodiment of the author's intent and the director's interpretation (the director here was Joshua Logan). The leads were Claudia McNeil, Alvin Ailey, and Diana Sands, but the rest of the company moved around and through their focal struggle with a grace and power for which the conventional word "supporting" is inadequate.

In terms of melodrama the play intensified, and provided overt symbols for, a familiar enough experience—the masks of accommodation we wear to make personal relationships tolerable. *Tiger, Tiger, Burning Bright* is melodrama, not realism, because it transforms proclivities into deeds and inadequacies into vices. Factually, the house of illusion constructed by Feibleman could never have stood; symbolically, though, such houses stand on every street. In more specific terms the play offered a series of tableaux in high melodrama: the noble son exposed as a thief, the prim maiden discovered in her whore's raiment, the dream of honor on which the mother has built her matriarchy

212

THE MILK TRAIN DOESN'T STOP HERE ANYMORE

shattered by a word. But the melodrama here is also in the service of tragedy, for good does struggle with good, and the fate of the family is not irrelevant to our general condition.

Whatever swamps and miasmas Tennessee Williams may still have in store for us, his tone from *Period of Adjustment* through *The Night of the Iguana* to *The Milk Train Doesn't Stop Here Anymore* has been relatively free of horrors. By comparison with the dramatist's past, the mood of these plays is almost benign.

In *The Milk Train Doesn't Stop Here Anymore* (Morosco Theatre, Broadway) Williams essays the device, technically interesting and theatrically exciting, of presenting a conventionally tragic situation in the vocabulary of comedy. The tension thus built can, I think, be called melodrama; to laugh in the teeth of death is surely a melodramatic, not to say heroic, extravagance. (I understand that Eugène Ionesco develops a variation of the same theme in a recent play titled *Le Roi se meurt* [*The King Expires*].)

Like Belle Poitrine of Patrick Dennis's novel *Little Me*, Flora Goforth in *The Milk Train Doesn't Stop Here Anymore* has risen from dubious obscurity to wealth and social power by a lively and judicious commerce in husbands. Also like Dennis's heroine, she is now writing her memoirs and for that purpose has installed in her complex of Italian coastal villas a battery of tape recorders and an intercom system that gives her instant command of her secretary at any hour of the day or (more frequently) night. But unlike Belle, Flora Goforth is dying, dying most painfully and in full knowledge of the nearness of the hour. Flora is a clown, and she is dying to an accompaniment of bells and slapstick; nevertheless, there is the fact of the matter.

She has planned to spend her last summer in virtual retirement, repaying herself for the loss of society by tormenting her secretary, a Vassar girl with a bun, who is a particularly suitable target in that she is mourning her late husband. Mourners are Flora's natural victims, the more so since she foresees that she will have none. This routine of dictation and rabbit-punching is upset by the unannounced arrival of a young man clad in *lederhosen*, wearing a knapsack, and holding a somewhat scuffed volume of his poetry in hand.

As Flora soon learns from her sharp-taloned chum Signora Condotti (formerly Mrs. Ridgeway), this Chris Flanders, an itinerant constructor of mobiles, has been present at the demise of so many rich and lonely ladies that he is known the length of the French and Italian coast as the Angel of Death. This does not much daunt Flora, who is aware in any case that her course is run, but she is determined not to be duped. She will take on Chris as an ultimate lover, but for free-

REVIEWS

loaders bent on exchanging spirituality for room and board, the milk train no longer stops at Casa Goforth.

As long as Williams keeps to the purgative exchanges between a pair of dragons too old to bother with hypocrisy, as long as he shocks us out of complacency toward such matters as individual morality and universal mortality, he is pertinent and very funny. And since Hermione Baddeley and Mildred Dunnock were handling his foils, the stage sparkled like a bowl of rhinestones.

Chris, the transcendental beachboy, is a more uneasy element. He could be as bitingly droll as the two harridans, with their costume wigs and cosmetic smattering of Italian, but it is not clear that the author intends Angel of Death as an entirely ironic nickname. Paul Roebling played the role as hygienically as a young man can when he must expose to maximum view a pair of legs that are a little too shapely and a little too evenly tanned to elicit the unreserved admiration of males in the audience. But he was made to say some very silly things in the manner of eastern mysticism, and I got the strong impression that he was about to bestow apotheosis on Flora Goforth when the final curtain cut off my view.

If so, this is carrying melodrama to the point of blasphemy—by which I mean an offense against the God-given sanity of the audience. It is enough that Williams should make us feel for Flora: when he implies that her death will be an assumption (and what else is that mobile, glittering in the light of the last scene, meant to imply?), he falls into bathos. For Flora has great relevance as a bitch and none at all as a saint. But whatever its deficiencies as philosophic tragedy, *The Milk Train Doesn't Stop Here Anymore* was a theatrical evening of wit and pertinent exaggeration.

Melodrama, then, abides; it can be found in almost any play that cuts beneath our skin. It is the embodiment in action of what we know our secret lives to be. For the secret life is not so much a self-delusion as evidence that few people can make art of their personal histories. Melodrama is the armature that a man would need to give his days and years some communicable shape—and that, finally, will have to rest as the definition.

But for Whom Charlie, by S. N. Behrman (1964)

S. N. Behrman's *But For Whom Charlie*, with which the Repertory Theatre of Lincoln Center completes its first season, is concerned with integrity, the particular need for it in our quicksand society.

BUT FOR WHOM CHARLIE

Mr. Behrman frames this thought in major and subsidiary contexts and undertakes to embody it in dialogue of such wit, topicality, and emancipated naughtiness that we shall not notice that the proposition is self-evident. His two acts froth with seeming jokes and pseudo-paradoxes; the atmosphere is as heady as a *New Yorker* fashion ad come to life. *But For Whom Charlie* may be banal, but no one can complain that it is unprofessional.

I don't mean to depreciate integrity as a dramatic theme. It has often been the source of stunning surprises and tantalizing dilemmas, and it will provide these pleasures again. However, it is a theme demanding some individuality of viewpoint; it must be approached obliquely. What cannot be done, outside the pages of *Boy's Life*, is to declare that integrity is splendid and its absence a great pity. But Mr. Behrman's villain announces his venality with the complacence of an Ivy League Iago, and his hero fairly glows with spiritual honesty, inhibited only by a diffidence so grotesque that anyone experienced in stage conventions knows he will firm up in the last act like properly calculated *blancmange*. "Isn't injustice the essence of everything?" someone asks early in the evening, to which the play replies with a resolute "Heaven forbid!"

Mr. Behrman has always been responsive to current social vibrations, and he astutely sets his new play on the premises of the Seymour Rosenthal Foundation, endowed by the guilt-ridden son of a Hollywood vulgarian for the support of talented writers of slight commercial promise. Seymour (Jason Robards, Jr.) lives upstairs, whence sounds of Bach are frequently heard, but the place is run by Charles Taney of the play's title (Ralph Meeker), who drinks, fornicates, bullies, and schemes all over Jo Mielziner's split-level, Castro Convertible set with an extrovert assurance based on the fact that, back in the days when they were both Yalies, he had defended Seymour against the anti-Semites. Never having had a friend, it takes Seymour twenty years to get the hang of Charlie.

Foundations have had many and confusing effects on our intellectual life, and in themselves raise vexing problems of integrity. Unfortunately, the play shows no deeper interest in the ambiguities of institutionalized benevolence than it does in the moral stamina of its characters. Mr. Behrman introduces an aging novelist (David Wayne) who has learned to tap Seymour like a sugar maple, but the cynicism is too blatant to be arresting. (Wayne plays the part with a deft relish that is easily the most gratifying ingredient in the production.)

Also prominent on stage are Charlie's feminine counterpart (Salome Jens), who tells us that her first job, which led to her first

REVIEWS

marriage, was performing in the nude in pornographic movies; and a thoroughly decent girl (played by Faye Dunaway with as much flavor as the insipid invention permits) who sleeps where her fancy suggests, but who is steadily devoted to getting a Rosenthal grant for her talented, alcoholic, sado-suicidal brother (Clinton Kimbrough). The play is full of references to literary works that verge on genius, but as is usual in such cases no documentation is provided.

Elia Kazan has instructed everyone to ham it up (Mr. Meeker grins like a shark, Mr. Robards dithers and gulps and wriggles like a puppy, Miss Jens gives us recollections of Theda Bara) and to speak their lines as though they were reciting gems from Bartlett's *Familiar Quotations*. The punchy delivery elicits a good deal of reflexive laughter and made me feel as though I were glumly sitting through a farce in a language unknown.

So now the initial Lincoln Center repertory is complete, and the three plays will continue in rotation for the rest of the season. It is good that the venture has been born, but thus far it is not nearly good enough. All this talent, all this money, all this attention has not added one cubit to the stature of the New York theater. Messrs. Whitehead and Kazan have dared little and dreamed small: they have revived one of the less effective plays by the much revived O'Neill (*Marco Millions*), and they have offered new works by Arthur Miller (*After the Fall*) and S. N. Behrman that any producer would eagerly have launched in the West Forties. Quite aside from the merits of these particular plays, it is utterly pointless for Lincoln Center to do what Broadway is competent and clamoring to do. The idea is to augment and surpass, perhaps to challenge and inspire, the commercial theater—not to imitate it. Or if I am wrong, what is the idea?

Dutchman & *The Baptism*, by LeRoi Jones (1964)

It is altogether likely that the folks who go down to the Cherry Lane Theatre (Off-Broadway) to see the one-act play now being produced there are witnesses to a signal event—the emergence of an outstanding dramatist, LeRoi Jones. His is a turbulent talent. While turbulence is not always a sign of power or of valuable meaning, I have a hunch that Jones's fire will burn ever higher and clearer if our theater can furnish an adequate vessel to harbor his flame. We need it.

He is also very angry. Anger alone may merely make a loud noise, confuse, sputter, and die. For anger to burn to useful effect, it must be

216

DUTCHMAN & THE BAPTISM

guided by an idea. With the "angry young men" of England one was not always certain of the source of dissatisfaction or of its goal. With LeRoi Jones it is easy to say that the plight of blacks ignited the initial rage—justification enough—and that the rage will not be appeased until there is no more black and white, no more color except as differences in hue and accent are part of the world's splendid spectacle. But there is more to his ferocity than a protest against the horrors of racism.

Dutchman, the first of Jones's plays to reach the professional stage, is a stylized account of a subway episode. A white girl (Jennifer West) picks up a young black (Robert Hooks) who at first is rather embarrassed and later piqued by her advances. There is a perversity in her approach that finally provokes him to a hymn of hate. With lyrical obscenity he declares that murder is in his and every black's heart and were it to reach the point of action, there would be less "singin' of the blues," less of that delightful folk music and hot jazz that beguile the white man's fancy, more calm in the black soul. Meanwhile, it is the black man who is murdered.

What we must not overlook in seeing the play is that, while this explosion of fury is its rhetorical and emotional climax, the crux of its significance resides in the depiction of the white girl, whose relevance to *Dutchman*'s situation does not lie in her whiteness but in her representative value as a token of our civilization. She is our neurosis. Not a neurosis in regard to blacks, but the absolute neurosis of American society.

She is "hep": she has heard about everything, but understands and feels nothing. She twitches, jangles, jitters with a thin but inexhaustible energy, propelled by the vibrations from millions of ads, television quiz programs, newspaper columns, and intellectual jargon culled from countless digests, panel discussions, illustrated summaries, smatterings of gossip on every conceivable subject (respectable and illicit), epithets, wisecracks, formulas, slogans, cynicisms, cures, solutions. She is the most "informed" person in the world and the most ignorant. (The information feeds the ignorance.) She is the bubbling, boiling garbage cauldron newly produced by our progress. She is a calculating machine gone berserk; she is the real killer. What she destroys is not men of a certain race but mankind. She is the compendium in little of the universal mess.

If *Dutchman* has a fault, it is its completeness. Its ending is somewhat too pat, too pointed in its symbolism. If one has caught the drift of the play's meaning before its final moment, the ending is supererogatory; if one has failed to do so, it is probably useless.

REVIEWS

Anyone wishing to check further on LeRoi Jones's sudden and commanding intrusion upon the theater may be able to see *The Baptism*, which is now being presented, on a week-to-week basis, Monday nights in Off-Broadway houses that are otherwise dark—but for which one-act backing is being raised for a regular production.

In this black Mass version of a Passion play, Jones converts his rage to slapstick blasphemy. A homosexual Satan and a cant-singing Negro preacher war for the soul of the young feckless Son of God. The real evil is hypocrisy, the sin of euphemism, and the devil drives it from the stage with a coruscating flow of obscene vernacular.

This is not a finished or carefully thought-out play. It is rough work, in every sense: the purging outrageousness of a fine poet. It is also wildly funny, both in its essential comment and from the shock of incongruity. Jones has the gift of vivid economy, which sparks his scene into instant activity.

In *The Baptism*, he gets the invaluable cooperation of Taylor Mead as the campy Fallen Angel. Mead, who was one of the antic cast of the film *Hallelujah the Hills* (1963, Adolphas Mekas), has a mocking intelligence, superb timing, and a face and body of indescribably mobile depravity.

On the night I was present, Mead also played the title role in Frank O'Hara's *The General*, a vaudeville in which an exceedingly great leader returns to his scenes of Pacific glory. There is not nearly enough substance to the series of loosely integrated skits, yet Mead holds it together by main force of ingratiating corruption.

Hamlet, by William Shakespeare (1964)

On Sunday evenings at the 13th Street Theatre (Off-Off Broadway), a troupe assembled and directed by Michael Alaimo (he was the dumb-show King in Joseph Papp's Central Park *Hamlet*) is prancing through the First Quarto version of the play in, of all things, *Commedia dell'arte* style. This farcical view of *Hamlet* and his playmates, running so counter to the carefully focused, introspective offerings of recent experience, seems, at first, sacrilegious. But acceptance and utter enjoyment follow hard upon, for the play emerges, from this unaccustomed vantage, in a broad antic humanity that the audience explores and enjoys on its own, freed by *Commedia* from the constricting, interpretive definitions to which it has become so conditioned.

The style is obviously appropriate to Hamlet's assumed antic air, but when the Hamlet who knows a hawk from a handsaw is

218

HAMLET

nevertheless portrayed *à la Commedia*, and when uncle, mother, prime minister, and the rest are played in pratfall, amazing, unfamiliar personalities appear. The slapstick entices a whole-human response, and the tragedy of Hamlet's, and his fellow inmates', loss of life's potential is mourned anew in sardonic, capering caricature.

Relieved of psyche-probing and redemption, the brother-murderer King is a crude, crooked cracker who snatches what he wants and belches it. His Queen is a hard, fun-loving broad who's been around and likes it, and who's going to wiggle her way into more of the action, whatever and wherever it is. It's lots of fun, but it also makes a lot of good sense. I'll venture that this thirsty Queen, who thoughtlessly drains the poison cup, is closer to the Queen the first Elizabeth saw than are our recent repentants. Horatio as buffoon-foil and Polonius (Corambis in the First Quarto) as Ass and Ophelia as Blondie are comic and ring true. And these sensible, palatable truths stand delectably apart from any attempt at interpreted Truth, for which fact, among others, I loved the evening.

But, most interestingly, the off-beat perspective of *Commedia* allows us to view Hamlet himself through an ancient lens that has become all but forgotten. Our modern glass has been carefully curved to center upon Hamlet as aspect. We are shown finely rendered but angrily restricted, or else indecisive, or else Oedipus-complexed Hamlets, in contexts so specialized, so individually and preciously interpreted that Richard Burton found them obstructive to his own aspect, and therefore deleted the "stamp of one defect" lines that Laurence Olivier stressed as the very theme and center of his interpretation. The wide-view lens of *Commedia* displays a clay-footed Hamlet, a fumbling, Chaplinesque character who can no more overcome the foibles of his mind and body than can you or I. There is life and fun and comic beauty and softly bleeding tragedy in his plight, even as there is in yours and mine. I relish this view of Hamlet as I relish Chaplin and Molière because all of life is there. Nobody is screwing a lens into tight focus on the surrounding view.

The choice of the First Quarto as vehicle for this revealing exploration was apt. Theories regarding this version abound. But whether the First Quarto is, as some say, an abbreviated version approved by the master for his provincial following, or an early version later embellished by Shakespeare in the manner so deplored by Ben Jonson, or simply an inept piracy, it does provide a perfect platform for this *Commedia* rendition of Hamlet in his underwear.

What language is there is poetry, sayeth the soliloquy, so garbled in this text that dumb show is substituted by the players; but the First

REVIEWS

Quarto omits, of course, a great many of the beloved, fulsome passages, and they are sorely missed. Let no reader misunderstand. This *Commedia* version of the First Quarto is not the *Hamlet* with which one wants to live one's theatrical or poetic life. It is not preferred, from any literary standpoint, to the complete play as we know it. But there is available to our view, on 13th Street, an anachronistic view of *Hamlet* that even in this abbreviated, de-tuned version is most illuminating.

The *Commedia* style was certainly well known in Elizabethan England. It grew out of and as a part of the humanistic upsurge in Italy that was the precursor of England's own Renaissance. Shakespeare's players' own style may have been much closer to *Commedia* than to the Method, and it may well be that the Alaimo troupe's version of *Hamlet* gives us a unique opportunity to taste an ancient flavor.

But *Hamlet*'s historical or dramatic relevance *à la Commedia* is secondary to the sheer fun of the portrayal. All else aside, the players offer an entrancing evening of theater. They are individually welltrained in the *Commedia* art, and they play well in ensemble. They prove, anew, that there is more in Shakespeare and in *Hamlet* than is dreamed of in some philosophies.

Baal, by Bertolt Brecht (1965)

The most difficult years in an artist's life come in the decade after his death. Unmaliciously, even unconsciously, fashion, segmentation, and cult implacably enforce a second and final death—that of his art. Bertolt Brecht died nine years ago. Fashion now puts printed signs on our stages, or lines lights about our proscenia. It narrates over loudspeakers; it throws titles and slogans onto screens; it projects slides. We call these already fossilized relics Brechtian.

But how are we, today, to know the real nature of the art these devices memorialize? There was a Brechtian school, but it was like that of Frank Lloyd Wright. The genius-leader gathering his *Bund* brooks no competition. When he is gone there remain only bereaved and leaderless followers—sponge-type intellectuals who had never found for themselves how much they had contributed to the leader's processes and how much they had leaned on him. After he is gone, they may ritualize or categorize or deify. But the cult rarely furthers, or even explains, the master's art.

Relatively few of Brecht's plays have been undertaken anywhere outside East Germany in the last decade. When they have been

BAAL

attempted, critics who knew Brecht's Berliner Ensemble have seen only glimmerings of the master. His theater is not easily transferred into a repertory or into a contra-cultural style and attitude; it is not a cloak or a stance that can be donned or discarded at will. It is a way of theatrical life.

Brecht's plays have been successful in America only when they have been segmented or de-fanged. *The Threepenny Opera* ran for years— but an "enjoyable" version, in which Mack the Knife's switch-blade protruded from its sheath only enough to scratch and tickle. We "liked the music." We found *Brecht on Brecht* more palatable than the plays. The few productions that have attempted to replicate Brecht's own have not been successful, artistically or financially.

Therefore, Theodore Mann and Paul Bibin's decision to stage *Baal* at the Martinique Theatre (Broadway) is fortunate. Their choice is good primer: Brecht for America. It is closer to the American "Method" than Brecht's later "alienated" or "epic" plays. It embodies the *Angst* to which citified Americans are attuned these days. Being Brecht's own Goethe-esque *Young Werthe*r, as well as his Kafkaesque *Trial*, it is probably the easiest of his works for Americans to comprehend. (Our attitudes in the 1960s are more akin to those of pre-World War I than post- World War I Germany—let alone to the Continent of post-World War II.)

Brecht was twenty when he wrote *Baal* in 1918. It was his first full-length play. He had just returned from service with the defeated German army. All Germany was reeling in disbelief at the disintegration of all that had been supposed indestructible and forever true. Not only their military but their civilization and their art and their culture had been shown up as fraudulent. And Brecht was a German poet who knew how fully the wracked culture had fed his soul. The writing of *Baal* became the first of a series of efforts to excoriate the spirit of Goethe and Schiller from his being.

Brecht denied and denounced the possibility of individual moral choice in this world. His rage at cultural and personal romanticism was as great as his own inner compulsion to strain the limits of his human periphery toward the God-like. In *Baal*, he undertook to mock religion and humanity and morality out of his being—to eviscerate the "heavy elephantiasis of conscience," as he put it. With Rimbaud he saw earth as infernal and viewed morality as a "weakness of the brain." With Georg Büchner, he saw the defeat of the Gothic culture by the Gallic as individuality's death knell. Men would now become worker-ants. A young folk poet, Baal moves among the intelligentsia in the cafés and among the workers, among the moral and the

REVIEWS

immoral. But he is consistent in his human relations. He gives nothing; he only feeds. He fills his belly and uses his women. Then having drunk his fill of women, he will drink of men. He becomes his friend Ekart's lover. Having used Ekart, he kills him in a fit of lover's jealousy. Having used his own life, he dies. His final jealousy is leveled at the God-like—at the stars. Baal, mouthpiece of Brecht's own yearnings and agonies, has swilled in the gutter, and he has soared to and fallen from the stars.

Forced, as he saw it, by intransigent history to discard his own longed-for likeness to God, Brecht fastened his German bent for religion upon personal animalism. The human body became his real protagonist and hero—the amorally incoherent, animalistically assertive, ecstatically enduring life force of raw, naked, muscled man. For Brecht, life embodied the conflict between supermen fighting for their bodies' joys with the strength of savages and the impersonal, passionless agents of social usefulness. Yet the animal hedonist is coward and rogue. He is likable, charming, and sexually submissive. He is Baal; later he is Macheath. He is not only passive, he is also masochistic because he can atone to himself for the God-likeness he has lost only by wishing for and seeking his animalistic death.

The enemy of the rogue is the knave—the doer. The socially effective man is the implacable enemy of the animalistic. The Brechtian doer (like Peachum) is sadist. The knaves' sadism does battle with the rogues' masochism in Brecht's theater, and the standard ending of his plays is the total victory of cruelty. The good is passive, masochistic—the bad is active, sadistic, and victorious. Brecht knew his people and knew his tune. He did not need to wait for the Nazis. He had already invented them.

Gladys Vaughan's direction of the Martinique *Baal* is, on the whole, perceptive and evocative. Since this is pre-abstract—even pre-Brechtian (as to systemology) Brecht—questions of empathy versus alienation were not immediately pertinent. (For Americans who are still at least vestigially puritanical, the voyeurism induced by the play's sexuality creates a sort of empathy Brecht would least desire.) James Earl Jones's Ekart is magnificently libidinal. But Mitchell Ryan's Baal falls short. Brecht's Baal needs to alternate on stage between the gross sensuality and licentiousness of the Baal of ancient Semitic legend and the moral, socially aware man of conscience. Ryan is simply unable to evoke hedonism, unable to become stallion. Consequently, Baal's duality is not adequately expressed.

The *Baal* company (alternating in repertory with *Othello*) plays well in ensemble, and there are no weak performers in the supporting cast. Will Holt's direction of Stephen Wolpe's musical arrangements adds substantially to the mood and the flow. This is a staged work of which its producers and participants may be justly proud. It provides America with its first real opportunity to see a Brecht play done very much as Brecht would have it. But *Baal* is the earliest, most American Brecht. When will we see, for example, *Saint Joan of the Stockyards* presented not as a charade but as relevant social commentary? For Americans, there is no greater challenge over the entire theatrical spectrum than that of Brecht. Brecht wanted from his actors all that Stanislavsky and Strasberg have wanted and, in addition, Brecht wanted them to fully understand and create a stage commentary upon the social meaning of the characters and interactions they were portraying. This, coupled with his demand that the actor not engage the audience's empathy in such a way as to rob it of its intellectual objectivity, is the famous Brechtian "alienation." (In a sense it is "supra-theater," but it is just as true to say that this alienation is nothing different from that innate to the *Commedia dell'arte*. W. C. Fields, simultaneously creating and commenting upon the Bank Dick, himself exemplifies Brechtian "alienated" theater.)

Brechtian commentary for an American audience would be attuned to our own culture; it could not possibly be equivalent to the commentary of the Berliner Ensemble. The current Greenwich Mews Theatre (Off-Broadway) production of *The Exception and the Rule* illustrates the problem. It is "authentic" in that it tries faithfully to re-create what had been socially meaningful at another time and in another place. It is un-Brechtian in that it does not expose and cauterize today's American exceptions and rules.

Troubled Waters, by Ugo Betti, & *Live Like Pigs*, by John Arden (1965)

Despite a reputation in Italy that spires above that of Luigi Pirandello, Ugo Betti has been mostly ignored by the American theater. When we have seen his work, it had the appearance of dry and heavy pedagogy. One thinks particularly of the seemingly pseudo-literary, boringly earnest, and interminably windy 1963 production of *Corruption at the Palace of Justice* at the Cherry Lane Theatre. The more recent production of *The Queen and the Rebels* at Theatre Four was given an expressionist interpretation; thus humanized, it became acceptable to us as something on the order of good melodramatic Arthur Miller or Clifford Odets.

REVIEWS

Betti was not a theatrical theorist like Bertolt Brecht, but he did state clearly his view of the actor's role, describing his players as "pawns in the author's chess game." He specifically warned against temptations toward bathos and sentimentality, and his apprehensions proved valid. It has been his unfortunate history that typical American acting exaggerates his weaknesses and smothers his virtues. To keep Betti's drama intact, the cultural climate from which he evolved needs to be understood. The Greeks invented drama, but the Italians perfected comedy. It has become an innate Italian predilection to turn the most tragic happening into a game of decisive rumination, culminating in an irrational but perennial faith in the morrow.

If there is one qualitative difference between American and continental European playwriting in our time, it is that while our dramatists are still crying over their fall, the Europeans have, however bitterly, risen and begun again to use their splintered crutches. Betti himself wrote that "every writer represents a path, which begins at the I and leans toward the world." European dramatists relate the family to the world; Americans are still trying to relate the individual to the family. (It is no historical accident that introspective Method acting should have become so American a theatrical stance, for we, of all the current cultures, are most sorry for ourselves.)

It remained for a British director, Eric Salmon, to unveil Betti for Americans. Mr. Salmon's interpretation of *Troubled Waters* (the Italian title would be translated as *The Brother Who Protects and Loves*) at the Gate Theatre (Off-Broadway) shows us a Betti who is, of all things, Chekhovian. Seen through the eyes of European cynicism, and with the heavy hand of American Method acting lightened, the perverse and derisive irony of the conflicts Betti portrays becomes intensely human, recognizable as our very own, and playfully, even liltingly engaging. The complex thematics of the story and of the intellectual interactions is made secondary to the play's sense of mystery and its poetic, bittersweet aura of life.

Like the other recently produced Betti plays, *Troubled Waters* is concerned with the psychology of the winning and losing power-seekers, their actions and emotions, their recantations and degeneration, their catharsis, and the struggle of a few of their number for moral enlightenment and transcendence. An initial Kafkaesque atmosphere of obsession and mystery underlies an action that explores, octopus-like, the effects of man's recently enhanced libidinous self-knowledge.

Troubled Waters begins just after the bureaucrat Gabriele (played to near perfection by Harris Yulin) has defeated his compatriot

224

TROUBLED WATERS & LIVE LIKE PIGS

Giacomo in a struggle for political power. Alda, sister of the deposed politician, "saves" her brother from exile by reassuming an earlier prostitute-role, this time with her brother's conqueror. The balance of the play exposes the multitudinous aspects of a three-power struggle: that of an almost incestuous brother-sister relationship that competes with the sister's penchant for whoredom; that of the victor for his nihilistic, bestial freedom; and that of the brother not only to retain and maintain his earthly power and love relationships, but also to pierce through to a moral understanding of the dilemmas of the drama's major characters.

Brecht and Betti were alike in addressing themselves to the incongruity between mankind's desire for order, harmony, justice, the godlike, and moral identity and its animalistic, accidental, iniquitous existence. But while Brecht was depreciating the possibility of human moral choice, Betti was celebrating its newest, albeit provisional, rebirth. And while Brecht and Bernard Shaw avoided contemplating the inner man, and provided "answers" through simplistic, topical social preachments, Betti had the courage and resolution to cope with the core of human fallibility and guilt, and to reaffirm the resurrective aspects of the human spirit as well as human faith.

The Betti shown us at the Gate is in the mainstream of the world's dramatists, and for this revelation we owe its producers and director great thanks. (The production was presented as part of Memphis State University's dramatic program and thus constitutes a notable contribution by a regional institution to the New York theater.)

John Arden, roughly the contemporary and easily the peer of Harold Pinter and Arnold Wesker, is almost unknown in America. The block to his arrival here may have been that his early masterpiece, *Serjeant Musgrave's Dance*, is a great dirge-like morality play, involving a large cast and elaborate sets, costumes, and stage effects. It needs, thus, Broadway staging, yet its acrid, terrifying theme is not one to attract producers of happy plays. (My private test for the validity of the Repertory Theater of Lincoln Center, under its new management, is how soon it schedules *Serjeant Musgrave's Dance*.) But *Live Like Pigs*, as its name implies, can be staged in any alley; it is a boisterous, driving outburst of human spirit under compression, it plays like a roller coaster—swooping and diving and screaming at the tight corners—and it is a wonder that Off-Broadway did not seize upon it earlier.

The Theatre Company of Boston, with David Wheeler directing, has brought into New York (Actors' Playhouse, Off-Broadway) a

REVIEWS

production worth waiting for. The cast has accent trouble, as usually happens when Americans are asked to play lower-class English: the difficulty is not so much that lines are occasionally lost in phonetic accidents as that the speech sometimes takes on a virtuoso quality that becomes an irrelevant act in itself. But this technical obstacle aside, the company understands the content and atmosphere of *Live Like Pigs* and virtually flings the action at the heads of the stunned and delighted audience. We haven't lived so raucously on the New York stage in many a season. Arden has said that when he wrote *Live Like Pigs* (in 1958), he "was more concerned with the 'poetic' than the 'journalistic' structure of the play." This is the secret of his play's vitality and immediacy—he is dealing with people, not problems. Americans need to stretch their imaginations a little to engage the Sawneys, who are the principal people of *Live Like Pigs*; we have no one quite like them in our country. The British Isles had them until quite recently because in the sixteenth century, the landlords fenced their fields and put their peasants out on the roads. They have been there ever since, traveling by caravan, living by their wits, known to the settled folk as tinkers and gypsies. They never called themselves gypsies, and the gypsies (whom they called Romany) they feared and fought.

But the Sawneys can roam no more. England is too built up, too bureaucratic, simply too modern a state to provide leeway for the chaotic, larcenous, unbeholden nomads. The Sawneys had come to roost in an abandoned tramcar, from which, as the play opens, they have been ousted by the town council and removed to a semi-detached house in a bleakly respectable lower-class cooperative. They hate what has been done to them; they know nothing of living with neighbors, nothing of the paternalism of a welfare state, nothing of caring for the shelter it has provided them. And since the change is not of their making, they have no intention of learning.

The ménage, to give it the only possible name, consists of Sailor, an old man, and if you believe him—which nobody much does—a killer; his present woman, Rachel, a bawd; his daughter, Rosie, with her two children; and Rachel's wild and handsome son, Col. The half-gypsy Blackmouth, father of Rosie Sawney's children, soon arrives from a jailbreak, bringing with him the nymphomaniac and half-insane Daffodil and Old Croaker, her quite mad mother.

The Jacksons, father, mother, and a daughter who clerks in lingerie, live next door and are appalled. Why not? The Sawneys are literally impossible—they are filthy in word and deed, casually disruptive of all amenities, and basically dangerous to life and property. They are wild and only half-caged.

226

So the play develops along two lines: the orchestrated violence, passion, threats, blows, and drunken affection that is the normal life of the Sawneys, and the outlashing of this chaos on the Jacksons, for whom it is not even a conceivable way of life. Mr. Jackson is seduced (and revolted, at least in retrospect, by Sawney sexual deportment); Doreen Jackson has her clothes half ripped off and is half disposed to resent it; and Mrs. Jackson suffers abuse, obscenity, jostling, and the loss of her laundry. The Jacksons, of course, win in the end, for though the Sawneys are more lusty, the Jacksons are more powerful. They have allies, they own something (not much) worth fighting for, and they are not an extinct breed, fighting with its back to the tar pits.

The cast is large and I cannot call the roll. Most of the performances are excellent, both as individual conceptions and in the group interplay; two or three are brilliant; from two I wished for a little more bite than I got on second night. The overall impact matches one's expectations from reading the play, with a proviso. The Sawneys bluster, but they differ in one respect from the town-bred bully boy: they are really lethal. It is hard for an actor to portray a braggart without also suggesting a straw man, and the production did not quite drive home the real violence beneath all the noise.

The measure of Arden as a poet and the reason for the play's stage vigor is that he can genuinely side with both the Sawneys and the Jacksons. He does not quite approve of either; he could not possibly turn his back on the one or the other. What he does regret is the circumstance under which they have been forced to come together. That is the real topic of this beautifully human play.

Leonce and Lena & *Danton's Death*, by Georg Büchner (1966)

Georg Büchner had but one true love in his short life—and his love object was death. However much scholars or directors discuss the extent to which that passion determines and dominates *Danton's Death* and *Woyzeck*, Büchner unquestionably woos surcease with unabashed abandon in his first play, *Leonce and Lena*. Director Ken Costigan captured the essence of the affair in his production of the play for the Clark Center Drama Company at the West Side YMCA.

Taking his cue from the fact that Büchner placed Death on stage as a speaking character, Mr. Costigan worked out opening and bridging sequences of music and choreography that conveyed a vivid sense of fascination with the beckoning unknown. The siren Death is played—

REVIEWS

it would be more accurate to say mimed and dance—with captivating effect by Valerie von Volz. Under flowing black vestments, her entire figure was clasped in flesh-colored tights. Her seemingly naked challenge thus unsparingly argued the ultimate seduction.

But she does not need to expose her appeal to Prince Leonce, for he begins the play as her willing accomplice. Leonce's mutual involvement with Death is almost too convincing. If the Prince has indeed succumbed to oblivion's charms, how can there be a play? With the born showman's sense of timing, Büchner sounds a counterpoint to his constant and crescendo-less theme of doom sought and chosen. For all his fascination with death, Leonce is also not a little in love with the heady, God-miming fun of creating sardonic spoofs of his times and his life.

So, just as the players of our nineteenth-century melodramas broke up the heaviness of a portentous act with intermission interludes of *She's Only a Bird in a Gilded Cage*, Büchner interrupts Death's strumpet-solicitation with a series of playful caricatures of the tragic hero. The spoofs begin when his Prince mimics that aspect of Hamlet who was the drama's first Angry Young Man, and his Lena celebrates her mad reaction to loss of her Prince's love with rosemary in her hair. Then, after a brief return to his séance with Death, Büchner shows that not even Goethe is immune from his young laughter by sending Prince Leonce on a long spree with a Mephistophelean compatriot. In this sequence, the ambisexual Leonce is shared by his male and female companions, and Lena is an innocent Gretchen whom he seduces along the way. After another, almost ritualistic courting of Death, Schiller and the *Sturm und Drang* (Storm and Stress) movement come in for a turn of vaudeville. Leonce converts the Romantics' exaltation of the emotions of the individual hero into an exaggerated depiction of the self-pitying anguish of the individual anti-hero. The Prince enacts a preview of *Woyzeck*; the language is a perversion of Schiller's rhetoric.

Implicit in *Leonce and Lena*'s ambivalences and dichotomies is a qualitatively new and different genre of drama. For the first time in the history of the stage, Aristophanes' style of incisive commentary upon his society and his contemporaries has been joined to a baring of the author's psyche. For man is never more animal than in those periods when he feels newly deprived of godhood. Such a time was Büchner's. He was, in a sense, a victim of the Napoleonic heresy; he had thought to find, but had unaccountably lost, a deity. His reaction was a desire to foul this earth as he arranged his exit from it. His exposure on stage of the inner self he deprecated was a part of

228

LEONCE AND LENA & DANTON'S DEATH

this process. Schopenhauer expressed the mood of the times philosophically, but Büchner expressed it viscerally.

Leonce and Lena is, as would be expected, an imperfect first work. But in terms of drama, not of politics, it is a revolutionary work. It is the first of the essentially interior dramas of psychological self-indulgence, and leads, in an unbroken line, to Jarry, Strindberg, Tolstoy, Joyce, and O'Neill (and, of course, to the currently most self-indulgent of the self-indulgent genre, John Osborne's marathon *Inadmissible Evidence*). Brecht's most rampant play, *Baal*, is modeled after *Leonce and Lena*, and most of what is seen today at the New York coffeehouses is artistically less-valid *Leonce and Lena*.

Mr. Costigan's direction of the Clark Center production did not comment upon the play. Instead, it made way for Büchner's own comment. And it did so in a spirited and delightful manner. The confrontation with death's mystique became both awesome and knavish fun. Matters of state were ridiculed In high style, but their absurdity was not made silly. The sexual imagery was handled with imaginative finesse. Only in the final act did Mr. Costigan's direction falter. In this act, the dichotomies between Büchner's social farce and his masochistic poetry become, at least to American eyes, extreme. A dash of sustained European cynicism might have narrowed the gap. The playing itself was highly satisfactory throughout. Russell Horton as Prince Leonce quite properly refused to add his own self-indulgence to that of the playwright, and Beverly Luckenbach as Princess Lena was an evocative foil to Büchner's many moods. Jan McElhaney's choreography added to the mood and flow of the show.

Comparison of this Büchner production with that of *Danton's Death* at Lincoln Center a few weeks ago is unavoidable. For me, at least, the spirit of Georg Büchner permeated Clark Center, after having been unable to so much as buy a ticket at Lincoln Center. It is almost impossible to believe that Büchner—a man who was so completely disillusioned with both the rationalism of Voltaire and the polemicism of Schiller—could have become absorbed in the realistic and single-minded preachments of Herbert Blau's version of *Danton's Death*. It is equally difficult to believe that a Büchner who was enticed by the psychoticism and suicide of Kleist, and who was a progenitor of the spirit of Baudelaire and Rimbaud, could have become as purged of the love of death, and as unambiguously committed to uplifting social commentary, as Mr. Blau's "adaptation" would imply.

For a part of Büchner must have loved the death of Danton and thanked Robespierre vicariously for opening the welcome door. Mr. Blau's production at Lincoln Center (Vivian Beaumont Theater,

REVIEWS

Broadway) showed New York only one chord of Büchner's melody of ambiguities. No—on second thought, it would seem that another aspect of Büchner was demonstrated. For, however Mr. Blau may have failed to play Büchner's orchestration of human ambivalence, he did follow the playwright's lead with respect to self-indulgence.

San Francisco Mime Troupe (1967)

The San Francisco Mime Troupe opened a three-week New York stand on Thanksgiving Day, playing in the new loft home of the Filmmakers' Cinematheque on Wooster Street. The piece they chose from their repertory to show on the Lower East Side was Carlo Goldoni's *L'Amant Militaire* (*The Soldierly Lover*), a *Commedia dell'arte* chestnut that, set in Italy during a time of Spanish "pacification," lends itself well to the troupe's satiric improvisations.

This handsome, impertinent young company has drilled and polished itself with a diligence it would never have endured from its elders. (One gathers from the context that the mimers see fifty as that incredibly remote age when body and mind crumble into senility.) They sing, dance, strut, rant, and defy the crummy gods with a disciplined exuberance that sweeps an audience into their power. Their costumes (the men in half-masks) are flamboyant; the backdrops to the platform on which they gambol are stylized to a witty, pretty simplicity; and the production is flung on stage with the chaotic efficiency of a good tumbling act. You feel convinced that the mountebanks have come to the fair, which is the idea. Only the diction needs grooming—it is no good being outrageous in a variety of ludicrous accents if what you say is half lost in the hubbub.

It is also a question just how outrageous the Mime Troupe's contemporary interpolations now sound. The times, I felt, have been sneaking up on them. The political dialogue of the general community has itself turned rancid and, at least within the audience the San Francisco players can hope to attract, the nation's leaders are seldom mentioned without the ritual application of abusive adjectives. The Mime Troupe has a reputation for running afoul of the legionnaires and the watch-and-warders wherever it plays, but it sounded to me more naughty than wicked. Perhaps what the company needs is a script-writer old enough to fight dirty. These young men and women are no doubt intent on raising hell, but they get so quickly caught up in celebrating the joy of life that their bite has no poison. You need to be a little decayed yourself to fight corruption.

Soldiers, by Rolf Hochhuth (1968)

Rolf Hochhuth's didactic purpose in life is to bring certain dominant figures of World War II to the dock of public esteem. Pope Pius (*The Deputy*) was cold to the fate of Europe's Jews; Winston Churchill (*Soldiers*, now playing at the Billy Rose on Broadway) was indifferent to the lives of the citizens of Hamburg and Dresden, and capable (whether or not culpable) of assenting to the murder of General Władysław Sikorski, the Polish Prime-Minister-in-Exile. An examination of Franklin D. Roosevelt is in progress.

Hochhuth, it will be seen, does not waste his energies (and in research he is prodigious) on obvious villains. He is disturbed, rather, by the good man's compromise with evil under the pressure of war. Or, perhaps, he traces war to the fact that men called good are capable of such compromises. In any case, he has an instinct for the inconvenient thesis, and his plays move toward the stage in a storm of controversy that guarantees maximum attention for their pronouncements and minimum examination of their form. (The British censors, with the folly of their peculiar vocation, banned *Soldiers* and thus made it an object of national curiosity.)

It is not to be presumed that Hochhuth has plotted this road to theatrical fame, but it may well have been the only one open to him. His gifts are almost entirely polemical. He appears to understand the theater, not as, a stage on which things happen but as a platform on which things are said. His characters are not created, they are summoned; they do not unfold, they are displayed.

Thus the three acts of *Soldiers* (I ignore the fact that it is a play-within-a-play, since the surrounding envelope is no more than a tedious attempt to lend contemporary force to events whose continuing relevance is self-evident) take place aboard a warship in the North Sea; in Churchill's bedroom, presumably at 10 Downing Street; and in the garden at Chequers Court. But these locations, or the Prime Minister's appearance from scene to scene in a nautical jacket, boisterous pajamas, and an Royal Air Force uniform, have no bearing on the playback of statements made (or judiciously assumed to have been made) by Churchill and certain of his close associates in 1943. The purpose of locale and dress is visual variety, not dramatic movement.

The interest to be derived from this work is in historical detection and the significant juxtaposition of texts; it has nothing to do with drama, and is indeed so inappropriate to the stage that its content can be grasped only imperfectly under conditions of exhausting concentration. The only play offered here by Hochhuth is an affection that

REVIEWS

grows between Churchill's secretary and a young Polish officer, and is destroyed by the actions of their superiors; a playwright would of course have brought these two bit parts to the center of the work. Aside from this, the spectacle is a waxworks wired for sound—but sound that is innocent of any knowledge that if lines are to prevail on the stage they must be written for the stage.

The museum ghoulishness of the piece is accentuated by the appearance of the principals, and particularly of Churchill. By use of very heavy (and perfectly apparent) make-up, John Colicos is made to look a good deal like Churchill (in some poses, disconcertingly like W. C. Fields). But no one who ever saw or heard Churchill could be fooled for a moment. The tone of voice, the attitudes, the stature are insufficient—I had to fight the (at least melodramatic) supposition that the real Churchill had been disposed of by the Gestapo. As for Lord Cherwell and General Alan Brooke, they are given the presence of junior masters at a boys' school. But suppose the impersonations had been faultless, suppose this was Churchill miraculously returned, what would that have to do with acting? It would be mere mimicry, a trick, a mechanical duplication at the pole opposite to creating a stage image.

The truth is that real playwrights do not put public figures of world renown at the center of their canvases because to do so would be to frustrate the invention of character development and human relations that impels them to write plays. Shakespeare? But Henry V died in 1422, Richard II in 1485, and Shakespeare was born in 1564. Nor did those monarchs write memoirs, appear in newsreels, or record their speeches with the B.B.C. There is a great deal still to be said about Churchill—and, whether correct or not, Hochhuth has added his opinion to the conversation. But there is nothing to be done with him on the stage, and there won't be for 100 years.

Now, for the good of the theater, if not of history, I trust that Hochhuth is not amassing evidence to demonstrate that Roosevelt planned Pearl Harbor. True or false, it won't play.

The Memorandum, by Václav Havel (1968)

The socio-political high spirits that characterize so much of the news coming now from Czechoslovakia are to be found in full voice at the Public Theater, where Joseph Papp has staged *The Memorandum* by Václav Havel, a young Czech playwright and the literary manager of the Balustrade Theater in Prague. The Czechs today seem able to generate an impressive amount of reformist zeal without developing

232

THE MEMORANDUM

the self-righteousness and intolerance that customarily accompany such housecleaning. But distance makes this impression unreliable, and it is pleasant to have it supported by Mr. Havel's bureaucratic burlesque.

Not that *The Memorandum* is to be taken as a metaphoric reading of the readjustments now taking place within Czech Communist forces. Indeed, it was written some time back, and before the current positions had emerged. Rather, Mr. Havel entertains himself, and his audience, with some speculation as to what usually lies behind the more passionate ideological disputes. Chiefly, he finds, it is a matter of whose initials will validate a chit—a dominance too loosely guarded by those who enjoy it and hungered for with exaggerated appetite by those who do not.

In a true bureaucracy, any pretext will serve to test the nerves and resourcefulness of the reigning manager. In this case, the showdown comes over the adoption of Ptydepe as the official language for inter-office memoranda, the peculiar virtue of the tongue being that it can express with utter accuracy every nuance of every idea habitually transmitted in such communications (with the considerable side benefit that it is incapable of expressing other ideas in any form at all). The shocking fact is that the manager does not read Ptydepe, and his position is made no more tenable by the fact that neither does anyone else, with the exception of one very minor clerk who takes to the pigeonhole pidgin with Bartleby-like assiduity. He would obviously "go far" if the revolution were to prevail.

Alas for him, Ptydepe is mere pretext, and when the rubber stamps have changed hands Its hour of ascendancy is done. A chief clerk has been found wool-gathering, an assistant chief clerk has been rewarded for excellent generalship in the lunchroom—so empires topple and mutations of power spur the social evolution of the species.

All this is performed with excellent wit by a cast that Mr. Papp has schooled to crisp speech, elliptical gesture, and rapid movement. (Their agility is both improved and enforced by the revolving stage on which Douglas Schmidt has placed his office set. It spins, not only to change scenes, but also to place the hierarchic positions of the contestants in jeopardy—they must skip nimbly to stay in one place.) I do not know how much Mr. Papp has done to Americanize the atmosphere, but if his direction has been neutral in this regard, the universality of office types suggested by Mr. Havel's play is impressive. In addition to the expectable yea-sayers and rule-watchers, there is the stenographer who repeatedly prays leave to run out for light refreshments; the loud and bawdy administrative assistant, a sort of den

233

REVIEWS

mother to the young bachelors; the fattish boy who always knows what's on for lunch.

The members of the cast who make the sharpest impression—if only because they have the best opportunities—are Paul Stevens, John Heffernan, Sudie Bond, William Duell, and Olympia Dukakis. Brad Sullivan has a rewarding, if cramping, part as an official spy hidden in the ventilating system—a position he compromises by an inability to stifle outbursts of protest against breached protocol. The theater of moral instruction is not often this much fun.

A Midsummer Night's Dream, by William Shakespeare; *Tartuffe,* by Molière; & *The Seagull,* by Anton Chekhov (1968)

Look at the license plates. Now completing its sixteenth season, the Stratford Festival in Ontario draws from what has become probably the world's most extensive theatrical watershed; the paid attendance was more than a quarter-million in 1967, and will be bigger this year. Stratford treats its customers well: the small city smiles with discreet prosperity; the swans on Lake Victoria are endearingly insistent about picnic scraps; the huge theatrical company has become a phenomenon of integrated skill, trained to the top of its form, utterly at ease with one another and with its two stages, maneuvering the repertory with the dexterous snap of a cup-defender racing crew. One friend tells another, from Missouri to Manitoba, and Stratford is a great deal more than a success—it is an institution.

And a going institution. There is no hint of smugness, no arrogance about the place. This company knows how good it is, but knows as well what vigilance and character are required to remain that way. One of the joys, perhaps the great joy of the Festival, is the depth of its excellence. No one on its stages is there to fill space; everyone down to the page carrying a candelabrum is acting with every nerve of his body and according to the demands of the production. The commercial theater can almost never elicit or afford such dedication, and I had almost forgotten the richness and intensity of life that can pour from a stage when every fragment of its complexity is switched on.

Yet there is a blandness at the center of the enterprise. Stratford can confidently guarantee no to disappoint any reasonable man's expectations: I am less sure that it can surpass them. At least, what I saw there this year confirmed the ideas I had brought with me more

234

MIDSUMMER'S NIGHT DREAM, TARTUFFE & THE SEAGULL

than it expanded them. (I am told that in past seasons there have been occasions of astonishment, and in fairness it must be said that astonishment is a theatrical experience that the most superb of troupes cannot create at will.) It occurs to me that the Festival may have trouble relating to its public. Though its following is enormous, it has almost no audience at all. An audience goes to the theater as part of its life; people go to Stratford as part of their vacation. They are relaxed, nomadic, overwhelmingly benevolent; they are also almost exclusively middle-aged and more than moderately well heeled. They recognize that it is meritorious to attend plays endorsed by the wisdom of time; applauding the excellence they find at Stratford, they applaud also their excellence for being there. It is a friendly house, but a self-protected one.

Bending perhaps to that mood, the Festival is less a rite than a course of instruction. I have rarely seen productions so lucid, so informative as to the playwright's intentions, so solicitous of the spectator's comprehension. The effect, when the works offered are somewhat demanding, is to make the audience feel pleasantly bright. But wholehearted lucidity does not always work to the advantage of the piece; a degree of bafflement, a sense of reaching but not quite grasping, is also characteristic of the theater.

Thus the only Shakespeare I saw (the repertory this year also includes *Romeo and Juliet*) was at once the oddest and most explicit *Midsummer Night's Dream* of my experience. John Hirsch, the associate director, has dressed and staged the play to indicate that its subject is lust—with Athenian youths and maidens disporting in attitudes that in no way suggest Dresden china, and with Oberon, Titania, and their courts pawing one another in the undiscriminating pre-genital sexuality of the underground cinema. Puck has the rasping voice and knowing eye of a costermonger's child; sprites and elves, self-absorbed, sway to modified rock; and you can almost smell the pot in fairydom.

In this atmosphere, the "mechanicals," played more or less according to tradition, seem even more innocent than usual, and everyone laughs boisterously at their antics, relieved to be quit for a moment from the amorous damp of the main actions. It can all be justified readily enough; we've known for some time that Shakespeare's Greek idyll cloaks some dubious business. For one thing, there is that changeling boy over whom Oberon and Titania squabble, and for another the uneasy permutations of obsessed infatuation. But Shakespeare rarely took single views of human behavior, and there are hazards in showing exactly what he meant. Thus if one introduces

235

REVIEWS

Theseus as a senile—or seminal—admiral out of Gilbert and Sullivan (I don't understand why the Athenians are made to appear in Victorian garden-party rig, unless it is done as a tribute to Tyrone Guthrie, founding genius of Stratford, who likes to stage Shakespeare in fancy dress), it may serve to advance the intuition that the playwright saw lechery as man's most persisting itch. But a doddering Theseus can scarcely deliver his Act V lines in support of the comic thespians, and the actor must abandon the device out of respect for the words.

Similarly, the somewhat rancid concept of Oberon may accord to a degree with Shakespeare's suspicion of love's witchcraft (after all, its most conspicuous victim here is an ass named Bottom), but what of the Oberon who so tenderly blesses the house in which the lovers sleep? Shakespeare was not a very simple man, and it is imprudent to resolve his enigmas for him. I will say, though, that a steamy *Midsummer Night's Dream* is a relief of sorts from the lavender-water masques of countless Christmas holidays.

Tartuffe, staged by Jean Gascon, the new artistic head of Stratford, comes across fast, funny, sharp, and relentless. It is so marvelously acted by all hands that William Hutt's Tartuffe does not seem the virtuoso performance that it undoubtedly is. But again the play lacks shadows; it is flat good and flat evil. Tartuffe is a joyless villain, a Protestant sort of sinner, and I have seen actors far less gifted than Hutt who got a Catholic lyricism into the role. Tartuffe can be thought to hug himself in an ecstasy of hypocrisy that is not without religious overtones. Orgon is certainly his dupe, but whose dupe is Tartuffe? The question does not arise at Stratford; it is all subversive slapstick and domestic irony. I don't much like the Richard Wilbur translation. Its rhymes clang with an insistent accuracy that is particularly jarring when your ears have been made sensitive by Shakespeare's subtle chiming.

The company's *Seagull*, again directed by Mr. Gascon, gave me the most pleasure during my stay at Stratford. You could almost justify the formation of permanent companies on the single ground that only such groups can perform Chekhov. Players who don't know and trust one another will never surrender themselves to Chekhov's dangerous intimacy. This cast did so, and the performance glowed. Again, though, it appeals more to the mind than to the heart, ambiguity being what Chekhov found in life and what makes his plays so demanding of one's conscience. In this production, weakness is made manifest, stupidity asserts itself, Arkadina is a bitch (Chekhov never lets you call his people names), and Treplev is a little too much the British schoolboy in love. I have never seen the idea of the play interpreted

236

WE BOMBED IN NEW HAVEN

more succinctly—maturity is a disease that poisons the young—but there have been times when I felt the play itself more deeply.

That leaves Alexandre Dumas's *The Three Musketeers*—and I am content to leave it. It is this season's circus turn, and I guess a festival needs one such dependable crowd-rouser. They do it with wonderful leaps, thrusts, and brandished bottles, and it is a tribute to the physical training of the company. I'm sure everyone moves better in the other plays for having been through the exercise of Dumas's sword opera, but it contains too little substance for its quota of noise.

Waiting for Godot opened after I left Stratford. I regret missing it, for I should have liked to see what moves they make to clarify Beckett's misanthropic word magic. The exegetes have been at work on this conundrum for some time, which is possibly why the Festival chose it as this year's contemporary presentation. There is by now plenty of background for interpretation.

I don't want to be misunderstood: any of the productions I saw at Stratford (well, perhaps not the Dumas) would embellish a season in New York or London or Paris. The Festival is hallmark theater: it is a standard against which other companies may measure themselves, if they have the nerve. If it were not so good, one would not be so sensitive to its possible flaws. What I sense—this tendency to instruct rather than to transport—may also have been detected by Mr. Gascon and his colleagues long before I hit town. If it worries them a little, that is good. The one thing that might diminish Stratford would be a failure to worry.

We Bombed in New Haven, by Joseph Heller (1968)

Out in Brooklyn, the Becks (The Living Theatre) have been employing ritual, yoga, the mass chanting of slogans, and group therapy on the stage and in the house to purge the audience of its militarist and capitalist devils and restore it to communal grace. Now on Broadway (Ambassador Theatre) Joseph Heller, in *We Bombed In New Haven*, seeks much the same goal through wit, schmaltz, buffoonery, scenic legerdemain, and a preoccupation with the ambiguities allegedly induced by the fact that actors are real people who impersonate fictions.

Mr. Heller is much less experienced in the theater than are the Becks—indeed, this is his début—but I think he has a better grasp of its dimensions. He seems to understand that a playwright's most

237

REVIEWS

important creation is the audience, a fragile and ephemeral entity that takes shape in the house from the matrix of what takes place on the stage. "Audience Involvement," that article of faith in the modern theater, does not consist in roughing up the cash customers, a self-defeating form of aggression that only fragments the assemblage into individuals acutely aware that they have private dignities to protect. Involvement is achieved by giving the audience a line to follow, a form to perceive, so that for an hour or so the minds of a considerable group of people are aligned, their disparate experiences brought to bear on a coherent set of events. When this works, the audience is magnetized to a state of perception that may be considerably superior to its individual talents. It is nothing new in the theater, Lord knows, but I suspect the sin of pride is involved in supposing that it is not enough— the playwright's sin of wanting to manipulate the audience, not by his art but in his own person.

Mr. Heller knows all this and gets off to a good start. We are somewhere with a bomber crew that is about to bomb Constantinople because the script says that is what comes next. The script also tells who will die and where, and the men jockey for fatter, "more secure" roles. Jason Robards is the operations captain, Diana Sands the coffee-and-doughnuts Red Cross girl (beautiful and bouncy in an ugly costume). They sleep together at night and, in this double-focus context, offstage. On duty and in the play, they jibe at each other with the sharp humor of people not quite sure that they have committed themselves as far as their bodies have carried them. "I want you," he says. "For very long?" she asks.

Captain/stage manager Robards (Mr. Heller gives scrupulous credit to Thornton Wilder) employs the ingratiating informality of an insecure man to get the flight in the air and the show on the road, nervously conscious all the while of his major (William Roerick), the agent of delegated authority and keeper of the text. It is a fault, perhaps of Mr. Heller's stage inexperience, perhaps of John Hirsch's direction, that you know from the moment he walks on the set that Robards will leave anyone in any lurch. One of the real ambiguities of stage "reality" is that an actor is burdened with a foreknowledge that a man does not have to carry.

More generally, though, I am less seized than Mr. Heller by the fascinations of the play-within-life device. I have seen it tried fairly often, and it usually strikes me as being more a tangle than a mystery. On this occasion, too, faults in direction have caused the crewmen— who are "the people"—to cavort when out of character, so that they are less impressive as "themselves" than as "actors." Nevertheless,

238

WE BOMBED IN NEW HAVEN

Mr. Heller has a use beyond intellectual décor for his bifocal approach. It creates a tension between men as citizens (actors), villains and victims of the state, and men as individuals, with pasts to complete and futures to anticipate. "They told me it would disrupt my life less If I got killed sooner," says a young replacement, and the audience applauds its recognition of the gap between official cant and private truth. The ambiguity between role and fate induces a parallel ambiguity between audience and public, so that the major who commands according to "their" script may be felt to be quoting from "our" script as well.

The problem is how to resolve a play so bifurcated, and in this Mr. Heller is not so successful. As the evening works into its second half, the split becomes increasingly overt, with actors refusing to go on in their parts, with Miss Sands beseeching Mr. Robards to get her out of the theater, with everyone shouting that he, at least, has no intention of dying, and with one recalcitrant actor being suddenly shot dead onstage because he will not pretend to die offstage. But of course he is not really killed, the two aspects of the play do not really coalesce, the edges of the mirrors have become apparent, and the audience starts to squirm.

That squirming is the giveaway. It always happens when the spectators begin to suspect that they are being lectured, that the play is no longer the thing, and they have become it. A theater is not a pulpit: it is a place where you must show, not tell, what you believe. Like all serious playwrights, Mr. Heller has something he wants to show, and he begins promisingly enough with metaphor and paradox, wit and romance, to create a body for his conviction. But I get the impression that he had a much clearer image of the moral than of the work, so that in the end he loses control of his play and falls back on exhortation. The characters become witnesses, the developments become predictable, the action loses plausibility, there is not enough incident left to reach to the final curtain. The play dies and the message takes over.

It is disappointing, because although I doubt that Mr. Heller is up to writing *The Trojan Women*, he knows war well enough to loathe it, and he knows the theater well enough to realize that you cannot make that loathing real by inventing new epithets for Lyndon Johnson. For quite a space he maintains the distance and expectancy that make a play work, but he had not enough invention to get the job completed and ends up chanting with the Becks in Brooklyn. It is the more serious because his *Catch-22*, that spectacular mockery of martial heroics, suffered a similar collapse into strident exhaustion in the homestretch.

239

REVIEWS

Little Murders, by Jules Pfeiffer (1969)

Jules Feiffer's first play, *Little Murders*, has arrived at Circle in the Square, Off-Broadway in Greenwich Village, after vicissitudes on Broadway and out of town. It is an excellent evening in the theater; that it is an excellent play I would not be so quick to say, but it has been directed by Alan Arkin to resemble a most eventful one. Actually, not a great deal happens. Happens, that is, in terms of human intercourse. Feiffer's stock in trade is the multiple-frame cartoon in which a contemporary type thinks aloud, his ruminations rising, station by station, from specious rationality to veritable dementia. That, basically, is the device he has adapted to the stage, both for the overall development of the play and in its individual scenes.

By his title, I take Feiffer to mean that we are killing one another, institutionally and interpersonally. Gunfire can be heard in the streets at the opening, and it has risen to a pandemonium of urban violence at the close. Meanwhile, within the depressed but almost classless apartment that is the single set, familial guerrillas are at work. The father is a pugnacious loser, the mother a believer in the power of aphorisms to uphold standards; there is a disheveled son, stewing in idleness, who confides that what he wants to do, really, is direct movies.

A daughter comes home with her latest fiancé ("another of those fags," her father fears in advance), and these two set the domestic soundtracks in motion. It is a cacophony between the generations, but also intragenerational. The daughter is a revolting combination of two repellent types: Daddy's best girl and the competent American female. She can spar three rounds with anything in pants, she is Little Miss Fixit, and she is determined that everyone shall live up to what she sees as the best in them. She is perfectly miserable in her frustrated need to be bossed around, but unhappily her young man (and apparently all the previous young men) is supine in combat, passive in love, disengaged from tradition, and bored with his own professional success.

These nonentities in a vacuum aggress at one another according to their several humors, but it is here that Feiffer's gift for lampooning his age in isolated boxes works against his aspirations as a playwright. *Little Murders* never generates an organic life; there is a good deal of physical contact, but almost no intellectual or emotional reaction. The characteristic episode is a monologue on a rising pitch, with the speaker flinging himself into a chair or out the door at the climax, and his recipients left gazing at their shoes. Indeed, three persons—a Jewish judge who blesses America for having allowed his immigrant parents

240

LITTLE MURDERS   PROMENADE

to wreck their health on his behalf, a Greenwich Village pastor to the hippies, and a paranoid police captain—are brought on to give just one long monologue apiece. The interplay on stage is so minimal that I could not understand why, after the girl is killed by a sniper's stray bullet, her husband (there has been a marriage) should be suddenly transformed into a relentless operator.

If you were to ask me what the play is about, I should be reduced to ticking off the illusions, prejudices, and perversions that Feiffer cites as disfigurements of our society. More comprehensively I could not say, because plays are about what people do to one another, and these people do nothing. That, I have no doubt, is how Feiffer sees us—a multitude of isolated mouths praising poisonous nonsense—and he has a point, if a somewhat simplified one. It may be, though, that the stage is not the best place for stating it. One comes from *Little Murders* feeling more beaten upon than enlightened.

Nevertheless, the script is funny—dangerously funny, because Feiffer drags his characters from among his audience, and his lines can be heard in the lobby during intermission; more humiliatingly, they can be heard coming from your own lips on the way home. Feiffer is one of those artists who compel life to conform to their visions.

Linda Lavin is a small-boned girl who has some trouble living up to the physical specifications of the daughter; otherwise, the cast gets itself well set in Feiffer's uniforms. The three walk-on monologists, Shimen Ruskin, Paul Benedict, and Andrew Duncan (in the order mentioned above), have obviously been polishing their lines for weeks before audiences of delighted friends. Each of them now possesses a sure-fire nightclub turn.

Promenade, by María Irene Fornés (1969)

At the Judson Poets' Theatre (Off-Broadway), *Promenade* (book and lyrics by María Irene Fornés; music by Al Carmines) is a rainy day in the attic with Mother's old clothes, Mother's old enthusiasms, and a pile of vintage dance records. Here are Erich von Stroheim, Mr. Hyde, John Held, Jr., girls (all necks and beads), zebra-striped convicts with hearts of gold, pert servants for whom their masters are not heroes, and a little old lady who has lost her babes and found the wisdom of the world. They sing and dance, change partners, and grind right and left for some two hours of crafted innocence (otherwise camp) to a cascade of music that sounds as though one's ears were afflicted with total recall.

REVIEWS

Mr. Carmines is a musical chameleon; he can recapture the quality of every popular musical style of this century, endowing it with just enough self-mockery to make evident his recognition that what he has is a talent, not an art. That is disarming of him, and to be sure his scores sound better than many that claim to be creations; but this is the third Carmines show I have heard (*In Circles* and *Peace* were the others), and I've come to feel that the law of diminishing returns is taking hold. His songs are composed not of notes but of nostalgia—as soon as you listen they vanish.

A number of pleasant people are responsible for *Promenade* (among others, Lawrence Kornfeld directed and Rouben Ter-Arutunian designed the set, which is principally bicycle wheels), and I am pleased that they have a hit; I am also somewhat puzzled. The show seemed to me a little bleak and a little stiff from straining. More serious, it had trouble getting its footings in place, establishing its base of assumptions. Anything offered on a stage, from Sophocles' *Oedipus Rex* to Brandon Thomas's *Charley's Aunt*, has to make clear, and quickly, what premise it starts from. It need not be tangible—the seacoast of Illyria will do well enough—but unless it is manifest the audience gapes at flies.

I decided finally that *Promenade* was operating from a set of values that prevailed before we plucked the forbidden atom and came to realize that the birth rate was a worse scourge than Attila the Hun. The rich were listless parasites, the poor (even when criminal) were the salt of the earth, and a witty waitress could steal the show from any coupon clipper. But before this came to me I had sat morosely (it is always depressing to hold your applause when huzzahs are booming all around you) through a dozen scenes that seemed dedicated to *non sequiturs* and connected by random association. And when I did catch on, I remembered, too, that the entertainments *Promenade* was resuscitating had themselves been the thinnest possible slices of life. I wondered at so much deadpan effervescence for so meager a memory.

Everyone coached by Al Carmines sings with a big, operatic voice—always the same operatic voice, which is another of his impressive tricks. This simulation of superb vocal cords (something, I have no doubt, achieved by diaphragm control and a small auditorium) is nothing to get depressed about, but I went home in that state. The *papier-mâché* sundaes in drugstore windows used to put me in the same funk; my mouth got gritty thinking of them.

The Trial of A. Lincoln, by James Damico (1970)

At last, and at least, the American theater no longer assumes that if what we used to call "the Negro problem" is ignored, it will go away. More "race plays" by black authors and white ones are being produced in this country nowadays than ever before.

They seem to fall into four main categories (and all four categories include plays by white authors as well as black). First of all, to get them out of the way quickly, there are the delusively optimistic, brotherhood-is-just-around-the corner shows, such as Ossie Davis's *Purlie Victorious* and Leonard Spigelglass's *Look to the Lilies*, which are still to be found (with music!) on Broadway. Second are the plays that simply try, without emphasizing a particular polemical point, to express what it feels like and is like to be a black man in modern America. This is probably the most distinguished group: it includes *A Raisin in the Sun*, by Lorraine Hansberry; *Ceremonies in Dark Old Men*, by Lonne Elder III; and *No Place to Be Somebody*, by Charles Gordone, the last of which recently won the Pulitzer Prize. (White authors do not write much in this category anymore, but if you want to go back far enough there is *Porgy and Bess*, by DuBose Heyward.) Things being how they are, and always have been, in the United States, the second category inevitably overlaps with the third: the oppression/persecution plays, which include *The Great White Hope*, by Howard Sackler, and *Slave Ship*, by LeRoi Jones.

The fourth category is the newest and the most "relevant" of all. The increasing interest in plays about the black presence in America is beginning to combine with an increasingly agonized sense of racial crisis to produce a group of plays that evoke the racial wrath to come, plays which suggest that at the basis of black-white relations in this country is hatred: deep, dangerous, and mutual. After the plays of persecution, we are beginning to see plays—not all of them by LeRoi Jones—that attempt to show what persecution leads to when the persecuted begin to retaliate. Some such plays have been, and will be, merely black revolutionary propaganda; some will not.

One such (non-propagandist) play was recently given its world premiere by the Hartford Stage Company, the local resident professional theater of Hartford, Connecticut. The play is by a young writer named James Damico, and it is titled *The Trial of A. Lincoln*. It is set in the basement of a police station in an American city; the time is the present. A very odd sort of mock trial is going on: Abraham Lincoln, no less, is suing a black militant named I.A.T. (for "I Am The") Best for slander, because Best has called him a racist.

REVIEWS

But just what are we supposed to make of Lincoln's reappearance in 1970? And why is this trial, which is evidently not really a trial, being held in a police-station basement? Mr. Damico does not choose to make things clear until his play is nearly over—at which point the police station is suddenly transfixed by the spearhead of a black uprising. It turns out that the "trial" is a sort of group-therapy exercise, to allow black and white police officers to work off their mutual hostilities; but the hostilities remain. The ending is a trick ending, and I had better not give it away; but it is fair to say that the only comfort it offers is the grim satisfaction that comes from confronting the possibility that there is no comfort to be had.

Damico never tells us what city he is writing about, but there are special reasons for doing a play like this in Hartford, which suffered serious riots only last summer. While the play was actually in production this spring, a story from Hartford in the *New York Times* indicated that racial tensions there were still very high. *The Trial of A. Lincoln* attempts to mirror just the sort of tensions, the deep and desperate hatreds between the races, that cause riots and that result from them. (Damico even suggests that these hatreds can underlie what look like close friendships.) The presentation of this play in this place at this time was a serious attempt to assist the community in the difficult task of realizing its own situation: something that the touring companies that stop in Hartford for one-night stands will never accomplish.

Unfortunately, the best way to make any community realize anything is not by boring it, and Damico's play is highly ingenious— but it is also badly misproportioned. There is endless haggling over mock legal technicalities, and then more haggling over what Lincoln really thought about the blacks, a matter that could easily have been settled by printing a few quotations in the program. The play comes to life only near the end, when the uprising breaks in upon the trial: but by then it is too late.

In spite of a few excesses here and there, *The Trial of A. Lincoln* was pretty well performed at Hartford, under Paul Weidner's direction. Mel Winkler was particularly good—relaxed, yet dangerous—as the black militant defendant, I.A.T. Best. Santo Loquasto's setting and Joe Pacitti's lighting turned the thrust stage of the Hartford company into a convincingly subterranean basement. The standard of professionalism was encouraging, although it could not save the play.

What is even more encouraging is the attempt on the part of the theater to speak to the community about itself—to notice what is

244

THE TRIAL OF A. LINCOLN

happening, and to become involved in it—not as a vessel of propaganda but as an agency for dispassionate understanding. This will probably not be the last time that such an attempt produces an image of mutual hatred and racial violence. It seems to be time to stop talking about oppression, with its neat opposition of villain and victim, and start talking about its consequences. There are dangers in this—honorably avoided in *The Trial of A. Lincoln*—dangers of sensationalism, dangers that the play will contribute to irrational alarm and increase tension rather than alleviate it. I am afraid that we shall have to take that risk, along with a great many others.

Bibliography of Robert Hatch's Writings on Theater and Drama

The New Republic
The New Republic, May 15, 1950
A Phoenix Too Frequent, by Christopher Fry, & *Freight*,
by Kenneth White
pp. 21–22

The New Republic, November 3, 1950
Julius Caesar, by William Shakespeare
p. 22

The New Republic, March 15, 1951
Billy Budd, by Herman Melville
p. 23

The New Republic, May 28, 1951
Stalag 17, by Donald Bevan & Edmund Trzcinski; *Dream Girl*,
by Elmer Rice
p. 23

The Nation
The Nation, January 23, 1954
Mademoiselle Colombe, by Jean Anouilh
pp. 77–78

The Nation, February 26, 1955
The Desperate Hours, by Joseph Hayes
p. 186

The Nation, March 12, 1955
The Dark Is Light Enough, by Christopher Fry, & *Silk Stockings*,
by George S. Kaufman & Abe Burrows
p. 226

246

BIBLIOGRAPHY

The Nation, March 19, 1955
Bus Stop, by William Inge, & *The Master Builder*, by Henrik Ibsen
pp. 245–246

The Nation, April 2, 1955
The Three Sisters, by Anton Chekhov
pp. 293–294

The Nation, April 9, 1955
Cat on a Hot Tin Roof, by Tennessee Williams
pp. 314–315

The Nation, April 30, 1955
Champagne Complex, by Leslie Stevens
p. 381

The Nation, May 7, 1955
Inherit the Wind, by Jerome Lawrence & Robert E. Lee; *Trouble in Tahiti*, by Leonard Bernstein; *27 Wagons Full of Cotton*, by Tennessee Williams
p. 410

The Nation, May 14, 1955
The Honeys, by Roald Dahl
pp. 430–431

The Nation, May 21, 1955
Damn Yankees, by George Abbott
p. 449

The Nation, May 28, 1955
The Maids, by Jean Genet
pp. 469–470

The Nation, June 11, 1955
Once Upon a Tailor, by Baruch Lumet, & *Seventh Heaven*, by Stella Unger & Victor Wolfson
p. 510

The Nation, June 25, 1955
The King and the Duke, by Francis Fergusson
p. 590

BIBLIOGRAPHY

The Nation, July 2, 1955
The Trial, by Franz Kafka
p. 18

The Nation, November 5, 1955
The Cherry Orchard, by Anton Chekhov
p. 406

The Nation, November 12, 1955
The Bourgeois Gentleman, by Molière, & *The Chalk Garden*,
by Enid Bagnold
pp. 426–427

The Nation, November 26, 1955
A Hatful of Rain, by Michael Gazzo
pp. 455–456

The Nation, December 3, 1955
The Lark, by Jean Anouilh
pp. 485–486

The Nation, December 17, 1955, & May 19, 1956
Pipe Dream, by Richard Rodgers & Oscar Hammerstein; *The Most
Happy Fella*, by Frank Loesser
p. 544 & p. 439

The Nation, May 26, 1956
The Iceman Cometh, by Eugene O'Neill
pp. 458–459

The Nation, June 9, 1956
The Littlest Revue, by Ogden Nash & Vernon Duke
p. 497

The Nation, July 21, 1956
Measure for Measure & *King John*, by William Shakespeare
pp. 64–66

The Nation, November 17, 1956
Johnny Johnson, by Paul Green
pp. 439–440

BIBLIOGRAPHY

The Nation, December 8, 1956
Girls of Summer, by N. Richard Nash, & *The Happiest Millionaire*,
by Kyle Crichton
p. 506

The Nation, January 5, 1957
The Good Woman of Setzuan, by Bertolt Brecht
p. 27

The Nation, January 12, 1957
Troilus and Cressida, by William Shakespeare
p. 46

The Nation, January 19, 1957
Purple Dust, by Sean O'Casey
pp. 65–66

The Nation, February 2, 1957
The Waltz of the Toreadors, by Jean Anouilh
p. 106

The Nation, March 16, 1957
A Hole in the Head, by Arnold Schulman
pp. 241–242

The Nation, March 23, 1957
Good as Gold, by John Patrick
pp. 262–263

The Nation, March 30, 1957
Exiles, by James Joyce
p. 281

The Nation, April 6, 1957
Orpheus Descending, by Tennessee Williams
pp. 301–302

The Nation, May 11, 1957
Livin' the Life, by Dale Wasserman & Bruce Geller; *The First
Gentleman*, by Norman Ginsbury
p. 427

BIBLIOGRAPHY

The Nation, May 18, 1957, & June 1, 1957
A Moon for the Misbegotten, by Eugene O'Neill, & *New Girl in Town,* by George Abbott
p. 446 & p. 486

The Nation, February 8, 1958
Summer of the 17th Doll, by Ray Lawler, & *The Music Man,* by Meredith Wilson
pp. 126–127

The Nation, February 15, 1958
Endgame, by Samuel Beckett
pp. 145–146

The Nation, May 17, 1958
The Visit, by Friedrich Dürrenmatt, & *The Firstborn,* by Christopher Fry
pp. 455–456

The Nation, October 25, 1958
A Touch of the Poet, by Eugene O'Neill
pp. 298–299

The Nation, November 22, 1958
Epitaph for George Dillon, by John Osborne
pp. 394–395

The Nation, May 23, 1959
The Nervous Set, by Jay Landesman & Theodore J. Flicker; *Once Upon a Mattress,* by Jay Thompson, Dean Fuller, & Marshall Barer
pp. 483–484

The Nation, June 6, 1959
Gypsy, by Arthur Laurents
pp. 521–522

The Nation, July 23, 1960
The Tempest & *Henry V,* by William Shakespeare
pp. 58–59

The Nation, March 25, 1961
Roots, by Arnold Wesker
p. 272

BIBLIOGRAPHY

The Nation, October 14, 1961
Purlie Victorious, by Ossie Davis
pp. 254–255

The Nation, March 3, 1962
Fly Blackbird, by C. Bernard Jackson & James V. Hatch
pp. 201–202

The Nation, July 14, 1962
The Merchant of Venice, by William Shakespeare
pp. 17–18

The Nation, March 30, 1964
But for Whom Charlie, by S. N. Behrman
pp. 335–336

The Nation, April 13, 1964
Dutchman & *The Baptism*, by LeRoi Jones
p. 384

The Nation, November 2, 1964
Hamlet, by William Shakespeare
p. 312

The Nation, June 7, 1965
Baal, by Bertolt Brecht
pp. 625–628

The Nation, June 21, 1965
Troubled Waters, by Ugo Betti, & *Live Like Pigs*, by John Arden
pp. 681–682

The Nation, January 3, 1966
Leonce and Lena & *Danton's Death*, by Georg Büchner
pp. 26–27

The Nation, December 11, 1967
San Francisco Mime Troupe
p. 637

The Nation, May 20, 1968
Soldiers, by Rolf Hochhuth
p. 678

BIBLIOGRAPHY

The Nation, May 27, 1968
The Memorandum, by Václav Havel
p. 709

The Nation, September 2, 1968
A Midsummer Night's Dream, by William Shakespeare; *Tartuffe*,
 by Molière; & *The Seagull*, by Anton Chekhov
pp. 189–190

The Nation, November 4, 1968
We Bombed in New Haven, by Joseph Heller
pp. 477–478

The Nation, January 20, 1969
Little Murders, by Jules Pfeiffer
p. 94

The Nation, June 30, 1969
Promenade, by María Irene Fornés
p. 837

The Nation, June 15, 1970
The Trial of A. Lincoln, by James Damico
pp. 733–734

Horizon
Horizon, March 1960
Vol. 2, No. 4
"Circle in the Square"
pp. 95–99, 119–121

Horizon, September 1960
Vol. 3, No. 1
"Theater: Laughter at Your Own Risk"
Krapp's Last Tape, by Samuel Beckett
pp. 112–116

Horizon, November 1960
Vol. 3, No. 2
"Theater: This Blessed Plot, This Shakespeare in the Park"
The New York Shakespeare Festival
pp. 116–118

BIBLIOGRAPHY

Horizon, January 1961
Vol. 3, No. 3
"Theater: The Roaring Presence of Brendan Behan"
The Hostage, by Brendan Behan
pp. 113–114

Horizon, March 1961
Vol. 3, No. 4
"Theater: Human Beings and Substitutes"
Period of Adjustment, by Tennessee Williams, & *A Taste of Honey*,
by Shelagh Delaney
pp. 102–103

Horizon, July 1961
Vol. 3, No. 6
"Theater: Arise, Ye Playgoers of the World"
The Death of Bessie Smith & *The American Dream*, by Edward
Albee; *Roots*, by Arnold Wesker
pp. 116–118

Horizon, November 1961
Vol. 4, No. 2
"Theater: The Terrifying Jean Genet"
The Blacks, by Jean Genet
pp. 98–102

Horizon, January 1962
Vol. 4, No. 3
"The Persistence of Ibsenism"
pp. 106–108

Horizon, March 1962
Vol. 4, No. 4
"Where There Is Total Involvement: The Living Theatre"
pp. 106–109

Horizon, May 1962
Vol. 4, No. 5
"The Hunt for Heroes"
A Man for All Seasons, by Robert Bolt, & *The Caretaker*, by Harold
Pinter
pp. 110–112

253

BIBLIOGRAPHY

Horizon, July 1962
Vol. 4, No. 6
"Theater: A Coming Talent Casts Its Shadow Before: John Arden"
pp. 91–94

Horizon, September 1962
Vol. 5, No. 1
"Theater: On Being Upstaged by Scenery"
pp. 110–112

Horizon, November 1962
Vol. 5, No. 2
"Theater: the Actors' Studio Goes Legit"
pp. 106–108

Horizon, January 1963
Vol. 5, No. 3
"The Case for Repertory"
pp. 106–108

Horizon, March 1963
Vol. 5, No. 4
"Laugh Now, Pay Later"
A Man's a Man, by Bertolt Brecht; *Oh Dad, Poor Dad, Mamma's Hung You in the Closet and I'm Feelin' So Sad*, by Arthur Kopit; & *Who's Afraid of Virginia Woolf?*, by Edward Albee
pp. 106–109

Horizon, May 1963
Vol. 5, No. 5
"Melodrama on Broadway"
The Dumb Waiter, by Harold Pinter; *Desire Under the Elms*, by Eugene O'Neill; & *The Milk Train Doesn't Stop Here Anymore*, by Tennessee Williams
pp. 106–109

Horizon, July 1963
Vol. 5, No. 6
"Adult Prodigy: Orson Welles"
pp. 84–91

BIBLIOGRAPHY

Horizon, November 1963
Vol. 5, No. 8
"Tyrone Guthrie: The Artist as Man of the Theatre"
pp. 35–41

Index

Abbey Theatre (Dublin), 61, 66, 148
Abbott, George, 106–107, 115, 140, 147–149, 203
Absurdism, 10, 53, 100, 107, 152, 184, 190, 209, 210
Actors' Playhouse (New York), 225
An Actor Prepares, 57–58
Actors' Studio, 10, 12, 55–61, 254
Actors' Studio Theatre: see "Actors' Studio"
Act Without Words I, 168
Adams, John Quincy, 158
Adaptation, 21–22, 24, 57, 69, 72, 95, 109, 128, 131, 138, 144, 204, 229, 240
Adler, Stella, 137
Aeschylus, 65, 157
After the Fall, 216
Ailey, Alvin, 212
Alaimo, Michael, 218, 220
Albee, Edward, 11, 50, 60, 86, 121, 123, 183–188, 200, 203–208
Aldredge, Theoni, 202
Aldredge, Thomas, 166
Alexander the Great, 168
"Alienation" (Brecht), 223
Allegory, 129, 185, 199–200
L'Amant Militaire (The Soldierly Lover), 230
Amato Opera (New York), 18
Ambassador Theatre (New York), 210, 237
The American Dream, 11, 50, 121, 183–188
American Gothic, 20, 25
American Negro Theatre, 90
American Shakespeare Festival (Stratford, Conn.), 12, 51–52, 67, 133, 136, 163, 165, 170
Amphitheater, 29, 51, 201
Anderson, Maxwell, 25, 65
Anderson, Robert, 12

Andreyev, Leonid, 65
Anglophilia, 7, 45
Angry Young Men (U.K.), 174, 186, 217, 228
Animalism, 222, 225
Anna Christie, 148–149
Anouilh, Jean, 11, 27, 94–95, 116, 128–129
Anspecher, Florence, 31
ANTA Theatre (New York), 96–97, 196
Anti-drama, 26, 210
Anti-heroism, 199–200, 228
Anti-Saloon League (Oberlin, Ohio), 183
Anti-Semitism: see "Judaism"
Appia, Adolphe, 51, 54–55
The Apple, 42–44
Apron stage, 51, 134, 244
Archer, William, 4
Arden, John, 11, 45–50, 112, 223–227, 254
Arena theater, 18, 21–23, 51, 84, 91, 133, 211
Aristophanes, 228
Arkin, Alan, 240
Armistead, Horace, 51
Aronson, Boris, 95, 99, 101, 144, 147
Around Theatres, 10
Arsenic and Old Lace, 105
Association of Performing Artists (A.P.A., University of Michigan), 62
As You Like It, 29
Atkinson, Brooks, 4
Attila the Hun, 242
Auden, W. H., 39
Austen, Jane, 106, 164
Autobiography, 40, 57, 60, 74, 78, 177, 190
Avant-gardism, 4, 26, 39, 53
Awake and Sing!, 57

Baal, 11, 220–223, 229
The Bad Seed, 25

INDEX

Baddeley, Hermione, 214
Bagnold, Enid, 125–127
Balanchine, George, 60, 64
The Balcony, 183, 192–193, 203
Balustrade Theater (Prague), 232
Balzac, Honoré de, 65
Bancroft, Anne, 60
The Baptism, 216–218
Bara, Theda, 216
The Barber of Seville, 79
Bardophilia, 33
Barker, Margaret, 100
Barnes, Clive, 5
Baroque, 76
Barrymore, Ethel, 58
Barrymore, John, 5, 58
Barrymore, Lionel, 58
Barrymore Theatre (New York), 96, 113, 126
"Bartleby, the Scrivener" (Melville), 233
Bartlett's *Familiar Quotations*, 216
Bates, Alan, 200
Bay, Howard, 96
B.B.C. (British Broadcasting Corporation), 78, 232
Beardsley, Aubrey, 32
Beck, Julian, 38–44, 237, 239
Beckett, Samuel, 10–11, 53, 119–120, 136–137, 152–153, 155, 166–175, 183–185, 200, 203, 237
Beerbohm, Max, 3, 10
Begley, Ed, 104
Behan, Brendan, 11, 23, 27, 45–46, 174–178, 253
Behrman, N. S., 12, 214–216
Belafonte, Harry, 148
Belasco, Leon, 98
Bel Geddes, Barbara, 103
Bell, Clive, 174
Benavente, Jacinto, 27
Benchley, Robert, 7
Benedict, Paul, 241
Bennett, Alan, 208
Bennington College (Vermont), 183
Bennion, Peggy, 29
Bentley, Eric, 3–4, 7–11, 139, 204, 209
Bérard, Christian, 52
Berliner Ensemble (Germany), 221
Bernays, Edward, 31
Bernhardt, Sarah, 58

Bernsey, William, 18
Bernstein, Leonard, 103–105
Bernstein, Maurice, 70, 74
Best, Edna, 94–95
Betti, Ugo, 11, 223–227
Bevan, Donald, 93–94
Beyond the Fringe, 207–208
Bibin, Paul, 221
The Bible, 38, 48, 103, 156, 208
Biddle, Anthony J. Drexel, 138
Biddle, Cordelia Drexel, 138–139
Big Fish, Little Fish, 86
Bijou Theatre (New York), 118, 147
Bikel, Theodore, 129
Billy Budd, 11, 92–93
Billy Rose Theatre (New York), 123, 205, 231
Biltmore Theatre (New York), 207
Blackburn, Robert, 29
The Blacks, 53, 121, 189–196
Blau, Herbert, 229–230
Blitzstein, Marc, 71
Blossom, Roberts, 166
Boleyn, Anne, 197
Bolt, Robert, 12, 52, 56, 196–200
Bond, Sudie, 50, 234
Booke, Sorrell, 189
Booth, Edwin, 58
Booth Theatre (New York), 212
Born Yesterday, 94
Borstal Boy, 177
Bosco, Philip, 32
The Bourgeois Gentleman, 11, 125–127
Bovasso, Julie, 108
Bowles, Jane, 22
Box set, 23–24, 41, 51–54, 81, 83–84, 134, 220
Boy's Life, 215
Boyt, John, 145
Braham, Horace, 91
Braine, John, 186
Brand, 34, 37–38
Brando, Marlon, 58, 96
Breasted, James H., 70
Brecht, Bertolt, 10–11, 26, 39, 41–42, 46, 139–140, 183, 203–208, 220–225, 229
Brecht on Brecht, 221
Brigham, Constance, 104
Britton, Don, 139

257

INDEX

Broadway (New York), 2, 4, 11–12, 20, 22, 24–28, 38, 44, 48, 55, 61–63, 67–68, 78, 80, 87, 90–91, 93–99, 102–105, 107, 126–128, 130–131, 137–138, 140, 142–143, 145, 147, 149, 151, 153, 156–157, 160–161, 174–175, 179, 182, 188, 196, 198–199, 205–207, 210, 212–213, 216, 221, 225, 230–231, 237, 240, 243, 254

Broadway Theatre (New York), 126, 161

Broderick, James, 137

Brontë, Charlotte, 72

Brook, Peter, 154–155

Brooke, Alan, 232

Brooks, Van Wyck, 158

The Brothers Karamazov, 107

The Brother Who Protects and Loves: see *Troubled Waters*

Browne, Roscoe Lee, 194

Brustein, Robert, 1, 3, 9–12

Bryan, William Jennings, 103

Buchan, John, 72

Büchner, Georg, 11, 221, 227–230

Building a Character, 57–58

Burlesque, 49, 98, 139, 162, 233

Burns, David, 144

Burrows, Abe, 96–98

Burton, Phillip, 142

Burton, Richard, 219

Bus Stop, 99–101, 114

But for Whom Charlie, 214–216

Caesar, Julius, 38

Cage, John, 40

Calculated Risk, 210

Caldwell, Zoe, 81

Call, John, 166, 202

Cambridge, Godfrey M., 188–189

Cambridge Drama Festival (U.K.), 26

Cambridge University (U.K.), 174

Campbell, Douglas, 81, 85

Canadian Broadcasting Company (C.B.C.), 78

Canadian National Railways, 78

Cannery Row, 130

Cannon, Jack, 28

Cantril, Hadley, 73

Capalbo, Carmen, 148

Čapek, Karel, 65

Capitalism, 237

Capote, Truman, 25, 27

The Caretaker, 11, 122, 196–200

Carmen, 79

Carmines, Al, 241–242

Carnegie Hall Playhouse (New York), 117, 137

Carnovsky, Morris, 101, 136, 164–165

Catch-22, 239

Catherine of Aragon, Queen, 197

Catholicism, 22–23, 178, 278, 236

Cat on a Hot Tin Roof, 11, 102–103, 114, 128, 146

Cavalleria Rusticana, 22

Cavanaugh, Jr., Edward Francis, 25

CBC-Radio (New York), 73

CBS-TV (New York), 34

Central Park (New York), 2, 29, 31, 33, 66, 165, 201–203, 218

Ceremonies in Dark Old Men, 243

The Chairs, 183

The Chalk Garden, 125–127

Chamberlain, Neville, 73

Chambord, Jacqueline, 166

Chaney, Frances, 101

Chaplin, Charles, 219

Chapman, Robert, 92

Charley's Aunt, 63, 242

Chekhov, Anton, 5, 10–11, 34, 53, 61, 65–66, 82–84, 101–102, 113, 125, 138, 144, 189, 224, 234–237

Chelsea Theater Center (New York), 4

Cherry Lane Theatre (New York), 20, 53, 119, 123, 141, 152, 210, 216, 223

The Cherry Orchard, 11, 125

Cherwell, Lord (Frederick Alexander Lindemann), 232

Chicken Soup with Barley, 182, 186

Children of Darkness, 27

The Chili Widow, 12

Christianity, 178, 196, 202

Church, Sandra, 161–163

Churchill, Winston, 231–232

Cimino, Leonardo, 101, 165

Cinemiracle International (Los Angeles), 60

Circle in the Square Theatre, 18–27, 53, 111, 132–133, 192, 211, 240, 252

Citizen Kane, 73–76

City Center (New York), 93

258

INDEX

Civic Repertory Company (New York), 64, 67
Clark, Bobby, 85
Clark, Kendall, 136
Clark Center Drama Company (New York), 227, 229
Classicism, 20, 27, 29, 57, 63, 67, 79–80, 82, 84, 176, 188
Cleveland Playhouse (Ohio), 65
Clurman, Harold, 22, 57, 95, 99–100, 130–131, 143, 146, 159
Cocteau, Jean, 39–40
Cohn, Roy, 83
Colicos, John, 232
The Collection, 211
Collins, Michael, 177
Colonialism, 194
Columbia University (New York), 10
Columbus Circle (New York), 162
Come Back, Little Sheba, 99
Comédie Française (Paris), 55, 61, 95, 125
Comedy, 10–11, 32, 45, 93, 97–98, 105–106, 125, 130–131, 135, 139–140, 142, 144, 149, 153, 155, 176, 179–181, 185, 203–204, 208, 211, 213, 219, 224, 236
Commedia dell'arte, 218–219, 220, 223, 230
Communism, 186, 196, 233
Compulsion, 76
Confederacy (U.S.), 189
Congressional Record, 62
Congreve, William, 53, 79
The Connection, 4, 38–41, 44, 111
Connell, Leigh, 19, 24–27
Conrad, Joseph, 73
Constructivism, 51
Conventionalism, 8, 21, 24–25, 82, 84, 106, 108, 130, 136, 149, 186, 195, 211–213, 215
Cook, Peter, 208
Cooper, Gladys, 126
Cooper, James Fenimore, 66
Copeau, Jacques, 39
Coriolanus, 65
Cornell, Katharine, 70, 97–98, 101, 156
Coronet Theatre (New York), 142, 149, 156
Corruption at the Palace of Justice, 223

Corsaro, Frank, 60, 128
Cort Theatre (New York), 174, 188
Corzatte, Clayton, 164
Costigan, Ken, 227, 229
Cotsworth, Staats, 34
Cotten, Joseph, 210
The Country Girl, 162
Coward, Noël, 141
Coxe, Louis O., 92
The Cradle Song, 20
The Cradle Will Rock, 71, 75
Craig, Gordon, 51, 54–55
Crawford, Cheryl, 56, 60
Creighton, Anthony, 160
Crichton, Kyle, 137–139
Crimean War, 47
Criticism, Film, 1, 8–10
Criticism, Theater, 1–15, 29, 211
Cromwellianism, 48
Cronyn, Hume, 81, 85, 87, 106
Crosby, Bing, 162
Cummings, Vicki, 90
Cusack, Cyril, 148
Cyrano de Bergerac, 86

Dahl, Roald, 105–106
Dailey, Irene, 139
Damico, James, 243–245
Damn Yankees, 106–107, 115
Danton's Death, 227–230
The Dark Is Light Enough, 96–98
Dark of the Moon, 18
Darrow, Clarence, 76, 103–104
Darwin, Charles, 104
David Copperfield, 159
Davies, Robertson, 79
Davis, Bette, 54
Davis, Donald, 169–171
Davis, Ossie, 12, 188–189, 243
The Death of Bessie Smith, 183–188, 206
Death of a Salesman, 82, 86
Dee, Ruby, 188
De Gaulle, Charles, 86
Dekker, Thomas, 71
DeKoven, Roger, 101
Delaney, Shelagh, 12, 45, 178–181
Dennis, Patrick, 213
Denton, Crahan, 99
Depression, Great, 67, 70
Derr, Richard, 90

259

INDEX

Desire Under the Elms, 208–214
The Desperate Hours, 86, 95–96, 113, 210
Devine, George, 181
Dewhurst, Colleen, 28, 211
Dickens, Charles, 72, 159
Dinner at Eight, 86
Disher, M. Wilson, 209
Documentary, 41
A Doll's House, 37, 206, 212
Dostoevsky, Fyodor, 107, 159
Douglas, Paul, 144
Douglass, Stephen, 107
The Drama Observed, 3
Dream Girl, 93–94
Dreiser, Theodore, 66
Dr. Faustus, 71
Drury Lane Theatre (London), 18
Du Bois, Raoul Pène, 161, 163
Dudley, John Stuart, 60
Duell, William, 234
Dukakis, Olympia, 234
Duke of York Theatre (London), 39
Dumas *père*, Alexandre, 237
The Dumb Waiter, 11, 208–214
Dunaway, Faye, 216
Duncan, Andrew, 241
Dunnock, Mildred, 103, 136, 214
Dürrenmatt, Friedrich, 11, 119, 153–157
Duse, Eleanora, 58
Dutchman, 123, 216–218

Eberling, George, 101
Ebert, Joyce, 164
L'École des Femmes (*The School for Wives*), 52
Edinburgh International Festival (Scotland), 78
Edison Theatre (New York), 91
Edwardianism, 140
Edwards, Ben, 143
Edwards, Hilton, 70
Eisenhower, Dwight D., 188, 204
Elcar, Dana, 106
Elder III, Lonne, 243
Elizabethanism, 76, 80–81, 155, 163, 191, 201
Emerson, Faye, 62
Emery, John, 136
Emperor and Galilean, 38

The Emperor Jones, 148
Endgame, 11, 119, 152–153, 167–169, 183, 203
An Enemy of the People, 36
Ephron, Henry, 207
Ephron, Phoebe, 207
Epic theater (Brecht), 139
Epitaph for George Dillon, 160–161
Epstein, Alvin, 137, 142, 153
Ericson, John, 93
The Eumenides, 65
Euripides, 65
Evans, Maurice, 93
Ewell, Tom, 58
The Exception and the Rule, 223
Exiles, 12, 144
Experimentalism, 5, 20, 24, 26–27, 44, 51, 63, 71, 169
Expressionism, 51, 223

Falstaff, 79, 125, 166
Farce, 38, 85, 94, 105, 141–143, 145, 148, 188, 203, 206, 208–210, 216, 218, 229
Fascism, 71, 174
Faulkner, William, 66, 76
Federal Theatre Project, 71
Feibleman, Peter, 212
Fergusson, Francis, 10–11, 20
Festival Theatre (Cambridge, U.K.), 78
Festival Theatre (Stratford, Ontario), 24, 78–79, 87, 234–237
Field, Betty, 159
Fields, W. C. 223, 232
Filmmakers' Cinematheque (New York), 230
Fine, Aaron, 109
Finney, Mary, 106
The Firstborn, 153–157
"First Person Singular" (radio series), 72
The First Reader, 109
First World War: see "World War I"
Fiske, Minnie Maddern, 58
Fitzgerald, F. Scott, 14
Fleischer, Richard, 76
Foch, Nina, 90, 136
Fontanne, Lynn, 59, 154–155
Forbes, Meriel, 143
Forbes, Scott, 62
Ford Foundation (New York), 62

260

INDEX

Fornés, María Irene, 124, 241–242
48th Street Theatre (New York), 93
46th Street Theatre (New York), 107, 115, 149
Fosse, Bob, 149
4th Street Theatre (New York), 34, 52, 101, 125
Franciosa, Anthony, 128
Frankel, Gene, 189
Franklin, Benjamin, 76
Freedman, Gerald, 31
Free State Army (Ireland), 177
Freight, 90–91
Freud, Sigmund, 35, 96
Freudianism, 36, 133, 209
Froehlich, Rico, 132
Fry, Christopher, 12, 89–90, 96–98, 153–157
Frye, Northrup, 12
Fulton Theatre (New York), 90
Fundamentalism, 104
Furstenberg, Betsy von, 127

Gale, Shirley, 101
Gallicism, 100, 221
Gallup, George H., 180
Gam, Rita, 81
Gardner, herb, 206
Garfein, Jack, 137
Garfield, John, 60
Garrick Gaieties, 56
Gascon, Jean, 236–237
Gate Theatre (Dublin), 70
Gate Theatre (New York), 224–225
Gazzara, Ben, 58, 103, 128
Gazzo, Michael, 12, 116, 127–128
Geiringer, Robert, 29
Gelber, Jack, 4, 38–39, 42–43, 111
The General, 218
General Motors (Detroit), 149
Generation of Vipers, 238
Genet, Jean, 11, 40, 53, 107–109, 115, 121, 147, 174–175, 183–184, 189–196, 203, 208, 253
The Gentle People, 57
Gershwin, George, 204
Gestapo (Germany), 232
Ghostley, Alice, 104
Ghosts, 4, 34, 36
Giant's Causeway (Ireland), 55

Gibbs, Wolcott, 7, 98
Gibson, William, 40
Gilbert, Benjamin A., 162
Gilbert, W. S., 203, 236
Gill, Brendan, 7
Gilman, Richard, 1, 3, 9, 11
Giraudoux, Jean, 27, 208
The Girl on the Via Flamina, 20, 25
Girls of Summer, 137–139
Glanville, Maxwell, 90
The Glass Menagerie, 40
Globe Theatre (Broadway): see "Lunt-Fontanne Theatre"
Globe Theatre (London), 31, 51, 66, 165
Goethe, Johann Wolfgang von, 221
Gold Eagle Guy, 56
Golden Boy, 57
Goldoni, Carlo, 230
Goodman, Paul, 39
The Good Woman of Setzuan, 11, 139–140
Gordon, Glen, 90–91
Gordone, Charles, 243
Gothicism, 23, 190, 221
Gozzi, Carlo, 65
Graham, Billy, 43
Graham, Martha, 22–23
Grand Guignol, 50, 139, 185
The Grass Harp, 25
Gray, Charles, 141
The Great God Brown, 65
The Great White Hope, 243
Green, Paul, 12, 56, 117, 136–137
Greene, Bert, 109
Greenwich Mews Theatre (New York), 223
Greenwich Village (New York), 18–20, 25–26, 43, 53, 166, 191, 241
Grizzard, George, 81, 83, 86
Grotesque, 75, 100, 184, 215
Group Theatre (New York), 56–58, 136
Grove Press (New York), 47
Guitry, Sacha, 76
Gustafson, Carol, 101
Guthrie, Tyrone, 12, 28, 62, 67, 77–87, 140–141, 236, 255
Guthrie (Repertory) Theatre (Minneapolis), 62, 113
Guys and Dolls, 106
Gypsy, 161–163

261

INDEX

Habimah Theatre (Tel Aviv), 78
Hagen, Uta, 139
Hall, Willis, 45
Hallelujah the Hills, 218
Hamlet, 5, 11, 28, 68, 78, 82–83,
    85–86, 198, 203, 218–220,
    228
Hammerstein, Oscar, 106, 130–132
Hancock, John, 204
Hansberry, Lorraine, 243
The Happiest Millionaire, 137–139
The Happy Haven, 45, 49–50
Harris, Julie, 94–95, 128–129
Harris, Rosemary, 141
Harron, Donald, 98
Hart, Moss, 138, 176, 203
Hartford Stage Company (Conn.), 243
Hartigan, Grace, 41
Harvard University (Cambridge, Mass.),
    11, 208
Hatch, Gillian Gretton, ix
Hatch, Peter, ix
Hatch, Robert, 1–15
Hatch, Jr., Robert Littlefield: see
    "Hatch, Robert"
Hatch, Ruth Bower, ix
A Hatful of Rain, 116, 127–128
Havel, Václav, 12, 124, 232–234
Havoc, June, 60, 162
Hawthorne, Nathaniel, 66
Hayes, Alfred, 20
Hayes, Helen, 40, 157–159
Hayes, Joseph, 12, 86, 95–96, 113
Haymarket Theatre (London), 18
Hayward, Leland, 161
Hearst, William Randolph,
    73, 75
Heartbreak House, 71
The Heart of Darkness, 73
Heckscher Theatre, 29
Hedda Gabler, 34
Hedonism, 222
Heffernan, John, 234
Hegel, G.W.F., 11
Heine, Heinrich, 166
Held, Jr., John, 241
Helen Hayes Theatre (New York), 179,
    207
Heller, Joseph, 237–239
Hellman, Lillian, 2, 65, 128

Hemingway, Ernest, 66
Henritze, Bette, 202
Henry, Joyce, 108
Henry VIII (King of England), 197
Henry V (King of England), 232
Henry V, 31–32, 163–166
Henson, John, 132
Hepburn, Katharine, 164
Herlie, Eileen, 160
He Who Gets Slapped, 65
Heyward, DuBose, 243
Hiken, Gerald, 125, 139
Hill, Roger, 70
Hiller, Wendy, 148
Hingle, Pat, 137–138
Hippolytus, 65
Hirsch, John, 235, 238
Hitler, Adolf, 75
H.M.S. Pinafore, 164
Hochhuth, Rolf, 12, 231–232
A Hole in the Head, 143–145
Holland, Joseph, 91
Holliday, Judy, 93–94
Hollywood (Calif.), 63, 73, 75, 93, 96,
    143, 215
Holt, Will, 223
Homericism, 24
Homolka, Oskar, 100
The Honeys, 105–106
Hooks, Robert, 217
Hoover, Herbert, 204
Hopper, Hedda, 73
Horizon, ix, 1, 252–255
Horror, 45, 75, 77, 82, 96, 100, 105,
    127, 153, 160, 178–179, 181, 184,
    203, 206, 211, 213
Horton, Russell, 229
The Hostage, 174–178
Houghton, Norris, 92
Houseman, John, 71, 133, 135–136
The House of Connelly, 56
Howard, Sidney, 131–132
Huckleberry Finn, 24, 64
Hudson Theatre (New York), 198
Hugo, Laurence, 93
Hugo, Victor, 10
Huneker, James Gibbon, 7
Huston, John, 75
Hutt, William, 236
Hyman, Earle, 136, 164

262

INDEX

Ibsen, Henrik, 4, 11–12, 34–38, 53, 55, 60, 65–66, 79, 86, 99–101, 145, 183, 190, 253
Ibsenism: see "Ibsen, Henrik"
The Iceman Cometh, 11, 20, 23–25, 53, 111, 132–133, 157, 159
Idealism, 26, 28, 30, 35, 51, 53, 64, 94–95, 125, 137, 148, 156, 201
Illusionism, 21, 23, 39, 40–42, 50, 54, 80, 86, 105, 109, 139, 150, 158, 176, 193, 212
Imperial Theatre (New York), 98, 117, 131
The Importance of Being Earnest, 65
Impressionism, 23
I'm Talking about Jerusalem, 182, 186
Inadmissible Evidence, 229
In Circles, 242
Inge, William, 2, 11, 60–61, 99–101, 114
Inherit the Wind, 103–105
Internet, 13
In the Jungle of Cities, 41–42
In the Summer House, 22
The Invasion from Mars, 73
Ionesco, Eugène, 183–184, 203, 213
I Pagliacci, 22
Irish Nationalism, 175
Irish Republican Army (I.R.A.), 176
Irony, 1–2, 10–11, 75, 140, 154, 204, 208, 224, 236
Ives, Burl, 103

Jack, or The Submission, 184
Jackson, Andrew, 158
Jaffe, Sam, 95
James, Henry, 25, 66, 157
Jane Eyre, 72
Jarry, Alfred, 39, 229
J.B., 4
Jeffers, Robinson, 22
Jens, Salome, 215–216
Joan of Arc, 128–129
John Gabriel Borkman, 38
John Golden Theatre (New York), 160, 207
Johnny Johnson, 56, 117, 136–137
Johnson, Dots, 90
Johnson, Lyndon B., 239
Johnson, Susan, 132

Johnson, William, 130
Jones, James Earl, 202, 222
Jones, LeRoi, 12, 123, 216–218, 243
Jones, Robert Edmond, 40
Jonson, Ben, 86, 219
Jouvet, Louis, 52
Joyce, James, 12, 145, 173, 229
Judaism, 186–187, 202, 215, 222, 231, 240
Judson Poets' Theatre (New York), 124, 241
Julius Caesar, 11, 31, 51, 71, 75, 91

Kafka, Franz, 11, 68, 77, 109–110, 155, 221, 224
Kane, Whitford, 136
Kanin, Garson, 2, 94, 144
Karloff, Boris, 129
Kauffmann, Stanley, 1, 3, 6, 9–11
Kaufman, George S., 86, 96–98, 138, 176, 203
Kazan, Elia, 22, 56, 60, 62–63, 67–68, 103, 216
Keach, Stacy, 5
Kellin, Mike, 131
Kelly, George, 91
Kelly, P. J., 153
Kennedy, John F., 188
Kerensky, Alexander, 11
Kerr, Jean, 207
Kerr, Walter, 4, 11
Kesselring, Joseph, 105
Keynes, John Maynard, 174
Kimbrough, Clinton, 216
King, Dennis, 92
The King and the Duke, 20
King Henry V: see *Henry V*
King John, 133–136
King Lear, 55, 201
Kingsley, Sidney, 56
Kline, Franz, 41
Klugman, Jack, 161, 163
Kooning, Willem de, 41
Kopit, Arthur, 12, 203–208
Kornfeld, Lawrence, 242
Krapp's Last Tape, 11, 53, 120, 166–174, 185, 200
Krasna, Norman, 2
Kronenberger, Louis, 95
Krutch, Joseph Wood, 7

263

INDEX

Kubla Khan, 80
Kummer, Claire, 65
Kurnitz, Harry, 2

The Lady from Shanghai, 75
Lafayette Theatre (New York), 112
Lahr, Bert, 153
Landau, Jack, 133
Langdon, Harry, 64
Lansbury, Angela, 181
The Lark, 116, 128–129
Lascoe, Henry, 98
Laurents, Arthur, 161–163
Lavin, Linda, 241
Lawler, Ray, 12, 149–151
Lawrence, Jerome, 12, 103–105
Lawrence of Arabia (T. E. Lawrence;
   T. E. Shaw), 198
The League of Youth, 38
Leaves of Grass, 64
Lee, Robert E., 103–105
Lee, Gypsy Rose (Rose Louise Hovick),
   161–162
Lee, Ming Cho, 202
Le Gallienne, Eva, 62, 64, 67, 101
Leggatt, Alison, 160
Lenard, Mark, 145
Lenin, Vladimir, 11
Lenox Hill Theatre (New York), 92
Leonce and Lena, 227–230
Levin, Meyer, 29
Levy, Melvin, 56
Lewis, Robert, 22, 56, 58
A Life in the Theatre, 78
Life magazine, 62
Lincoln, Abraham, 158, 243–245
Lincoln Center (New York), 10, 60, 68,
   214, 216, 225, 229
Lincoln Center for the Performing Arts:
   see "Lincoln Center"
The Lion King, 4
Lippold Richard, 41
Little Eyolf, 37
Little Me, 213
Little Murders, 240–241
Little Theatre (New York), 157
Littlewood, Joan, 45, 176, 181
Live Like Pigs, 45, 47–50, 112, 223–227
Living Room Theatre: see "Living
   Theatre"

Living Theatre (New York), 10, 12,
   38–44, 53, 63, 111, 237, 253
Loeb, Philip, 101
Loesser, Frank, 106, 117, 130–132
Logan, Joshua, 212
Long, Shorty, 132
Longacre Theatre (New York), 94, 105,
   116, 128, 137
Long Day's Journey into Night, 25, 147,
   157
The Long, Hot Summer, 76
Look to the Lilies, 243
Loquasto, Santo, 244
Lorca, Federico García, 27
Lowell, Robert, 166
Lubitsch, Ernst, 98
Luckenbach, Beverly, 229
Lucullus, 75
Lund, Art, 131
Lunt, Alfred, 59, 154–155
Lunt-Fontanne Theatre (New York),
   119, 153
Lyceum Theatre (New York), 116, 122,
   127, 138, 179, 199

Macbeth, 26, 33, 68, 71, 75–76, 112, 135,
   203
MacGrath, Leureen, 34
MacLeish, Archibald, 4, 71
Macmillan, Harold, 207
Macready, William, 58
Mademoiselle Colombe, 94–95
The Magnificent Ambersons, 75
The Maids, 107–109, 115, 147, 191–192
Majestic Theatre (New York), 151
Malden, Karl, 96
Malet, Arthur, 165
Malina, Judith, 38–44, 237, 239
Malis, Fran, 108
Malone Dies, 167–168, 173
A Man for All Seasons, 52, 56, 196–200
Mann, Theodore, 18–19, 24–27, 221
A Man's a Man, 203–208
Many Loves, 39–41
Marchand, Nancy, 139
"The March of Time" (newsreel), 71, 73
Marco Millions, 216
Marino, Joseph, 34
Marlowe, Christopher, 71
Marre, Albert, 126

264

INDEX

Martin, Nan, 202
Martin Beck Theatre (New York), 118, 145
Martinique Theatre (New York), 221–222
Marx, Karl, 11
Mary, Mary, 207
Masochism, 222
Masque Theatre (New York), 204
The Master Builder, 11, 36, 99–101
The Matchmaker, 79
Maurer, Peggy, 101
Maxwell, Frank, 93
Mayer, Edwin Justus, 27
Mayfair Theatre (New York), 120, 182, 188
Mayro, Jacqueline, 163
McCarthy, Mary, 9
McClintic, Guthrie, 98
McConnell, Frederic, 65
McCormick, Myron, 105
McElhaney, Jan, 229
McKenna, Siobhán, 26, 126
McLiam, John 29
McNally, James B., 30
McNeil, Claudia, 212
McVey, Patrick, 99
Mead, Taylor, 218
Meara, Anne, 28
Measure for Measure, 11, 31–32, 133–136, 165
Medea, 22
Medford, Kay, 144
Medici family (Italy), 82
Meeker, Ralph, 215–216
Mekas, Jonas, 218
Melodrama, 12, 42–43, 56, 93, 95, 127, 144, 157, 176, 188, 208–214, 223, 232, 254
Melodrama, 209
Melville, Hermann, 11, 65–66, 92–93
Memling, Hans, 197
The Memorandum, 124, 232–234
Memphis State University (Tenn.), 225
Men in White, 56
Menotti, Gian Carlo, 132
The Merchant of Venice, 122, 201–203
Mercury Theatre (New York), 71–72
Meredith, George, 158
Merman, Ethel, 161–162

Merrick, David, 161
Merrill, Bob, 149
Method acting, 55–59, 220–221, 224
Method—or Madness?, 58
Metropolitan Opera (New York), 22, 61, 63–64, 68, 79
Meyerhold, Vsevolod, 39
A Midsummer Night's Dream, 69, 234–237
Mielziner, Jo, 131, 161, 163, 215
The Milk Train Doesn't Stop Here Anymore, 208–214
Miller, Arthur, 65, 82, 128, 216, 223
Miller, Henry, 40
Miller, Jonathan, 208
Mills, John, 198
Milne, A. A., 65
The Miracle Worker, 40
The Miser, 82, 85–86
Mitchell, Langdon, 65
Moby Dick, 65
Modigliani, Amedeo, 44
Moiseiwitsch, Tanya, 81
Molière (Jean-Baptiste Poquelin), 11, 52, 66, 82, 85, 125–127, 183, 219, 234–237
Molloy, 167–168, 173, 200
Montgomery, Robert, 96
A Moon for the Misbegotten, 11, 118, 147–149
Moore, Dudley, 208
Moore, Karen, 163
Moralism, 14, 97, 102, 150, 204, 221–222, 234
Morality plays, 26, 136, 177, 225
More, Thomas, 196–198
Morgan, J. P., 74
Morosco Theatre (New York), 102, 114, 213
Morris, William, 186
Morrison, Paul, 92
Mortimer, John, 45
Moscow Art Theatre (Russia), 55, 61, 66–67
Moses, Robert, 30
Moss, Arnold, 98, 136
Mostel, Zero, 139
The Most Happy Fella, 117, 130–132
Mother Courage and Her Children, 26
Mr. Arkadin, 76

265

INDEX

Muni, Paul, 103–104
Museum of Modern Art (New York), 40, 61
Musicals, 18, 62, 98, 106–107, 130, 132, 137, 139, 148, 151, 162–163, 223, 242
Music Box Theatre (New York), 99, 114
The Music Man, 62, 149–151
My Philadelphia Father, 138

NAACP (National Association for the Advancement of Colored People), 188
Napoleon (Bonaparte), 228
Nash, N. Richard, 12, 137–139
Nathan, George Jean, 3, 7
The Nation, ix, 1, 6, 9, 246–251
National Repertory Theatre, 62
National Review, 10
National Theatre (New York), 103
Naturalism, 209
Natwick, Mildred, 143
Nazism, 222
Neville, John, 141
New Girl in Town, 147–149
Newman, Paul, 58, 60, 96
New Republic, ix, 1, 9, 209, 246
Newton, Isaac, 167
New York City Ballet, 29, 55, 63–64, 66
New York City Theatre Company, 93
New Yorker, 7, 98, 215
The New York Idea, 65
New York magazine, 9
New York Parks, 30
New York Philharmonic, 61, 68
New York Public Library, 29
New York Rapid Transit System, 68
New York Shakespeare Festival, 12, 27–33, 63, 122, 165, 201, 252
New York Shakespeare Workshop: see "New York Shakespeare Festival"
New York State Department of Education, 33
New York Times, 4–6, 39, 56, 62, 179, 244
New York Times Magazine, 87
The Night of the Iguana, 54, 213
Nihilism, 42, 108, 152, 225
Ninotchka, 98
No Exit, 187, 203
Nolte, Charles, 92
No Place to Be Somebody, 243

O'Casey, Sean, 11, 27, 141–142, 144, 176
Odets, Clifford, 57, 162, 182, 186, 223
Oedipus complex, 219
Oedipus Rex, 242
Off-Broadway (New York), 12, 18, 20–21, 24–27, 34, 48, 52–53, 63, 67, 92, 100, 101, 109, 125, 132, 139, 141, 155, 162, 166, 182, 188–189, 192, 204–205, 210–211, 216, , 218, 223–225, 240–241
Off-Off-Broadway (New York), 11, 107, 189, 218
Of Thee I Sing, 204
O'Hara, Frank, 218
Oh Dad, Poor Dad, Mamma's Hung You in the Closet and I'm Feelin' So Sad, 203–208
Ohio State University (Columbus), 95
Oklahoma!, 106, 130
Old Vic Theatre (London), 55, 78, 140
Oliver Twist, 72
Olivier, Laurence, 64, 68, 219
O'Neill, Eugene, 4, 11, 20, 25, 27, 64–66, 111, 118, 132–133, 147–149, 157–160, 169, 182, 208–214, 216, 229
Opatoshu, David, 98
Open Theater (New York), 4
Oresteia, 157
Orlandi, Felice, 105
Orpheus Descending, 11, 118, 145–147
Osborne, John, 11, 45, 160–161, 174–175, 178, 184, 186, 208, 229
Othello, 57, 68, 75–76, 215, 222
Our Lady of the Flowers, 190
Our Theatres in the Nineties, 2–3
Own Town, 20, 27

Pacitti, Joe, 244
Page, Geraldine, 24, 58, 60
Paisan, 90
The Pajama Game, 140
Panic, 71
Papp, Joseph, 27–28, 30–31, 33, 63, 66, 165–166, 201–202, 218, 232–233
Paramount Hotel (New York), 182
Parody, 18, 43, 95, 145, 194
Parsons, Louella, 73
Pasolini, Pier Paolo, 76
Passion plays, 218
Paulee, Mona, 132

INDEX

Peace, 242
Pearl Harbor (Hawaii), 232
Peer Gynt, 38, 60, 65
Penguin Books (New York), 48
Penn, Arthur, 60
Père Goriot, 65
Pereira, I. Rice, 41
Period of Adjustment, 178–181, 213
Perkins, Anthony, 76–77
Peter Pan, 101, 129
Petronius, 90
Pfeiffer, Jules, 240–241
Phillips, Eddie, 107
Phoenix Theatre (New York), 18, 20, 26, 78, 100, 140, 205
A Phoenix Too Frequent, 90–91
Picasso, Pablo, 85
Pidgeon, Walter, 138
The Pillars of Society, 37
Pinter, Harold, 11, 45, 122, 196–200, 208–214, 225
Pipe Dream, 130–132
Pirandello, Luigi, 10–11, 39, 65, 223
Piscator, Erwin, 39
The Playboy of the Western World, 65
Playhouse Theatre (New York), 104
Pleasance, Donald, 199
Plowright, Joan, 181
Plummer, Christopher, 129
Plymouth Theatre (New York), 143
Podmore, William, 98
Polan, Lou, 99
Political theater, 38
Pollard, Percival, 7
Pope Pius XII, 231
Porgy and Bess, 243
Porter, Eric, 155
Portman, Eric, 158–159
Portrait of a Lady, 25
Power, Tyrone, 98
Presbyterianism, 106
Preston, Robert, 151
Pride and Prejudice, 106
Priestley, J. B., 79
Princess Theatre (London), 18
Princeton Observatory (N.J.), 72
Promenade, 124, 241–242
Propaganda, 35, 204, 243, 245
Proscenium arch: see "Box set"
Protestantism, 236

Proust, Marcel, 173
Provincetown Players (Mass.), 66
Provincetown Playhouse (New York), 53, 109, 120, 166
Prud'homme, Cameron, 149
Public Theater (New York), 124, 232
Pulitzer Prize (drama), 243
Puritanism, 7, 222
Purlie Victorious, 188–189, 243
Purple Dust, 141–142

The Quare Fellow, 23–24, 27, 178
Quayle, Anthony, 156
The Queen and the Rebels, 223
Quintero, José, 18–19, 22–27, 53, 133, 211
The Quintessence of Ibsenism, 35
Quinton, Albert, 166

Rabelaisianism, 147
Racine, Jean, 39
R.A.F. (Royal Air Force), 177, 198, 232
Ragin, John, 164
A Raisin in the Sun, 243
Rasumny, Mikhail, 95
Rathbone, Basil, 91
Rationalism, 30, 35–37, 109, 147, 157, 229, 240
Rattigan, Terence, 54, 159, 198
Rawlins, Lester, 153
Ray, Andrew, 181
Ray, James, 31, 165
Raymond, Guy, 131
Rea, Oliver, 80
Read, Herbert, 13
Realism, 10–11, 23, 76, 84, 91, 181–182, 212
Red Army (U.S.S.R.), 177
Redgrave, Michael, 150
Reed, Carol, 76
Reinhardt, Max, 51, 67
Renaissance, 156, 164, 220
Renata Theatre (New York), 20, 145
Repertory theater, 12, 26, 37–40, 42–44, 55, 61–68, 70, 77, 79–80, 82, 86–87, 93, 128, 136, 144, 153, 163, 165, 188, 201, 210, 221–222, 230, 234–235, 254
Repertory Theater of Lincoln Center: see "Lincoln Center"
Restoration (U.K.), 86

267

INDEX

Revolutionary War (U.S.), 157–158
Rewalt, Lothar, 93
Rhetoric, 44, 97, 157, 161, 217, 228
Rhinoceros, 203
Rice, Elmer, 11, 65, 93–94
Richard II (King of England), 232
Richardson, Howard, 18
Richardson, Lee, 202
Richardson, Ralph, 143, 159
Richardson, Tony, 181
Richard III, 83, 203
Richard III (King of England), 197
La Ricotta, 76
Rimbaud, Arthur, 221
Ritt, Martin, 76
Ritter, Thelma, 149
Ritualism, 39, 53, 80, 84, 86, 108, 139,
    150, 162, 189, 191–192, 220, 228,
    230, 237
RKO Pictures (Hollywood), 73, 75
Roach, Hal, 64
Robards, Jr., Jason, 24, 26, 215–216,
    238–239
Robbins, Jerome, 161, 163
Robertson, Cliff, 147
Robespierre, Maximilien, 229
Rockwell, Norman, 180
Rodgers, Richard, 2, 106, 130–132
Roebling, Paul, 129, 214
Roerick, William, 238
Rogers, Paul, 141
Rogoff, Gordon, 11
Le Roi se meurt (*The King Expires*), 213
Rollo's Wild Oat, 65
The Romance of Canada, 78
Roman Empire, 38
Romanticism, 2, 34, 61, 76–77, 98, 131,
    142, 198, 221, 228
Romeo and Juliet, 33, 212, 235
Roosevelt, Franklin D., 231
Roots, 120, 182–183, 186–188
Rose, George, 197
Rosenthal, Jean, 134
Rosmersholm, 36–37
Ross, 54, 198
Ross, Anthony, 99
Ross, David, 34, 52, 101
Rossellini, Roberto, 90
A Royal Affair at Versailles, 76
Royal Court Theatre (London), 45

Rubin, Arthur, 132
Runanin, Boris, 131
R.U.R., 65
Ruritanianism, 83
Ruskin, Shimen, 241
Ruy Blas, 10
Ryan, Eileen, 101
Ryan, Mitchell, 222
Ryder, Alfred, 91

Sackler, Howard, 243
Sadism, 222
Sadler's Wells Theatre (London), 55, 79
Saint Joan, 33
Saint Joan of the Stockyards, 223
The Saint of Bleecker Street, 132
Saks, Gene, 101, 137
Salmi, Albert, 99, 139
Salmon, Eric, 224
Sands, Diana, 212, 238–239
San Francisco Mime Troupe (Calif.), 230
Saroyan, William, 64
Sartre, Jean-Paul, 107–108, 155, 187,
    192, 203
Satire, 104, 137, 188, 207–208
Sayler, Oliver M., 67
Scenery, stage, 12, 51–55, 254
Schiller, Friedrich, 221, 228–229
Schine, G. David, 83
Schmidt, Douglas, 233
Schneider, Alan, 31–32, 169–170
The School for Scandal, 65
School of the American Ballet (New
    York), 55
Schopenhauer, Arthur, 229
Schubert Theatre (New York), 130
Schulman, Arnold, 143–145
Scofield, Paul, 196
Scott, George C., 28, 202, 211
Scottish National Players, 78
The Seagull, 65, 234–237
Second World War, 7, 79, 93, 174, 204,
    221, 231
Semitism: see "Judaism"
Sennett, Mack, 64
Sentimentality, 11, 47, 129–130, 144,
    174, 176, 211, 224
Serjeant Musgrave's Dance, 45–48, 50,
    225
The Seven Deadly Sins, 27

268

INDEX

Shakespeare, William, 9, 11–12, 27–33, 37, 51–52, 63, 66–70, 75–76, 82–84, 91, 112, 122, 133–137, 140–141, 144, 163–166, 170, 183, 201–203, 208, 218–220, 232, 234–236, 252
Shakespeare in Central Park: see "New York Shakespeare Festival"
Shaw, George Bernard, 2–3, 10, 12, 33, 35, 37, 65, 71, 126, 137, 183, 187, 225
Shaw, Glen Byam, 198
Shaw, Irwin, 57
Shaw, Robert, 200
Sheridan, Richard Brinsley, 65
Sheridan Square (New York), 19
Sherman, Hiram, 136
Sherwood, Robert, 65
She's Only a Bird in a Gilded Cage, 228
The Shoemaker's Holiday, 71
Show, 56
Show Boat, 106
The Show-Off, 91
Shubert Alley (New York), 10
Sierra, Gregorio Martinez, 20
Sikorski, Władysław, 231
Silk Stockings, 96–98
Silvera, Frank, 128
Simon, John, 1, 9–10
Simpson, N. F., 45
Six Characters in Search of an Author, 65
The Skin of Our Teeth, 40
Slapstick, 64, 141, 153, 164, 203, 213, 218–219, 236
Slave Ship, 243
Smith, Bessie, 183–188
Smith, Kent, 136
Smith, Loring, 164
Snow, C. P. 207
Socialism, 35, 182, 186
Soldiers, 231–232
Sondheim, Stephen, 161
Sontag, Susan, 9
Sophocles, 39, 79, 166, 242
South Pacific, 106
Sowing, 174
Spigelglass, Leonard, 243
Stalag 17, 93–94
Stamos, Theodore, 41
Stanislavsky, Konstantin, 101, 55, 57–61, 101, 223

Stanley, Kim, 99, 157–159
Stapleton, Maureen, 105, 146–147
State Department (U.S.), 40
Stein, Gertrude, 39, 109
Steinbeck, John, 130
Stephens, Robert, 160
Sterns, Gordon, 109
Stevens, Paul, 234
Stevens, Roger L., 60
Stevenson, Robert Louis, 72
Stewart, Fred, 60
Stickney, Dorothy, 106
Stiller, Jerry, 28
St. Mark's Playhouse (New York), 121, 189, 193
Stonehenge (U.K.), 55
Stowe, Harriet Beecher, 51, 188
Strachey, Lytton, 174
Strasberg, Lee, 223, 56–58, 60–61
A Streetcar Named Desire, 159
Strindberg, August, 39, 183, 190–191, 229
Stritch, Elaine, 99
Stroheim, Erich von, 241
Sturm und Drang (Storm and Stress), 228
Styne, Jule, 161, 163
Sullivan, Arthur, 203, 236
Sullivan, Jo, 132
Summer and Smoke, 20, 24
Summer of the 17th Doll, 149–151
Surrealism, 45
Swiss Guard, 177
Symbolism, 102, 192, 217
Synge, John Millington, 65–66

Take Her, She's Mine, 207
Taliaferro, John, 104
Tamburlaine, 79
The Taming of the Shrew, 31, 135, 165
Tandy, Jessica, 81, 87, 106
Tartuffe, 234–237
A Taste of Honey, 178–181
Taymor, Julie, 4
Television, 5, 7–9, 22, 28, 33, 43, 143, 145, 180, 202, 217
The Tempest, 135, 163–166, 201
Tempo Playhouse (New York), 107, 109, 115
Ter-Arutunian, Rouben, 51, 134–135, 149, 242

269

INDEX

Tetzel, Joan, 101
Thackeray, William Makepeace, 65
Thatcher, Torin, 92, 156
The Theater, 209
Theater-in-the-round: see "Arena theater"
Theater 12 (New York), 109–110
Theatre Arts, 64, 67
Theatre Company of Boston, 112, 225
Theatre De Lys (New York), 20
Théâtre des Nations Festival (Paris), 40–41
Theatre Four (New York), 223
Theatre Group (U.C.L.A.), 62
Theatre Guild (New York), 56, 70, 149
Theatre Workshop (London), 45, 176
They Knew What They Wanted, 131
A Thief's Journal, 190
The Third Man, 76
The 13th of March, 109
13th Street Theatre, 218, 220
The 39 Steps, 72
Thomas, Brandon, 63, 242
Thomson, Virgil, 135
Thorndike, Sybil, 50, 150
A Thousand Clowns, 206–207
Three Men on a Horse, 86, 203
Three Musicians, 85
The Three Musketeers, 237
The Threepenny Opera, 221–222
The Three Sisters, 11, 82–84, 86, 101–102, 113
Thrillers, 73–74, 93, 210
Thrust stage: see "Apron stage"
Tiger, Tiger, Burning Bright, 212
Times Square (New York), 162
Todd School (Woodstock, Ill.), 70
Tolstoy, Leo, 65, 229
Tom Sawyer, 64
Tone, Franchot, 148
Torn, Rip, 60, 211
Toscanini, Arturo, 169
A Touch of the Poet, 11, 157–160
Tragedy, 10–11, 36, 38, 64, 76, 84, 91, 100, 102, 104–105, 141, 144, 150–151, 157, 179, 198, 203, 206, 208–209, 211, 213–214, 219, 224, 228
Tragicomedy, 94

Traubel, Helen, 131
La Traviata, 79
Treasure Island, 72
The Treasure of the Sierra Madre, 75
The Trial, 11, 68, 74–77, 109–110, 221
The Trial of A. Lincoln, 243–245
Trilling, Lionel, 12, 14
Trinity College (Dublin), 174
Troilus and Cressida, 11, 140–141
The Trojan Women, 239
Trotsky, Leon, 11
Trouble in Tahiti, 103–105
Troubled Waters, 223–227
The Truth about Blayds, 65
Trzcinski, Edmund, 93–94
Turandot, 65
Tushar, James, 104
Twain, Mark, 64, 66
Twelfth Night, 164
27 Wagons Full of Cotton, 103–105
Two Gentlemen of Verona, 31
Tyers, John, 104
Tyler, Judy, 130
Tynan, Kenneth, 9, 185
Tyrone Guthrie Theatre: see "Guthrie (Repertory) Theatre"

Uncle Tom's Cabin, 51, 188–189
University of California (Berkeley), 18
The Unnamable, 167
U.S. Army, 69
U.S. Marines, 177
U.S. Postal Service, 67–68

Vanguardism: see "Avant-gardism"
Vanity Fair, 65
Vassar College, 213
Vaudeville, 42, 95, 162, 165, 170, 204, 218, 228
Vaughan, Gladys, 222
Vaughan, Stuart, 31, 165
Verdon, Gwen, 107, 148–149
Verse drama, 14, 71
Victorianism, 35, 164, 236
Village Voice, 11
The Visit, 119, 153–157
Vivian Beaumont Theater (New York), 62, 68, 229
Vlis, Diana van der, 139
Volpone, 86

270

INDEX

Voltaire (François-Marie Arouet), 156, 229

Von Volz, Valerie, 228

Voyeurism, 222

Wager, Michael, 60

Wagner, Richard, 55

Wain, John, 186

Waiting for Godot, 2, 4, 137, 152, 169, 173, 211, 237

Walker Art Center (Minneapolis), 81

Wallace, G. D., 131

Wallace, George, 149

Wallach, Eli, 58, 95

Wallop, Douglass, 107

Walston, Ray, 107

The Waltz of the Toreadors, 142–143

War and Peace, 65

Waring, Richard, 164

The War of the Worlds, 72, 75

Warriner, Frederic, 32

Washington Square (New York), 201

The Waters of Babylon, 45

Wayne, David, 215

The Way of the World, 53

Weaver, Fritz, 126–127, 136

We Bombed in New Haven, 237–239

Weede, Robert, 131–132

Weidner, Paul, 244

Weill, Kurt, 136

Welles, Orson, 12, 68–77, 254

Welles, Richard H., 70

Wells, H. G., 72

Wesker, Arnold, 11, 45, 120, 182–183, 186, 225

West, Jennifer, 217

West End (London), 78

Westman, Nydia, 153

Westminster Theatre (London), 78

Wheeler, David, 225

Wheeler, Hugh, 86

When We Dead Awaken, 34, 55

White, Dana, 139

White, Kenneth, 89–90

White, Tommy, 144

Whitehead, O. Z., 164

Whitehead, Robert, 62, 68, 216

White House (Washington, D.C.), 188

Whitman, Walt, 64

Who's Afraid of Virginia Woolf?, 11, 86, 123, 203–208

Wickwire, Nancy, 125

Widdoes, Kathleen, 166

Wilbur, Richard, 236

The Wild Duck, 65

Wilde, Oscar, 97, 126

Wilder, Thornton, 20, 27, 40, 64–65, 70, 79, 238

Williams, John, 98

Williams, Karl, 166

Williams, Tennessee, 11, 20, 27, 40, 54, 60–61, 65, 102–105, 114, 118, 128, 145–147, 159, 178–181, 183, 206, 208–214

Williams, William Carlos, 39, 41

Wilson, Edmund, 12

Wilson, Meredith, 62, 149–151

Wind, Edgar, 13

Windom, William, 95

Winkler, Mel, 244

Winter Garden Theatre (New York), 140

Winters, Marian, 98

Winters, Shelley, 128, 137

Wiseman, Joseph, 129

Witcover, Walt, 145

Wolf, Jutta, 145

Wolfe, Thomas, 157

Wolfson, Victor, 20, 25

Wolpe, Stephen, 223

"Wooden O": see "Globe Theatre"

Woodthorpe, Peter, 155

Woodward, Joanne, 58

Woolf, Leonard, 174

Woollcott, Alexander, 7, 70

Wordsworth, Richard, 141

Works Progress Administration (WPA), 71, 90

World War I, 69, 78, 158, 174, 208, 221

World War II: see "Second World War"

Worlock, Frederic, 62

Worsley, T. C., 82

Woyzeck, 228

Wright, Frank Lloyd, 220

Wylie, Philip, 138

Yale University (New Haven, Conn.), 10–11, 208, 215

Yeats, W. B., 157

INDEX

York Playhouse (New York), 121, 188

You Can't Take It with You, 138, 176, 203

Young, Stark, 3, 7, 209

Youngstein, Max L., 60

Young Werther, The Sorrows of, 221

YouTube, 13

Yulin, Harris, 224

Zeisler, Peter, 80

The Zoo Story, 185

Zorich, Louis, 166

Printed in the USA
CPSIA information can be obtained
at www.ICGtesting.com
CBHW070003170724
11682CB00008B/292